Imperial Potentate Dr. F. T. "Hogan" H'Doubler, Jr.
1980–1981

PARADE TO GLORY

The Story of the Shriners

and Their Caravan to Destiny

Revised and Updated by

ORVILLE FINDLEY RUSH

Original Author

FRED VAN DEVENTER

PARADE TO GLORY
Published for the Shriners by
William Morrow edition published July 1959
Copyright 1959
Revised 1980 by
The Imperial Council, A.A.O.N.M.S., an Iowa Corporation
Library of Congress Catalog Card No. 59–5505
Printed in the U.S.A.

Foreword

The Sands of Time trickle on endlessly and tell a continuous story.

The complete history of the AAONMS is a saga yet to unfold.

Born in an era very similar to that of today, with an economy wildly out of control, yet it offered solace to the founders as it does to members today. With the current economic morass and the seemingly striking failure to date of spontaneous recuperative forces to manifest themselves materially signals no lasting amelioration but the shrine has in its membership men of distinctive stature who are capable of leading us to a solution of the crisis as they have in numerous previous national and world difficulties.

In over 100 years of history, the shrine has enrolled some of the world's most distinguished citizens and is a real force in world affairs. It will continue to grow in prestige. Its history is important, imperviably fascinating. Early, effloresce was effected, followed by effulge, and finally efficacious endeavor. It burst into bloom to blossom.

This effusion should please the legions of buffs in the fraternity who devote their lives to the esoterica of history. "History encompasses time. The inaudible and noiseless foot of time. Winged time glides on insensibly, and deceives us; and there is nothing more fleeting than years." Ovid.

Orville Findley Rush

Table of Contents

IMPERIAL OFFICERS 1980–1981

**F. T. H'DOUBLER,
JR., M.D.**
Abou Ben Adhem
Temple
Imperial Potentate

**RANDOLPH R.
THOMAS**
Morocco Temple
Deputy Imperial
Potentate

**DANIEL E.
BOWERS, M.D.**
Mohammed Temple
Imperial Chief
Rabban

**RICHARD B.
OLFENE**
Kora Temple
Imperial Assistant
Rabban

GENE BRACEWELL
Yaarab Temple
Imperial High Priest
& Prophet

**WALKER S.
KISSELBURGH**
Al Malaikah Temple
Imperial Oriental
Guide

**THOMAS W.
MELHAM**
Tripoli Temple
Imperial Treasurer

JACK H. JONES
Egypt Temple
Imperial Recorder

**RUSSELL H.
ANTHONY, D.V.M.**
El Kahir Temple
Imperial First
Ceremonial Master

VORIS KING
Habibi Temple
Imperial Second
Ceremonial Master

**EDWARD G.
MCMULLAN, C.D.**
Al Azhar Temple
Imperial Master

**GEORGE W.
POWELL**
Crescent Temple
Imperial Captain of
the Guard

**JOSEPH P.
PADGETT**
Islam Temple
Imperial Outer Guard

**REV. WILLIAM H.
MAGILL**
El Jebel Temple
Imperial Chaplain

LIVING PAST IMPERIAL POTENTATES

THOMAS W. MELHAM
Tripoli Temple, 1957–58

GEORGE E. STRINGFELLOW
Crescent Temple, 1958–59

MARSHALL M. PORTER.
Al Azhar Temple, 1961–62

GEORGE M. KLEPPER
Al Chymia Temple, 1962–63

HAROLD C. CLOSE
Egypt Temple, 1963–64

O. CARLYLE BROCK
Zem Zem Temple, 1964–65

ORVILLE F. RUSH
Kena Temple, 1966–67

THOMAS F. SEAY
Medinah Temple, 1967–68

CHESTER A. HOGAN
Afifi Temple, 1968–69

**AUBREY G.
GRAHAM**
Khedive Temple,
1970–71

**C. VICTOR
THORNTON**
Moslah Temple,
1971–72

**JACOB A.
WINGERTER**
Salaam Temple,
1973–74

**JACK M. STREIGHT,
Q.C.**
Gizeh Temple,
1974–75

W. W. BENNETT
Ararat Temple,
1975–76

PETER VAL PREDA
Cairo Temple,
1976–77

**FRED R.
MORRISON**
Moslem Temple,
1977–78

**WARREN F. WECK,
JR.**
Zuhrah Temple,
1978–79

**CHARLES J.
CLAYPOOL**
Antioch Temple,
1979–80

1

Jolly Associates

The story of the Shrine is the story of men with reverent minds and merry hearts, men from every walk of life—from business, the professions, the arts, the sciences, sports, government, politics, labor, including some of the most prominent and distinguished world leaders. Ethos. It is a story worth the narration.

The story is replete with indisputable fact, coupled with legend and partial fiction, as one might assert of any organization over a century in age, but out of the welter of fact, fiction, fancy and legend has sprung the most colorful of all fraternal entities. The Shriners have played and marched their way into a glory of fraternalism hitherto unknown.

In the spring and summer of 1870, the "13" mania swept New York City and among its more ardent devotees were Walter Millard Fleming, M.D.; William J. Florence, actor; Charles T. McClenachan, lawyer; William S. Paterson, paper merchant; George Millar, printer; and William Fowler, restaurateur and wine merchant.

As much as anything else, the craze over "13" could be attributed to the aftermath of the War Between the States, a flouting of all omens of ill-luck in an effort to forget. There were those who insisted on sitting down to their luncheons at exactly 12:13 at tables set for thirteen. Games were invented in which "13" played the dominant role, and attempts were made not infrequently to have thirteen persons at social affairs.

Among the luncheon tables set for thirteen guests was one on the second floor of Knickerbocker Cottage located at 426 Sixth Avenue, a popular restaurant operated by Fowler and patronized largely by members of the Masonic fraternity, which was about to erect a new temple on nearby Twenty-third Street. Masonry was prosperous. There were many lodges

Knickerbocker Cottage

The Cradle of the Mystic Shrine in North America

of the first three degrees. The Ancient Accepted Scottish Rite was growing rapidly; and if the Knights Templar were a bit slower, it could be attributed to the cost of uniforms that every member had to own at that time.

There were thousands of Masons in the New York of 1870, many of them with businesses and offices that abounded in the vicinity of Twenty-third Street. Banded together as they were in the spirit of fraternalism, it was quite natural and customary that they should carry that spirit outside their lodge rooms, and many of them made it a habit to visit Knickerbocker Cottage, which was housed in the old Varian Homestead, a large white house in the Dutch style, erected at Twenty-eighth Street when that area was on the outskirts of the city. Its rooms were large and charming. The food was good and Knickerbocker Cottage had attained a certain renown because of both the size and quality of its cellars.

There were several Masonic luncheon tables in Fowler's place, mostly made up of the same groups, day after day. Fowler promoted the idea of little cliques and was a member, or an honorary member, of most of them, for he was a popular host. But the most popular of all of the luncheon tables was the one on the second floor in a room that overlooked Sixth Avenue, a table set for thirteen. Faces at the large round table might vary from day to day, and there were occasions when its thirteen chairs were not filled, but no matter how many sat down at 12:13, nor who attended on a given day, this table was one for fun. Perhaps the jokes were better. Perhaps there was more natural wit. Perhaps the select coterie was composed of the more natural extroverts who welcomed only those who could contribute to the merriment. Jolly associates.

Dr. Fleming was an accepted member of that table for thirteen, and so were Florence, McClenachan, Paterson, Millar and others; and Fowler himself spent more time in the "13" room than elsewhere for here was the gayest of all gay company. For Dr. Fleming to be admitted to this select group was something of an achievement. It testified to his personal charm and his developing practice as a physician, for Dr. Fleming had hung out his shingle on Twenty-eighth Street less than a year before.

Always, except in an emergency, Dr. Fleming made it a point to complete his morning rounds at nearby St. Elizabeth's Hospital and his morning calls at the homes of his patients before 11:45. Then, with his Homburg at a jaunty angle, he walked from his office to Fowler's in time to sit down with his cronies at exactly 12:13. He was just thirty-two years old, but already he had begun to develop an expanding waistline, across which dangled a heavy gold chain, attached to an equally heavy gold watch. He sported long, flowing sideburns that dropped below his massive jowls; and even in a day when the clean-shaven man was a rarity, they attracted attention. His clothing was of the very best and, all in all, he radiated strength, character, and joviality. He was exuberant and effervescent, but nevertheless he appeared to have a certain majesty about him. He was a large man, some five feet, nine inches tall and inclined to corpulence. The result was that he walked with a certain ponderousness, which belied his inner self.

Dr. Fleming was also a determined man. He had left a good practice in Rochester, New York, to become a part of this great city that was developing at the mouth of the Hudson and that even then—five years after Appomattox—was still celebrating the end of the bloodiest war in history. Parts of the Confederacy were still prostrate and sometimes starving, but in New York the only problem was to find new worlds to conquer. The French Empire was about to crumble before Bismarck and Victor Emmanuel would soon take over Rome and, in effect, restrict the temporal power of the Papacy to the Vatican grounds. But neither event would interrupt the flow of the finest wines and brandies to a city that was literally "living up" the preservation of the Union.

New York boasted of more than a million people, 900,000 of them on Manhattan Island, and was still growing. Factories sprang up almost overnight, and so did the splendid but architecturally grotesque mansions of the city's growing number of millionaires. The handsome, silver-mounted carriages of the new-rich were drawn by matched pairs of whites, grays, bays and blacks over cobblestoned Broadway and Fifth Avenue, carrying ostrich-plumed ladies to their milliners or to their favorite theaters, of which there were many. Show business was booming, and names still mentioned with awe in the history of the theater were just coming into full prominence.

Labor was scarce, but money was free and easy. When Fisk and Gould almost (but not quite) cornered the nation's gold supply in 1869 and thereby precipitated "Black Friday" on the New York Stock Exchange, the city staggered momentarily and then resumed its swagger. The golden spike had just been driven at Promontory, Utah, and now the millionaires could ride swiftly, if not comfortably, from New York to San Francisco. They wouldn't even worry about the Indians, for wasn't General George Custer, the dashing, flamboyant and perhaps inept hero of the Civil War, on guard? The scandals of Grant's administration were yet to come and if anyone at all gave the matter a thought, he could not have conceived of the panic of 1873. The economic situation of the early 1800s was similar to our economic situation of today. There was poverty, of course, and plenty of it, but even the poor had their beer, delivered by lumbering wagons and drank as often as not under the gaslights of the neighborhood saloon.

It was indeed a time to be alive. The past was gone and best forgotten. The present was for living, and Fleming, Florence, McClenachan, Paterson and all the rest believed in living it to the fullest. But for Fleming there was also the future; and so it was that, sometime in the spring of 1870, there came to him while he sat at the table for thirteen at Fowler's an idea which developed through various vicissitudes (including use of the figure 13) into the Ancient Arabic Order Nobles of the Mystic Shrine for North America.

No one knows the exact date when the idea come to the popular doctor. No one knows what germ of thought, what gem of wisdom, or what casual story by one of his comrades gave the doctor his inspiration. Still, the time is clear, and so are a few other essential facts, some of them contained in the Ritual of the Order, which now lies in glory and splendor in the Shrine rooms of the George Washington National Masonic Memorial in Alexandria, Virginia. Hand-lettered in flowing design and illuminated with a now fading red ink, is the title page. It reads:

> The First Complete Ritual of the Ancient Arabic Order of the Nobles of the Mystic Shrine. Written for the establishment of the Order in the Western Hemisphere by Walter Millard Fleming, M.D.

The Ritual undoubtedly is in Dr. Fleming's handwriting. It bears many corrections and, despite official changes, is in essence the same Ritual used in later years. The lodge room setting remains unchanged. There was succor then and now for weary Sons of the Desert. The robes and other paraphernalia follow the chart today as they were laid down by the versatile doctor, and even the ceremony and most of the words are little removed from the original.

In 1950, when the Shrine rooms in the George Washington National Memorial in Alexandria, Virginia, were created, Mecca Temple of New York City (the first in America) generously contributed the original Ritual along with other memorabilia belonging to Dr. Fleming and William J. Florence, one of America's truly great actors and comedians, who was credited by Dr. Fleming and others with being a co-founder of the Shrine. On the inside cover of the Ritual, there is a notation, handwritten and signed by Dr. Saram R. Ellison, the second Recorder of Mecca Temple, which says: "In the latter part of 1901, Noble George W. Millar and I visited Dr. Walter M. Fleming, at the Imperial Hotel, his wife being sick at the time. He presented us with this

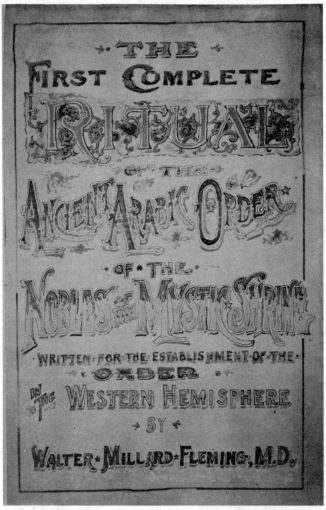

Cover page "The First Complete Ritual . . ."

Ritual, having found it in an unused trunk. He said it was the first complete Ritual of the Order. I had it mounted and bound, and it has been in our safe ever since."

These and no more are the incontrovertible facts of the origin and founding of the Shrine. The remainder is partly fact, partly legend, partly fancy, partly fiction. Thus the story of the Shrine begins to unfold.

GEORGE W. MILLAR

WILLIAM S. PATERSON

CHARLES T. McCLENACHAN

Dr. WALTER M. FLEMING

JOHN A. MOORE

The First 13 Masons
who received

WILLIAM J. FLORENCE

The Order of the Mystic Shrine

NOBLES FLORENCE & FLEMING AUG. 13-1870
THE OTHER 11 NOBLES JUNE 16-1871.

COPYRIGHT 1914 BY SARAM R. ELLISON, M.D.

DANIEL SICKELS

OSWALD M. D'AUBIGNE

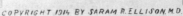

JOHN W. SIMONS

JAMES S. CHAPPELL

SHERWOOD C. CAMPBELL

EDWARD EDDY

ALBERT P. MORIARTY

2

Creation—from All of These

Many leaders of the Shrine, in the years since Dr. Fleming wrote his Ritual, have tried to describe just what the organization is. One of the best of these descriptions came from the pen of the late Dr. Hubert M. Poteat, Wake Forest University Professor and a Past Imperial Potentate. He wrote:

> The Shrine appeals to the strong manhood of North America for a variety of reasons. In the first place, the oriental pageantry and the magnificence of costumes and regalia appeal to men who may be old in years but who are still young in spirit. Little boys play cops and robbers; Shriners play Moslems and infidels.
>
> In the second place, the Shrine provides opportunity for fun and play and mirth on a truly magnificent scale. Shriners are apostles of good cheer and happiness and as such are performing a very vital function in this tragic modern world of ours. Indeed it may be said that we have been "called into the Kingdom for such a time as this."
>
> A further important principle of the Shrine is toleration in the field of religious opinion. One of the most tragic phenomena of our times is the endless warfare among the people of different faiths and beliefs. In other words we expend most of our energies fighting one another instead of the devil. The Shrine will have none of it and instructs its initiates that they are to recognize the right of every human being to worship God as he sees fit, without interference or even criticism from any man who walks this planet.
>
> If there is one thing our harassed world needs more than another today, it is brotherly love. This can be found nowhere in a finer or truer form than in the Mystic Shrine. This does not mean for a moment that all Shriners are

the perfect embodiment of this quality. However, Shriners in general do live by this principle.

Such is the weak and fallible nature of man that he needs all the spiritual strengthening he can get; and the Shrine teaches its initiates as all Masonic bodies do, that God IS and that it is our duty to worship and to obey Him, to esteem Him as the chief good and to fight with all our power against atheism.

Shriners play Moslems and infidels with reverent minds and merry hearts. Indeed! But Shriners are more than little boys grown tall. With all their fun, they have not forgotten charity. With all the splendor of their parades, they do not and cannot forget that first of all they are Master Masons with all the humility they are taught by the craft. For most of the more than nine hundred thousand Shriners in North America and all around the world, it is a matter of considerable pride that they wear the scimitar and crescent in their buttonholes as they go about their daily lives. It is with equal pride that they don the red fez with black tassel for more formal ceremonial occasions. But all of the fun, splendor and charity had to have a beginning, and this beginning must have come at some meeting in either 1869 or 1870 between Dr. Fleming and Billy Florence, both famous for aphorisms.

There is no record of that first meeting, but it is more than likely that it came about when the handsome, gay, devil-may-care actor called on Dr. Fleming for treatment of some minor ailment, which in itself was something of a plume in the hat of a doctor new in New York. Billy Florence in 1869 was established as the toast of the theatrical world. It might be said that he was the George M. Cohan or Jack Benny of his day. He lived in the better hotels that lined Fifth Avenue, and Dr. Fleming's house was just around the corner from the Fifth Avenue Hotel. Both were Master Masons and while Florence did not work at the craft with the same zeal as Dr. Fleming, he had, at that time, attained higher degrees. Once the business of medicine was out of the way, there was probably an inquiry about basic lodge, and after that an invitation to lunch and perhaps a bottle of wine. Thus are friendships born, and in truth Fleming and Florence were kindred souls, each with an insatiable zest for life. There was perhaps also some sort of adoration on the part of the young doctor for the handsome and popular star, for in reality Walter Fleming was a frustrated actor, whose life had been channeled by a doting father into the world of healing.

There were others too, in 1870, who undoubtedly contributed in some measure to the beginning of the Shrine, but just *who* contributed *what* is still subject to considerable controversy. Fifty years after the founding of the Shrine, James McGee, who became the twenty-eighth member of Mecca Temple, and was the last survivor of an original thirty, wrote from memory his history of the organization. In the light of subsequent revelations, it is more than likely that his story is nearer the truth than any other. All versions of the early and formative years of the Shrine are agreed, however, that four men carried the burden, with an assist from a fifth. These men were Fleming, Florence, McClenachan, Paterson and Fowler. Their backgrounds in life and in Masonry are important in the light of their contributions.

Walter M. Fleming was born in Portland, Maine, June 13, 1838, the younger of two sons of Dr. L. D. Fleming, who soon moved to Rochester, New York, and established a lucrative practice in a house on St. Paul Street in the heart of the thriving town. Both boys attended nearby Canandaigua Academy, and both boys matriculated at Albany Medical College.

The exact date when Walter entered Albany College is not known, for all of the early records of that institution have been destroyed by fire, but it must have been

during the years when Webster and Clay were trying
to save the Union and avoid the inevitable conflict between the North and the South. The best surmise is
that he enrolled in 1857, for the record shows that,
without even having been graduated, he was named
surgeon of the First Cavalry of the New York National
Guard in 1858. In 1861, he served as surgeon to the
Nineteenth Regiment of the same organization with
the rank of lieutenant or ensign.

The records of the Adjutant General's office show
that Fleming was "discharged in N.E.Va. dated August
3, 1861 on tender of resignation in consequence of
physical disability." The nature of the disability was
not explained and Fleming himself never mentioned
it, though in 1907 he applied for a pension. Undoubtedly his injuries were incident to the first movement
of Northern forces into Virginia, which began on May
24 and continued until after the Union disaster at Bull
Run in late July.

After his discharge, Fleming returned to the Albany
Medical College and received his degree in 1862. Dr.
Fleming then hung out his shingle in the same house
with his father on St. Paul Street in Rochester, and it
is apparent that in the ensuing years he developed
quite a following and an extensive circle of convivial
friends. In 1867 he was chosen by the city council in
a competitive election with other doctors as one of
two city physicians.

In that same year, his father died and Dr. Walter
assumed the entire practice, but life in Rochester grew
boring. Mrs. Mellan Lucas of Del Ray Beach, Florida,
Dr. Fleming's granddaughter, recalls that in his later
years he was an inveterate reader, so perhaps out of
the daily press or the periodicals of the time, there
came to him the desire to travel and participate in
some of the glamour of which he read. In any event,
the Rochester *Union and Advertiser* on April 3, 1869,
revealed that the doctor had sold his practice in order

to remove to New York City. Two days later the same newspaper reported a farewell party given for the doctor. The paper said: "It having been announced that Dr. W. M. Fleming was about to leave Rochester and take up his residence in New York, a considerable number of his friends decided to give a complimentary entertainment and invite him to accept the honor. . . . The party having gone through the courses of a splendid supper, moistened with sparkling wine, the feast of reason and flow of soul followed . . . and the evening was protracted until well toward midnight when the party separated."

And so the doctor cut his ties in Rochester and moved toward his destiny with the Shrine.

When Dr. Fleming arrived in New York in 1869, he had just received his symbolic Masonic degrees from Rochester Lodge No. 660. He was initiated an Entered Apprentice December 14, 1868, passed to Fellowcraft the following day and raised to the sublime degree of a Master Mason January 11, 1869; and it is apparent that from that time, Masonry more and more dominated his life.

But he had an active practice in New York for almost forty years. At the 1902 meeting of Albany's class of 1862, Dr. Fleming reported that he had become a qualified examiner in insanity in the Supreme Court of the City of New York, that he was a member of the New York County Medical Society, the Medical-Legal Society and the Physicians' Mutual Aid. In addition, of course, he practiced extensively among the members of the theatrical profession and was one of the first physicians to be attached to the Actors Fund of America. He wrote extensively on insanity and related subjects, including drug habits and dipsomania. Strangely enough, the only medical paper written by him still on file in New York's extensive medical library concerns diseases of the chest, including asthma, for which he believed snuff was not a suitable treatment.

Dr. Fleming's growth in Masonry is almost unbelievable, and most of it can be traced to his interest in and his love of his own Masonic child, the Ancient Arabic Order Nobles of the Mystic Shrine. For example, it is notable that at its official birth, the founders of the Shrine decreed that it would be available only to those Masons who had attained the 32° in the Scottish Rite or the Knight Templar degree in the York Rite. Yet, when he wrote the original Ritual, Dr. Fleming had received only his first three basic Masonic degrees.

There can be little doubt that private and informal agreements on the prerequisites for Shrine membership were made among the men who sat at the table for thirteen in Fowler's restaurant and that formal creation of the fun organization would be delayed until Dr. Fleming had obtained them. Accordingly, he received the 4th to 32nd degrees in Brooklyn's Aurora Grata Consistory on May 31, 1871. Two weeks later, June 16, 1871, the initial meeting of the founders of the Shrine was held officially in New York's Masonic Hall. On March 19, 1872, Fleming signed the bylaws of Columbian Commandery No. 1, thus completing all of the Masonic degrees prior to the official founding of Mecca Temple on September 26, 1872.

Indicating his zeal for Masonry is Fleming's own account, written for the one-hundredth anniversary conclave in 1910, when he was the oldest living past commander and too ill to attend, of how he literally saved Columbian Commandery from extinction in 1873.

The Commandery was at a low ebb, largely in debt and scantily attended. The proposition of my acceptance of the office of Commander was an astounding surprise. However, through the influence of my official comrades in arms and their persistent insistence, I acceded to their wishes to rescue the oldest Commandery in the state. . . . These ambassadors and advisory council comprised several enthusiastic members of both Commandery and the several bodies of the Ancient Accepted Scottish Rite. I was at this time an enthusiastic worker in all of the grades of Scottish Rite Masonry, and became enthused with the same spirit of perseverance and success in the Order of Knighthood. I at once proceeded to resuscitate Columbian. Had a "calling of the clans" from all the departments, and supported it to the full with both my counsel and my purse and with renewed zeal devoted all my energies to newly equip the Commandery, increase the roll of membership, arouse a new interest that would defy the angry waves of time and the storm of persecution. . . .

I then proceeded to make the paraphernalia and the work interesting and attractive. I then personally assumed the responsibility of all the monetary requirements. I resumed the usual banquets which had been long abandoned because of lack of funds required to sustain that interesting part of the ceremony. I then proceeded to equip the entire official corps in a full coat of mail armor, helmets, swords, staves, spears, hawbucks, leggings and gauntlets, all of which was strictly authentic and produced by the best costumers in the City of New York. Popularity and success following on the new regime, both officers and members seemed at once to take a new and splendid interest.

Fleming then goes on to relate that he equipped Columbian with a superb silver service and that he spared no expense to obtain the finest in every kind of equipment to make Columbian the acknowledged leader. At the same time he continued to work in the Scottish Rite, and for the three consecutive years that he served as Commander of Columbian was responsible for Knights becoming Scottish rite Masons and vice versa with the result, as he puts it, that "two separate series of rites or orders ultimately became almost a united family."

With all of this, he said, "I found it rather an arduous task to keep pace with all of the requirements in all the complicated ritualistic renditions, official and subordinate, for the several years during which I struggled to equip myself commendably in somewhere near a dozen prominent official positions, including at the same time instituting and fathering of the Order of the Mystic Shrine, the formation of Mecca Temple, first in the City of New York, and many temples following, also the Imperial Council of the Order for the entire jurisdiction of the United States and adjacent territories."

The fact is, of course, that Fleming needed Columbian and the Scottish Rite in order to get his own brain child in operation.

The second of the four men who created the Shrine was William Jermyn Florence. He was a real personality. He romped and played across most of America and Europe from the time he first became smitten with the stage. Actor, producer, writer, poet, tune-smith, comedian, monologuist, playwright—he was everything in the theater. He loved it and the people loved him.

He was a roly-poly man—at least in his later years. He was described by one of his contemporaries as being above five and a half feet tall, and weighing perhaps two hundred pounds. His voice was gentle and musical and his eyes constantly twinkled with mirth. He was an ardent fisherman and made annual pilgrimages to Canada for the salmon.

Florence was born William J. Conlin on July 26, 1831, in Albany, New York, one of a large brood produced by Mr. and Mrs. Benjamin Conlin, who had migrated from Ireland. The record of his early life is at the least confusing. Not until he achieved success on the stage did that record attain anything resembling clarity.

Most of the reports of Florence's early life reveal that the Conlins moved to New York City from Albany about 1845, principally because of better economic opportunities. Eventually most of Florence's brothers obtained employment with the city government, as did many others of Irish descent in those days. One brother, Peter, eventually became a police inspector. Another worked in the street department. But young Billy Conlin would have none of it. At the time of his death in 1891 the *New York Times* reported that he worked at a mechanical trade, earning enough to help support the family and to provide tickets for the theaters and music halls that abounded. Another story of those years is contained in a book called *Songs of the Florences* published by Dick and Fitzgerald in 1860. This story undoubtedly had Florence's approval, and it revealed that "the popular delineator of Irish character was educated at Princeton, N. J., and assumed the active duties of life as a bookkeeper in a well known mercantile house in Burling Slip, New York City." But even though this revelation may have been approved by Florence, it is to be doubted. There are no records in Princeton that he ever attended any school there and indications are that the family was too poor to afford a private-school education even for so talented a youngster as Billy Conlin.

During the years from 1845 to 1849 young Conlin began building up for himself something of a reputation for Irish dialect and finally he joined the Murdoch Dramatic Association, a sort of touring stock company, and as Peter in *The Stranger* he made his first stage appearance in the Richmond Theater in Richmond, Virginia, on December 6, 1849. He was just eighteen years old. And thus began one of the most fabulous careers in all the history of the American stage.

At the close of the 1849 season, Conlin was transferred to New York. He appeared under the management of Brougham and Chippendale at Niblo's theater, Brougham's Lyceum, the Broadway and other theaters of the day, largely in Irish dialect parts, among them that of Dolley in *Rob Roy.* Sometime during this period, he changed his name to William Jermyn Florence, Florence being his mother's maiden name. Whether he changed his name legally or simply adopted it, was never revealed by Billy himself, but it was as Florence that he lived for the rest of his life, and it was as William J. Florence that he married Malvina Pray on January 1, 1853. Malvina Pray was a pretty little thing, and was recognized even then as the *premiere danseuse* of the New York stage. She had first appeared as one of the Pray sisters, but when her sister married Barney Williams, another luminary of the New York theater, Malvina continued alone. It is likely that Florence and Malvina met while they appeared on the same program at Niblo's theater. The marriage resulted in the formation of one of the most famous of all married teams in the theater, comparable today to Lunt and Fontanne. They created *The Irish Boy and the Yankee Girl,* with which they toured America and Europe for years, and it was while on such a tour that Florence first became a Mason in Philadelphia. The records of Mt. Moriah Lodge No. 155 show that William J. Florence was initiated, passed and raised by virtue of a special dispensation at a special meeting of the lodge on October 12, 1853. For youngsters, Mr. and Mrs. William J. Florence were doing all right. Their biography reports that on this same triumphal tour they received complimentary benefits and services of silver in Baltimore, Washington, New Orleans and Charleston. Pittsburgh also must have been on the itinerary, for on the following June 10, 1854, he received his Mark Master degree in Zerubbabel Chapter No. 162. He received his Royal Arch degree two days later. He is listed on the minutes of the chapter as a comedian and classified a sojourner. It was not until December 5, 1855, that he was admitted to Pittsburgh Commandery No. 1.

It is obvious from the record of Mt. Moriah Lodge that his interest in Masonry lagged in the ensuing years. He was suspended December 22, 1857, for failure to pay his dues, but was restored to good standing February 24, 1863. He was again suspended December 22, 1868, for failing to pay his dues, but once again paid up on December 26, 1871. It is notable that this restoration came after the first meeting of the original thirteen members of the Shrine and during that period when Dr. Fleming was equipping himself with advanced Masonic degrees. These dates are important in the light of later developments.

Professionally, success followed success for the Florences until, individually and as a team, they became the toasts of the theatrical world, both in the United States and in Europe. They made their first European appearance in London in 1856, playing at the Royal and Drury Lane, and their biographers report that they were frequently visited by the Queen and the royal family. Certainly the Florences received one and perhaps more gifts from the then Prince of Wales.

At home, even during the war years, their success continued, and thus in 1867 when it was announced that the Florences again would tour Europe, C. T. McClenachan conceived the idea of making the young actor an ambassador of good will to the Scottish Rite bodies of Europe. After an agreement with the actor, McClenachan and two other inspectors general of the Scottish Rite in New York conferred the degrees on him at the old Metropolitan Hotel on April 21, under special dispensation. Florence was accredited to Aurora Grata Consistory in Brooklyn, with the notation that the actor was about to travel abroad.

What, if anything, Florence ever did for the Scottish Rite is not known, but it was on that trip in 1867 that he set the stage for the famous lawsuit over *Caste*, a play by an English writer named Robertson. Florence himself related that he was so impressed with it that he visited the theater where it was playing four times, and during those four performances succeeded in memorizing the entire play.

Robertson had sold the American rights to the play to Lester Wallach, owner of Wallach's theater and from time to time Florence's producer and manager, but Florence returned to New York and succeeded in producing the play before Wallach could get it on the boards. Wallach brought suit for damages in a case that Florence eventually won by a Supreme Court decision, which hinged on the fact that there was no international copyright convention. Having won the suit, Florence in a condescending letter to Robertson sent the author a check for fifty pounds, not because he owed it, but because he wanted to be fair. Robertson returned the check with a scathing retort. Even that situation failed to dim his popularity—nor was it ever dimmed.

Charles T. McClenachan, the third important Mason to participate in establishing the Ancient Arabic Order Nobles of the Mystic Shrine, was a lawyer of some repute. He had been born in Washington, April 13, 1829, but had established his practice in New York, and it was there that he became known as one of the outstanding Masonic ritualists in America. He was an active participant in all branches of the fraternity, and was the active Deputy for the State of New York in the Scottish Rite.

Perhaps more important in the eventual scheme of the Shrine than he was ever given credit for was the fourth important Mason—William Sleigh Paterson, destined to become the first Recorder of Mecca Temple and of the Imperial Council when it was formed in 1876. Paterson was born at Haddington, Scotland, March 6, 1844, and thus was the youngest of all those Masons actively associated with the formation of the Shrine.

Paterson's family migrated to the United States in 1847 where he received his education, which included mastering the French, German, Spanish, Italian, Latin, Greek and Arabic languages, all of which he used as a proofreader in a rather large printing establishment. He received all of his Masonic degrees in New York. He served as secretary of the Scottish Rite bodies of New York from 1872 to 1889. Because of their intimate association over the years, Paterson perhaps knew Fleming better than anyone else and, because of his knowledge of Arabic, helped more than anyone else in creating the legends of the Shrine.

The fifth man who assisted in the founding of the Shrine was undoubtedly William Fowler the restaurateur, who was not one of the original "13" but rather carried card No. 24 of Mecca Temple. Fowler loved fun and the Shrine was created for fun. William Fowler, Jr., who succeeded to ownership of the famous restaurant, recalled in 1914 in a letter to Saram R. Ellison, Recorder of Mecca Temple, that "from about 1870 to 1880 when my father was proprietor of Knickerbocker Cottage, we had there the Masonic Club. The membership consisted of those prominent in the Scottish Rite, and the first duty of one joining the club was to send his picture to be hung upon the walls of the club room, and we finally had a very valuable collection of pictures. At this time, Dr. Fleming was in the height of his popularity—and was supported by Charley McClenachan, Henry Banks, George Millar, Bill May, Genl. Roome, D. Northrup and many others of note.

"I distinctly remember on a certain Sunday afternoon, my father coming downstairs and telling me that they were hatching, up in the club, a new order to be called the Mystic Shrine and that in his opinion unless they got rid of some of the 'barnacles,' they would find trouble in starting.

"I know my father was one of the original organizers of the Shrine and it was natural for all hands to meet at his place and 'talk it over.'"

Of course, after forty-four years, young Fowler's memory might leave something to accuracy. Dr. Fleming was new in New York, and he could not possibly have been at the height of his popularity. But there seems to be no doubt that it was at Knickerbocker Cottage that the Shrine was "hatched" and that it was around that table for thirteen that preliminary discussions were held until finally a formal meeting was held on June 16, 1871, at the old Masonic Hall on Thirteenth Street, a meeting at which they could not possibly have foreseen the glorious future of that which they were about to create.

This follows the formula in the creation of most organizations.

3

Imperial Council Formulated— Myths Begin

If any of the founders of the Shrine could have foreseen in 1871 that the organization eventually would grow to its present astounding size and importance, they would undoubtedly have kept better records. But they didn't and even those records that are available are subject to a certain amount of skepticism. For that reason, much is left to the imagination and a true picture of those early years can be drawn only by deduction from a few facts.

It is young Fowler's letter that really sets the stage for the story of the original "13" meeting around the table in his father's restaurant. It was there, then, that the first discussions must have been held concerning the new Ritual that Dr. Fleming says—in his own hand-writing—he wrote in August of 1870. How many times they discussed it, how many actual persons read the Ritual, how many were considered to be a part of the inner circle of even the nature of the discussions can only be left to speculation. But there appears to be no question that the first formal meeting of thirteen was held June 16, 1871. Fleming said so, and so did Paterson. The trouble is that their statements do not dovetail, and if any records of the affair were kept, they have been lost.

In his early history of the meeting, Paterson recalled that it was on that evening that it was decided to confine membership in the Shrine to men who had received advanced Masonic degrees, in either the York or Scottish Rite. On the other hand, Fleming reported to the second annual meeting of the Shrine's Imperial Council in 1877 that it was at the 1871 meeting that the Order was conferred on the thirteen Nobles, including Florence and himself. But at that time, Fleming was not a member of any of the Scottish or York Rite bodies, and it must be assumed that formal organization was delayed until he could acquire the higher degrees. That took something over a year to accomplish, and it was not until September 26, 1872, that Fleming called the original thirteen together again. Invitations were extended to Billy Florence, Sherwood C. Campbell, James S. Chappell, Oswald Merle d'Aubigne, Edward Eddy, Charles T. McClenachan, George W. Millar, John A. Moore, Albert P. Moriarty, William S. Paterson, Daniel Sickels, and John W. Simons. Of these thirteen, who according to Fleming had had the Shrine degree conferred on them at the first meeting in 1871, only eleven showed up. Florence was presumably on tour, but no reason is given for the absence of Sherwood Campbell.

The 1872 meeting, like the original one in 1871, was held at the old Masonic Hall on Thirteenth Street, and it was there that Mecca Temple, Ancient Arabic Order Nobles of the Mystic Shrine, was organized. Finally, at long last, Fleming's dream had come true. And even though vicissitudes of fortune might lie ahead, Fleming was so sure of success that minutes were kept in an old "order" book, still preserved in the Shrine Rooms of the George Washington National Masonic Memorial. These minutes are in Dr. Fleming's handwriting, but are signed by Paterson, who was elected Recorder (secretary) of the infant fraternity.

It was Fleming's Ritual and he called the boys together and thus he presided at the 1872 session. The object, he formally told them, was to form a temple to be known as Mecca, and he started the meeting by reading a letter of advice and instruction from Florence. Unfortunately, that letter or its contents have not been preserved—nor were its contents inserted into the minutes. If they had been, some of the controversy in later years might have been avoided. Of course the fact is that if such a letter ever existed, Fleming may simply have forgotten it when he wrote the minutes and turned them over to Paterson.

Eight of the eleven members present on September 26, 1872, were elected as officers of Mecca Temple. Fleming, of course, became the Grand Potentate, and it is likely that he had a slate of the other officers prepared. As the minutes show, those elected were: Charles T. McClenachan, Chief Rabban; John A. Moore, Assistant Rabban; William S. Paterson, Recorder; Edward Eddy, High Priest; James S. Chappell, Treasurer; George W. Millar, Oriental Guide; and Oswald M. d'Aubigne, Captain of the Guard.

The minutes record that the other offices were left vacant until a subsequent meeting "and there being no further business, the Temple was closed in harmony, subject to the call of the Grand Potentate."

Dr. Fleming now had his new Order underway. He must have gone home that evening with a sense of pride and fulfillment. But it was not to be easy sailing. Reporting to the Imperial Session in 1877, Fleming said that after that 1872 organizational meeting "the order remained quiet and inactive until within the past year or more, when on the return of Brother Florence from Europe, where he had witnessed the work exemplified in the most impressive form, he was exceedingly enthusiastic to promote the promulgation of the Order."

When Dr. Fleming reported that the Shrine had been quiet and inactive after its formation, he meant just that. The minutes of the meetings of Mecca Temple are quite revealing. The second session of the temple was not held until January 12, 1874, a year and a half after it was constituted. Again the meeting was held at Masonic Hall on Thirteenth Street, when McClenachan moved that a committee be appointed to revise and perfect the Ritual and to facilitate the exemplification of the Order. The third session was called for December 13, 1875, at the new Masonic Temple on Twenty-third Street, but a quorum failed to show up, according to the minutes, and so the meeting resolved itself into an informal discussion of matters relative to the Order and "the session closed in harmony."

From these minutes and Fleming's own statement that the Order had remained inactive until 1875, it might be presumed that the doctor was too busy with his private practice and his duties in the Columbian Commandery and Scottish Rite to give much attention to his own brain child. But this is not exactly true. According to James McGee, No. 28 in the Mecca Temple roster, Fleming was constantly busy creating new members. In a letter to Saram R. Ellison, Recorder of Mecca Temple, in 1914, McGee wrote that the Shrine "became general anteroom talk at all Scottish Rite and Commandery gatherings. Fleming kept tab at many of these occasions on scraps of paper, putting them down as regular meetings and in later years styling them as first and second meetings at Masonic Hall, 114 East Thirteenth Street. This was where the Scottish Rite held their meetings. . . . These crude memorandums were all in the handwriting of Noble Fleming and were passed over to Noble Paterson, who became Recorder, to dress up with some degree of regularity and arrange as best he could to make a creditable showing. . . . The same looseness prevailed in keeping a record of those on whom Noble Fleming had conferred the Order. The slips or memorandums, same as the so-called meetings, were handed to Paterson and he collated them the best he could to show connecting links. No fees were charged. . . . It was natural that errors should creep in, but no one complained, forgetting there was a hereafter."

Nevertheless, in the first report of membership, which was not rendered until September of 1876, there were only forty-three Nobles, all but six of them in New York City. Furthermore, Fleming reported on the lack of activity in the Shrine during the first four years of Mecca Temple, from the scene and at the time, while McGee wrote from memory when he already was an old man. McGee's letters to Ellison are important because they also reflect on the controversy which developed in later years on the true history of the Shrine. In any event, Fleming called a fourth meeting of Mecca Temple to be held June 6, 1876, at the Masonic Temple in New York, and it was at that meeting that the Imperial Grand Council came into existence. In the light of his own statement of lack of activity and the "exceeding enthusiasm" of Florence to promote the promulgation of the Order, it is to be presumed that Florence called on Fleming after his return from a European tour and said, in effect, "Hey, what gives? Let's get going or drop the whole idea." Fleming got going. As Ralph Waldo Emerson declared "Nothing great was ever achieved without great enthusiasm."

The proceedings of that meeting of Mecca Temple and the formation of the Imperial Grand Council are intact and are rewarding in the light of later developments. These proceedings record that: "Pursuant to a call of the Past Potentates and legally constituted Nobles of the Ancient Arabic Order of the Nobles of the Mystic Shrine, the following named Nobles of the Order assembled at Masonic Hall, corner of Sixth Avenue and Twenty-third Street, in the City of New York, N.Y., on Nahar et Talata, the sixteenth day of the fifth Arabic Month, Jamaz ul Awwal, [sic] 1293 A.H., answering to Tuesday, June 6, 1876 A.D., at two o'clock P.M., for the purpose of organizing the Imperial Grand Council ƒ the Ancient Arabic Order of the Nobles of the Mystic rine for the United States of America."

This was the first occasion in the four years since its formation that the Shrine had used any Arabic nomenclature except in the Ritual itself, and even in the Ritual some of the words, phrases and titles that were supposed to give connotations of the Orient were in fact Hebrew rather than Arabic. For example, the titles of Chief and Assistant Rabbans, the second and third highest offices, have no Arabic translation, but in the Hebrew tongue refer to teachers.

Only twenty Nobles attended that first session of the Imperial Grand Council. They were Fleming, Paterson, and McClenachan, of course; and, in addition, George W. Millar, John A. Moore, William V. Alexander, John E. Bendix, Edwin Du Laurens, Edward M. L. Ehlers, Peter Forrester, William Fowler, William D. May, Sidney P. Nichols, Aaron L. Northrop, James A. Reed, W. Wallace Walker, J. H. Hobart Ward, all of New York City; George F. Loder, Grand Potentate of Damascus Temple, Rochester, New York; Samuel R. Carter, also of Damascus Temple; and George Scott of Paterson, New Jersey. Mecca members absent at the first Imperial meeting were (according to the proceedings) William J. Florence, Bensen Sherwood, Philip F. Lenhart, Charles P. Marratt, and Angelo Noziglia.

Conspicuous by its absence from the list of those either present or absent is the name of James McGee; for according to the records of Mecca Temple, McGee was just as much a member at that time as any of the rest and around this very point hinges some of the controversy that was to develop in later years. In any event, McGee held card No. 28. Marratt held card No. 29, and William D. May, card No. 30. Also conspicuous by its absence from either list is the name of William T. Hardenbrook, who carried card No. 25 and who was the editor of a Masonic newspaper and participated with McGee and others in the controversy over the history of the Shrine.

The official proceedings of the first session of the Imperial Council then report: "A Temple was opened in due form, Illustrious Walter M. Fleming, Grand Potentate of Mecca Temple presiding." Fleming announced the deaths of Sherwood Campbell, James S. Chappell, Oswald d'Aubigne and Edward Eddy, after which "The Imperial Grand Council of the Ancient Arabic Order of the Nobles of the Mystic Shrine for the United States of America was then duly organized."

Yet that organization just possibly might have been premature. Officially, the only members of the Shrine present were from Mecca and Damascus Temples and on the face of it there was no real need for a national organization. But Fleming was prepared for any objections that might arise. He had created Nobles in several other cities, and had given them titles of "Past Potentates" so that they might create their own temples in other cities. And with that in mind, he submitted his slate of candidates for Imperial Grand officers. Those elected were: Walter M. Fleming, Imperial Grand Potentate; George F. Loder of Rochester, Deputy Grand Potentate; Philip F. Lenhart of Brooklyn, Grand Chief Rabban; Edward M. L. Ehlers, New York, Grand Assistant Rabban; William H. Whiting, Rochester, New York, Grand High Priest and Prophet; Samuel R. Carter, Rochester, New York, Grand Oriental Guide; Aaron L. Northrop, New York, New York, Grand Treasurer; William S. Paterson, New York, New York, Grand Recorder; Albert P. Moriarty, New York, New York, Grand Financial Secretary; John L. Stettinius, Cincinnati, Ohio, Grand First Ceremonial Master; Bensen Sherwood, New York, New York, Grand Second Ceremonial Master; Samuel Harper, Pittsburgh, Pennsylvania, Grand Marshal; Frank H. Bascom, Montpelier, Vermont, Grand Captain of the Guard; and George Scott, Paterson, New Jersey, Grand Outer Guard.

The first meeting of the Imperial Council didn't last long, but there was certain groundwork to be done, and the nobility got right to the task. The officers, or those who were present, were installed by McClenachan, the ritualist, who didn't take an office, presumably because he was too busy with other affairs.

The meeting then took care of the following business:

Established New York City as the Grand Orient, or headquarters of the Imperial Council;

Approved a plan to create five Past Potentates in each subordinate temple in order that they could be made honorary members of the Imperial Council;

Created a committee to write statutes and regulations for the government of the Imperial Council and its subordinate temples, whereupon Fleming appointed McClenachan, Ehlers and Ward to that task;

Established fifty dollars as the fee for a charter for a new temple, ten dollars as the annual temple tax to the Imperial Council, and ten dollars as the minimum initiation fee for each new member;

Passed a resolution making it official throughout the United States that all Shriners must be members in good standing of either the Scottish Rite or Knights Templar.

Business completed, the boys dispensed with the reading of the proceedings, closed their session and presumably retired for some of the fun they all expected to have when they became Shriners.

Thus was born an organization which, over the years, though not Masonic, would become the playground and the showcase of Masonry. Trials and tribulations lay ahead. There were days and even years of discouragement for Fleming, for in the infancy of the Shrine, he carried the burden almost alone. There was no exemplification of rites. There was no money, except what Fleming and a few others contributed from their pockets. There were no insignia by which Shriners could be designated. Very simply, Fleming and his associates didn't have much of an inducement for prospective members. Mostly, new members were obtained by personal contact where Fleming's magnetic personality would become the motivating force. But this was too slow. The Shrine would never become great under those circumstances.

Something new was needed, something that would attract prospective Nobles by its glamour and its promise for the future. Thus it was that sometime during the fall and winter of 1876, Fleming began to devise a plan and—perhaps with the help of Florence, Paterson, McClenachan and others—to create a legend. He surrounded the Shrine with mysticism as thrilling as the Ritual itself. It was real cloak-and-dagger stuff. And though the stories he told were to be challenged in later years and called figments of his own fertile imagination, they did attract members. Even Fleming changed his stories from time to time, and he made greater use of the great name of Billy Florence—originally for the single purpose of promoting the growth of the Shrine. But, since Fleming told his stories with such sincerity, there were many who accepted them as historic fact. Others did not. Ergo, Mark Twain's advice: "Truth if very precious, use it sparingly."

Even as late as 1892 when controversy over the legend reached its height, Charles T. McClenachan declared it made no real difference whether the stories might be true and that the Shrine Ritual contained no more myth or fiction than Blue Lodge Masonry, the Chapter, the Commandery or even the Christian religion. McClenachan, who was an authority, held that no ritual need be strictly the truth and that few ever were. But there are always those who insist on absolute truth. They are the ones who say George Washington never chopped down the cherry tree or threw a dollar over the Rappahannock; they are probably right, but history was not damaged by such legends, and if they placed a halo of honesty and strength about the head of Washington, which would reflect itself in the eyes of American youth for generations to come, who is to say the creation of the myth was wrong?

4

Ankh

The legend of the origin of the Ancient Arabic Order Nobles of the Mystic Shrine begins with the second annual session of the Imperial Grand Council, held at the Masonic Temple in Albany, New York, February 6, 1877. The legend was given voice by Dr. Fleming in his first annual address, reporting on his activities. The circumstances of how he arrived at the content of the speech delivered that cold winter day, climatically so different from the hot sands of the strange Islamic world of the Arabs, are lost, if they were ever known, but it was the first effort to surround the new American order with authentic antiquity.

"It is some five years," Dr. Fleming said, "since I came into possession of detached and mutilated sections of the translation of the Ritual of the Arabic and Egyptian Order of the Mystic Shrine, brought to America by one of the foreign members and representatives, through the hands of Brother Oswald Merle D'Aubigne, 32°. It was exceedingly imperfect and incomplete and to a great extent badly translated and filled with unintelligible symbolisms. Another portion was brought from Oriental Europe by Ill. Brother William J. Florence, 32° and some of the vague history and Ritualistic sections were brought from Cairo, Egypt, by Ill. Brother Sherwood C. Campbell, 32°. Those portions in the possession of Brother Florence were marked, and referred to certain sections of the Koran for notes and allusions, which greatly facilitated the compiling and revising of the Ritual to its present completion. And then there was Ankh, ancient Egyptian ring symbolizing good luck, fruitful growth, and prosperity to guide them.

"This was a task of no small magnitude, and was undertaken and completed through the efforts of Brother Florence and myself, aided by a professional linguist and Arabic scholar."

Just whom Fleming meant in his reference to a professional linguist and Arabic scholar is not known. It might have been Paterson, who did know some Arabic; but as it later developed, it probably was Albert L. Rawson, an artist who had illustrated several books dealing with early Mediterranean religions. Rawson was not a Shriner at the time but became one later and participated actively with Fleming in publicizing the Order.

Fleming, in his address, went on to relate the circumstances and dates of the founding of Mecca Temple and the formation of the Imperial Council, and then he said:

"The original plate engravings, for the production of Dispensations, Charters and Diplomas of the Imperial Grand Council, were executed in Paris, France, and the designs were taken from the arches and gateways of the Egyptian Temple of the Sun and Ankh. The printing and colored transfers were perfected in the City of New York, where also the Statutes and Ritual were printed and the Grand Seal procured."

Only a few copies of the original charters are still in existence. Some of them have been destroyed by fire, and others have been lost. Those extant are really works of art, and may well have been the product of Rawson, some of whose art work, illustrating a volume on the Eleusinian theory of esoteric religion, is similar in style to the original charters.

Fleming also reported in 1877 on more earthy problems. He said that the work since the formation of

Mecca Temple had involved both a large expenditure and accruing indebtedness; but, he said, a few hundred dollars would place the Imperial Grand Council out of debt for the obligations of the past. It is noteworthy that Fleming contributed most of the expenses of the formation of the Order, and that he was not to be repaid the advances for a number of years.

But the Shrine was growing, Fleming reported. The second temple to be formed was Damascus at Rochester, but dispensations also had been granted to Al Koran in Cleveland, Syrian in Cincinnati, Mount Sinai in Montpelier, Vermont, and Naja and Cyprus in Albany.

The good doctor may or may not have been slightly embarrassed by some of the report he had to make. He said, for example:

"All who have received the Order are evidently exceedingly well pleased with the impressiveness of the Ritualistic work and the sublime tenets of the Order. It could no doubt be made a most powerful Order, devoted to the welfare of Masonry in this country.

"Mecca Temple," Dr. Fleming said, "is not exemplifying the work at present, as the matter was left entirely to one or two others and myself, and my time has been so fully occupied with the duties of Most Illustrious Grand Potentate, in promoting the establishment of temples, and the various requirements of the Imperial Grand Council, that it was impossible for me to carry on the work at home in a subordinate temple."

Dr. Fleming also explained that he thought the Shrine should be exclusive.

"It has been the desire," he said, "of the Grand Council as well as the membership subordinate to make it a select Order, uncontaminated with discordant elements and unworthy membership. There should be at least one branch of Ancient Craftsmen, select and free of the inappreciative and the unworthy. We trust, therefore, that, as it is a consummation most devoutly to be wished for, all will proceed with care, caution and judgment, in regard to whom they honor with admission."

By and large, it was the most successful meeting of the Shrine to that time. It had taken Fleming six long years to bring the infant Order thus far, but he could return to his medical practice in New York, confident that the new fraternity was on its way. It was to grow beyond the wildest imaginations of its founders, who "builded better than they knew" in the early days. Certainly one of the factors of that building was the aura of Oriental mysticism that Fleming had injected at the Albany session.

A half-century later, McGee declared that Fleming eventually regretted having mentioned the story of the Ancient Arabic manuscripts; but upon his return to New York from Albany he wrote or with Paterson helped to write the "origin and history" of the Order, which was included in a brochure obviously designed to spread and build it. It contained the statutes and regulations which had been adopted in Albany and full particulars on how new temples could be established. But the important part of the brochure was the embellishment of the legend. This 1877 brochure, which was found among the Paterson papers, reports:

The Order of Nobles of the Mystic Shrine was established in Mecca, Arabia, and became an acknowledged power in the year 5459, equivalent to the year of Our Lord 1698.

The Ritual was compiled and arranged at Aleppo, Arabia, and issued by Louis Marracci, the great Latin translator of Mohammed's Al Koran. This mysterious Order continued to thrive in Arabia from that date to the present time. It was revised and instituted at Cairo, Egypt, in 5598, equivalent to June 14, 1837.

The Order was primarily instituted for the purpose of promoting the organization and perfection of Arabic and Egyptian inquisitions, to dispense justice, and execute punishment of criminals whom the tardy laws did not reach to the measure of their crimes. Being designed to embrace the entire pale of the law, and composed of sterling and determined men who would upon a valid accusation fearlessly try, judge, and if convicted, execute the criminal within the hour—leaving no trace of their acts behind. . . .

More recent history informs us that Oriental Europe is permeated with secret organizations, comprising a selection of the highest and best educated classes of the Mussulman nations; their ostensible object being "the strife of Islam or Mohammedanism against the infidels"; and among the latter are supposed to be included Christians, Israelites, Mussulman princes and potentates, who are suspected, together with the Khedive of Egypt, of being favorable to Christian institutions.

The most prominent and powerful of these orders is the Bektashy, or Nobles of the Mystic Shrine. Its offshoots and satellites are the Darkawy, Khowan, Abd el Kader El Bagdadi, and the Issawiye, similar in obligation and purpose. These are not altogether politico-religious societies as generally supposed by the outside world. Although ostensibly appearing as such there is a deep and hidden meaning beneath the exposed superficial exterior, as promulgated to the profane.

These orders are closely allied to the famous "Illuminati," which fraternity exercised such vigilant power during the reign of King Frederick William of Prussia.

The real object of all of these Orders is to gain all possible power of reign and rule; to exercise these powers for the best welfare of country or land; and to fearlessly purify it of all base and sordid element of whatever nature, independent of creed, sect or nationality; their foundation being the acknowledgment of Deity or one ever-loving and true God. . . .

The Bektashy, or Nobles of the Mystic Shrine, as it is known in America, is of necessity divested of its inconsistent Islam dogmas and its ritual adapted to the consistencies of Christian institutions and American laws, and is destined to become a powerful order here in America.

Its jewel of membership, or the insignia of the order worn by its disciples, is the Crescent, formed by the claws of a tiger, united at the bases and bound with gold, bearing the additional emblems of the head of a female Sphinx, on one side a pyramid, urn, and star upon the other, also bearing the date of the reception of the order and the

Latin motto "Robur et Furor"—signifying strength and fury.

This particular history then includes considerable detail concerning the origin of the Crescent as a symbol of power and authority, and it goes on to say:

In 1801 the Sultan Selim III, having previously presented Lord Nelson with a crescent richly adorned with diamonds, founded the Order of the Crescent, which, as Mohammedans are not allowed to carry such marks of distinction, has been conferred on Christians alone.

Temples of the Order of the Crescent, or Nobles of the Mystic Shrine, were instituted in various cities of Europe many years ago, and now, although possessing all the powers, material and paraphernalia of the Inquisition, if required, still continue to thrive as social and charitable organizations, impressing on its disciples its purifying tenets and attributes, while always on the alert to arouse into executive action should an emergency arise.

In 1871 the Ritual was brought to America by one of the transient foreign members and representatives with instructions to place it only in the hands of prominent highgrade Masons for establishment and exemplification as had been done in Europe. Owing to the fact of Masons being regarded as a choice of the best men in the land, and having already passed the ordeal of obligation, the Order of Nobles of the Mystic Shrine would be regarded as safer with them than with the unobligated masses, and make it, if necessity required, a deliberating and executive body of inquisitorial nature, as when originally inaugurated.

The 1877 history is similar in content, but not in style or spelling, to a history of the Order printed in 1893 which had been "compiled and collated" by Fleming and Paterson, and it is this latter "origin of the Order" which over the years has been most quoted. In 1902, Fleming wrote a letter to George L. Root of Mohammed Temple, Peoria, Illinois, authorizing him to use the later version in a book he was preparing. Fleming wrote: "I am in receipt of yours of the 13th inst. relative to using my 'History of the Shrine.' Personally I have no objections, especially if for distribution to the Nobles of the Order. I do not think Noble Paterson would object if credited to its authors."

The legend of the Shrine became permanent with the publication of this later history. It probably was written in 1883 while Fleming was still the Imperial Potentate, for it is mentioned in the official proceedings of that year, but the first known publication came in a pamphlet issued by Imperial Recorder Frank Luce, who had succeeded Paterson. It is dated 1893.

That history says:

> The Order of the Nobles of the Mystic Shrine was instituted by the Mohammedan Kalif Alee (whose name be praised!), the cousin-german and son-in-law of the Prophet Mohammed (God favor and preserve him!), in the year of the Hegira 25 (A.D. 644) at Mecca in Arabia, as an inquisition, or Vigilance Committee, to dispense justice and execute punishment upon criminals who escaped their just deserts through the tardiness of the courts, and also to promote religious tolerance among cultured men of all nations. The original intention was to form a band of men of sterling worth who would, without fear or favor, upon a valid accusation, try, judge, and execute, if need be, within the hour, having taken precautions as to secrecy and security.
>
> The "Nobles" perfected their organization, and did such prompt and efficient work that they excited alarm and even consternation in the hearts of evildoers in all countries under the Star and Crescent.
>
> The Order is yet one of the most highly favored among the many secret societies which abound in Oriental countries, and gathers around its shrines a select few of the best educated and cultured classes. Their ostensible object is to increase the faith and fidelity of all true believers in Allah (whose name be exalted!). The secret and real purpose can only be made known to those who have encircled the Mystic Shrine according to instructions in "The Book of the Constitution and the Regulations of the Imperial Council."
>
> Its membership in all countries includes Christians, Isra-

elites, Moslems and men in high positions of learning and power. One of the most noted patrons of the Order was the late Khedive of Egypt (whose name be revered!) whose inclination toward Christians is well known.

The Nobles of the Mystic Shrine was sometimes mistaken for a certain order of the dervishes, such as those known as the Hanafeeyeh, Rufaeeyeh, Sadireeyeh, and others, either howling, whirling, dancing or barking; but this is an error. The only connection that the Order ever had with any sect of dervishes was with that called the Bektash. This warlike sect undertook to favor and protect the Nobles in a time of great peril, and have ever since been counted among its most honored patrons.

The famous Arab known as Bektash, from a peculiar high white hat or cap which he made from a sleeve of his gown, the founder of the sect named in his honor, was an imam in the army of the Sultan Amurath I, the first Mohammedan who led an army into Europe, A.D. 1360 (in the year of the Hegira, 761). This Sultan was the founder of the military order of the Janizaries (so called because they were freed captives who were adopted into the faith and the army), although his father Orkham began the work. Bektash adopted a white robe and cap, and instituted the ceremony of kissing the sleeve.

The Bektasheeyeh's representative at Mecca is a Noble of the Mystic Shrine, is the chief officer of the Alee Temple of Nobles, and in 1877 was the chief of the Order in Arabia. The chief must reside either at Mecca or Medinah, and, in either case must be present in person or by deputy during the month of pilgrimage.

The character of the Order as it appears to the uninitiated is that of a politico-religious society. It is really more than such a society could be; and there are hidden meanings in its simplest symbols that take hold on the profoundest depths of the heart.

Among the modern promoters of the principles of the Order in Europe, one of the most noted was Herr Adam Weishaupt, a Rosicrucian (Rose Cross Mystic), and professor of law in the University of Ingolstadt, in Bavaria, who revived the Order in that city on May 1, 1776. Its members exercised a profound influence before and during the French Revolution, when they were known as the Illuminati, and they professed to be teachers of philosophy. From the central society at Ingolstadt, branches spread through all Europe. Among the members, there are recorded the names of Frederick the Great, Mirabeau, a Duke of Orleans, many members of royal families, literary, scientific and professional men, including the illustrious Goethe, Spinoza, Kant, Lord Bacon, and a long list besides, whose works enlarge and free the mind from the influence of dogma and prejudice.

Frequent revolutions in Arabia, Persia and Turkey have obscured the Order from time to time, as appears from the many breaks in the continuity of the records at Mecca, but it has often been revived. Some of the most noted revivals are those at Mecca and Aleppo in A.D. 1698 (A.H. 1110) and at Cairo in 1837 (A.H. 1253), the latter under the protection of the Khedive of Egypt, who recognized the Order as a powerful means of civilization.

In the year A.D. 804, during a warlike expedition against the Byzantine emperor Nikephorous, the most famous Arabian Kalif, Haroon al-Rasheed, deputed a renowned scholar, Abd el-Kader el-Bagdadee, to proceed to Aleppo, Syria and found a college there for the propagation of the religion of the Prophet Mohammed (God favor and preserve him!). The work and college arose and the Order of Nobles was revived there as a part of the means of civilization.

The Order of Nobles of the Mystic Shrine in America does not advocate Mohammedanism as a sect, but inculcates the same respect to Deity here as in Arabia and elsewhere, and hence the secret of its profound grasp on the intellect and the heart of all cultured people.

The Ritual now in use is a translation from the original Arabic, found preserved in the archieves of the Order at Aleppo, Syria, whence it was brought in 1860, to London, England, by Rizk Allah Hassoon Effendi, who was the author of several works in Arabic, one of which was a metrical version of the Book of Job. His "History of Islam" offended the Turkish government because of its humanitarian principles, and he was forced to leave his native country.

In the year 1698, the learned Orientalist, Luigi Marracci, who was then just completing his great works, "The Koran in Latin and Arabic with notes," and "The Bible in Arabic" at Padua, Italy, was initiated into our Order of Nobles, and found time to translate the Ritual into Italian. The initiated will be able to see how deeply significant this fact is when the history of the Italian society of "Carbonari" is recalled. The very existence of Italian unity and liberty depended largely on the "Nobles" who were represented by Count Cavour, Mazzini, Garibaldi and the king, Victor Emmanuel.

Although Marracci was confessor to his Holiness, Pope Innocent XI, for several years, yet he was censored by the College of the Propaganda at Rome for having aided and abetted the work of a secret society, and the book was condemned to be burnt. A few copies were saved and one is still preserved in the library of the Synagogue, which stands just inside the ancient Roman gate of the City of Babloon, called by the Arabs Fostat, in the Middle Ages, and now known as Old Cairo.

In making the present version, the translator has had the benefit of the work of Alnasafi, of Marracci and of Hassoon. The rendering is literal where the idiom permitted, except where a local reference required the substitution of American for Oriental names of cities.

The work was perfected in August, 1870, under the supervision of Dr. Walter M. Fleming, 33°, Sovereign Grand Inspector General, A.A.S. Rite, and past Eminent Commander of Columbian Commandery No. 1, Knights Templar, New York, who received his instructions and authority from Rizk Allah Hassoon Effendee, who has competent jurisdiction for America.

The Ritual is known in Arabia as "The Pillar of Society," which is an honorary title given only to persons of very great distinction in the service of truth, justice and mercy, and the support of learning and culture, and was by courtesy attached to this work as originally written by the renowned Alnasafi Hafiz, the Persian poet.

The salutation of distinction among the faithful is: "Es Selamu Aleikum!" (Peace be with you!), to which is returned the gracious wish, "Aleikum es Selamu!" (With you be peace!).

The jewel of the Order is a crescent, formed of any substance. The most valued materials are the claws of a Royal Bengal tiger, united at their bases in a gold setting which includes their tips, and bears on one side of the center the head of a sphinx, and on the other a pyramid, urn and star, with the date of the wearer's reception of the Order, and the motto:

Arabic—"Kuwat wa Ghadab."
Latin—"Robur et Furor."
English—"Strength and fury."

The constitutional authority for promulgation of the principles and practice of the Order was confided to Dr. Walter M. Fleming, 33°, and his associates, William J. Florence, 32°; Edward Eddy, 33°; John W. Simons, 33°; Sherwood C. Campbell, 32°; Oswald Merle d'Aubigne, 32°; James S. Chappell, 32°; John A. Moore, 32° (the last seven have since entered the unseen temple); Charles T. McClenachan, 33°; Albert P. Moriarty, 33°; Daniel Sickels, 33°; George W. Millar, 33°; and William S. Paterson, 33°; together with Albert R. Rawson, 32° (the Arabic translator), all prominent Ancient Accepted Scottish Rite Masons and Knights Templar of New York, N. Y., who instituted the first temple of the Order in that city under the title of "Mecca Temple, Nobles of the Mystic Shrine," on Sept. 26, 1872.

Ill. Walter M. Fleming, 33°, was chosen its presiding officer, who is also called "The Shayk, or the Ancient," and also the Illustrious Potentate. He is known in the Persian temples as "The Shayk Alee," that is to say, the supreme Shayk. Ill. William S. Paterson, 33° was elected the Recorder.

On June 6, 1876, "The Imperial Council for North America" was formed, and the first officers elected (as in Arabia) for the term of three years. Ill. Walter M. Fleming became Imperial Potentate, and Ill. W. S. Paterson, Imperial Recorder.

The prerequisite for membership in Europe, Asia, Africa and America is the 32° A.A.S. Rite (18 in England), or a Knight Templar in good standing.

The generous proposition to make the Order of Nobles an organization for the exercise of charity, the improvement of the mind, and an ally of the Fraternity of Free Masonry in the United States, was primarily adopted by the Imperial Council.

This then was the history prepared by Fleming and Paterson. Fact? Well, hardly. Noted Arabic scholars in the United States in 1958 could find little if any fact in Fleming's report. Fancy, fiction, myth, legend? All of these. But what difference? The Shrine was formed as an organization where Masons might seclude themselves from the cares of the world and as Masons enjoy each other's company in good fun.

This then was the cloak-and-dagger stuff, but it is to be noted that in this rendition of the history of the Shrine, Billy Florence played a comparatively inconspicuous part. Yet Florence (with Fleming's help) had tried to get in the act a year earlier. In 1882 Florence wrote a letter for publication in the official proceedings of 1883:

> . . . I have long promised myself the task of writing a brief account of the first glimpses I had of the working of our Order, while on a tour in Europe some years since, and now give a portion thereof.
>
> In September, 1870, I was in the city of Marseilles, France, and having occasion to call on Duncan, Sherman & Co., Bankers, I was told by one of the gentlemanly clerks that there was to be a ceremony of an unusually attractive character, at a hall near the Grand Hotel de l'Univers, and knowing me to be a Mason, invited me to be present, offering to be my guide and voucher. My curiosity was excited by his glowing hints as to the Oriental wonders to be seen there, and I really cannot say whether I ate any dinner or not that evening, so anxious was I to keep the appointment.
>
> Having been introduced to the anteroom of the hall, in which the Mystic Shrine was concealed, I found a number of distinguished persons in animated conversation on the subject of our visit. One of these men was the British Consul at that port, another the Austrian Vice-Consul, and there were dukes and counts, bankers and merchants, scholars and artists, musicians and other professionals, all of whom seemed absorbed in the question of how the French of Marseilles had succeeded in getting possession of such interesting secrets.
>
> The Illustrious Grand Potentate of the evening was the celebrated Yusef Churi Bey, and the Temple was called Bokhara Shrine.
>
> Shayk Yusef had visited Bokhara, where he was a mem-

ber of the Mystic Shrine in that famous city of the Persians, and brought away a hastily written sketch of the Ritual and Laws of the Order. It would be impossible to give a complete narrative of the ceremonies of that Communication of the Nobles of Bakhara Shrine, and I must content myself with a mere outline.

The costumes were exact duplicates of Oriental patterns brought from Persia by Yusef Bey. In his long service as an attaché of the Persian Consulate, he had seen many countries, and profited by studies and observations in each, and was therefore well fitted to conduct such an institution.

The furniture of the Temple was the most peculiar I ever saw, and must have been gotten up by some one well skilled in stage scenery, for there were very well contrived dramatic effects, representing the sandy seashore, the rough, rocky hillside, the gloomy cavern, the solemn tomb, and a transformation scene which was at first a cemetery, full of tombs and monuments inscribed with the names of the departed, with epitaphs on their virtues and worth, when in an instant, the lights having been lowered, the scene changed to a sumptuous banqueting hall, with small tables for groups of 3, 5, 7, and 9.

I need not describe the work of the Temple any further than to say, that the intention is to enact a drama very much like our own, which had for its object the same lesson; and there can be no better or more zealous workers in a good cause than those French brothers who celebrated the Mysteries at Marseilles on that evening.

My duties prevented a sufficiently long stay in Marseilles to witness a second performance, and I therefore begged Yusef Bey to allow me to have a copy of the Ritual and Laws, which I received on the day I sailed for Algiers.

In Algiers the Shrine of the Mogribins was in full operation, meeting each week, on Friday evening. Abu Mohammed Baki was the Shayk, and among the members were nearly every one of the many consuls, vice-consuls, and other diplomats of the port, many of the most noted merchants and bankers, and not a few of the learned and gifted Mohammedans, who are passionately fond of perpetuating ancient customs which increase their social pleasures.

The Shrine is referred to by the Moslems generally as "The Order of the Unwritten Law," in distinction from the "Written Law," which is the Koran.

The costumes and furniture of the Shrine in Algiers were

gorgeous in silk, wool, and fine linen, decorated with embroidery in gold, silver and colors; and the swords, spears, and other articles used by the guards and officers in the work were genuine steel, many of which had been in actual service in the field of battle. . . .

There were many more letters in the same vein and as often as not in similar language. There was one addressed to Fleming from Abd-el-Makri, writing for the Shayk Mohammed Baki of the Shrine at Algiers, reporting that "during the past three months, many of the most wealthy and famous men of this province, including nearly every officer of the government" had become members. And quite modestly Florence reported that he had been made an honorary member of both the Shrine of the Mogribins in Algiers and the Bokhara Shrine in Marseilles.

Also printed in the official proceedings of the Shrine of North America for the year 1882 were letters, addressed to Fleming, reporting on Shrine activities in Cairo, Alexandria, Jerusalem and Damascus. And such reports revealed as much as anything else that not only in North America, but throughout the Islamic world there was a revival of the Shrine as originally created by the Kalif Ali.

"It is a pleasure to be able to inform you," said the letter from Cairo, "of the reestablishment of our order generally throughout the Eastern world, nearly every kingdom or sovereignty being now represented at the General Assembly of Nobles, which meets once in three years at Mecca." And there was one rather down-to-earth notation that "the banquets during the year have been catered by Ismail Tibneen, chef de cuisine, to His Highness the Khedive." Fleming learned from the letter that the Shrine at Alexandria held its meetings in the ancient palace of the Ptolemies.

Oh, there was more. Much more. And every word was designed to convince American Masons of high degree that membership in the Ancient Arabic Order

Nobles of the Mystic Shrine was of considerable importance. The translations printed in the Proceedings presumably were by Rawson the artist, but if the originals were ever preserved, they have not been discovered.

Between 1882 and 1892, there also appeared in the official Proceedings of the Imperial Council letters from John Worthington, a member of Mecca Temple and the United States Consul on the island of Malta in the Mediterranean. As it later developed Worthington was quite a personage and, perhaps inadvertently, the cause of much of the furor that was to come over the myths and legends that were being created.

Worthington's letters reported on visitations made to Shrine Temples throughout the Mediterranean area. They also reported expenses for the entertainment of visiting Nobles who stopped briefly at the island of Malta to obtain a pass which would gain them entrance to the various Shrines in that part of the world. For his work in entertaining the visiting Nobles and for visiting the various temples of the East on behalf of Fleming, and as his deputy, Worthington was paid five hundred dollars a year from the Imperial Treasury. But alas and alack, Worthington failed to report just which Nobles were entertained, and in so far as the records show, there was but one. Furthermore, in the light of later developments, the pass wasn't much to start with. Today's Arabic scholars declare its inscriptions are better as art work than as grammar and that they probably were made by some Algerian sailor who stopped off in Malta. Today's Arabic scholars go further. After reading the translations printed in the Proceedings, they state unequivocally that there is no historic fact to support any of the statements, places or names contained in all of the various letters. And perhaps most important of all is the fact that none of the Arabic originals has ever been found.

After Sam Briggs of Al Koran Temple in Cleveland succeeded Fleming as Imperial Potentate in 1886, he continued these reports from the East and continued to pay Worthington his five hundred dollars a year; but when William B. Melish of Syrian Temple of Cincinnati succeeded Briggs in 1892, he indicated forthwith that he was tired of all the "rot and rubbish" and intended to put an end to it, perhaps even going so far as to issue an official pronouncement proclaiming as false all matters that had pertained to the Oriental origin of the Shrine.

Augustus Peters, who had succeeded Fleming as Potentate of Mecca Temple, was upset, and to prevent any such action by Melish he sent Charles T. McClenachan and George W. Millar to Cincinnati to interview him. McClenachan penned the report of that interview.

"It appears," he wrote, "that the Imperial Potentate desires to make the organization of the Shrine a gentlemen's club on a Sunday School plan, which is entirely at variance with the views of your committee, and, as they believe, of the great majority of the Order. We believe we are in touch with the originators of the subordinate temples in this country, that the Oriental myth is one of the most essential portions of the institution, that to eliminate the myth is to emasculate the Order to such an extent that its progress would not only be stopped but that the society would fail and die out. Whatever there is of truth as well as whatever there is of myth, must be retained."

McClenachan said it was against all expediency to tell our youth that William Tell never shot the apple off the head of his son or that George Washington never chopped down the cherry tree, and that it was just as expedient to eliminate the myth of the Shrine.

Melish was unimpressed. He told his visitors that he understood and believed that Noble Florence and three or four others, sitting around a table in New York, had in a jolly way concocted the Ritual and started the Society. He asked McClenachan if he knew of a Ritual that Florence had brought to this country or if he believed Florence had ever been initiated in Beyrouth. Yes, indeed, said McClenachan. He firmly believed that Florence had been initiated in Beyrouth or somewhere else, and that he had brought a Ritual to this country.

Still unimpressed, Melish told the Mecca Committee that "all this Oriental and Eastern stuff was humbug and rot," that there were no Eastern temples, and in his opinion Worthington should be stopped from writing his rubbish; that we had better come down to a gentlemen's society and stop talking Oriental nonsense. He said Sam Briggs had told him that whenever a Potentate asked about the myth of the Shrine he always replied that there was no truth to the story.

McClenachan and Millar were generally unhappy about the interview with Imperial Potentate Melish and frankly said that the impression left on the committee was that Melish was not a Shrine enthusiast. Certainly there were to be repercussions of the visit at the Imperial Council session held in Cincinnati in 1893, when Mecca Temple and others joined hands to defeat Melish for reelection.

Amazingly enough, no mention is made in McClenachan's report of Dr. Fleming, who had only recently retired as Potentate of Mecca Temple. It would have been logical to assume that McClenachan and Millar, who had been so intimately associated with the founder of the Order, might at least have mentioned him in their conversations with Imperial Potentate Melish. But it was not to be. As a matter of fact, after Fleming had turned over the power in the Shrine to Sam Briggs in 1886, he attended only one imperial session of the Shrine. That was in 1893 when he helped organize the opposition to Melish.

After the death of Dr. Fleming in 1913, the battle over the truth or falsity of the Fleming-Florence tradition raged on. Dr. Saram Ellison, revered Recorder of Mecca Temple, and Louis N. Donnatin, who succeeded Ellison, acquired extensive collections in an attempt to prove that Florence was initiated into some Oriental mystery and conveyed that idea to Fleming. At the same time James McGee fought all the way to the floor of the Imperial Council in an attempt to disprove it. He even wrote his own history of the Shrine.

In essence, McGee simply contended that Fleming and Fleming alone created the Shrine, that Florence's only significant contribution was the use of his name and that eventually Fleming regretted having introduced the Oriental myths and legends concerning its origin. And some years later McGee was given concrete support by Charles P. Fleming, one of the doctor's two sons. But Fleming himself never publicly admitted that his history was fiction. As late as 1900, with considerable embellishment, he reiterated the ancient Arabic origin of the Order.

The battle continued privately and on the floor of the Imperial Council. At times it was bitter and personal. Louis Donnatin and Cyprian C. Hunt, the Potentate of Mecca Temple, even obtained statements from contemporaries of McGee to disprove his allegations. One of these was William Ten Eyck Hardenbrook, who carried Mecca's card No. 25, three ahead of McGee's No. 28.

Hardenbrook was a Masonic journalist, perhaps the earliest in New York, but like McGee, he was far along in years when his opinion was sought. But he was positive in his statement. "I hereby refute," he wrote to Potentate Hunt, "any statement made by any member of the Order to the effect that (it) is not founded upon a somewhat similar Arabian Order of ancient origin and existing at the time of the formation of Mecca Temple.

. . . It was through the efforts and instrumentality of William J. Florence who brought the original Arabic manuscript Ritual and its English translation to this country that the Order owes its institution and foundation in the United States. This document was on several

occasions the subject of discussion and debate with the
view of adapting its provisions to Masonic customs and
usages prevailing at that time. I often had the Ritual
in my possession for the purpose of study and suggestion for such arrangement as would make it useful and
adaptable for the initiatory work of Mecca Temple.
As the pioneer Masonic journalist in New York, being
the owner and editor of the Masonic Newspaper, this
work naturally referred to me. The adoption of the
insignia, jewels and paraphernalia of the Order was
also a matter of frequent consideration and the jewel,
consisting of the pyramid, Sphinx head, Star of Bethle-
hem upon the keystone uniting two claws of the royal
Bengal tiger in the form of the crescent was finally
adopted upon my recommendation and from a design
which I furnished Dr. Fleming."

That was a pretty definite statement, and by most
rules of evidence would have been considered final.
After all, he said, he had had the original manuscript
in his hands, but since it never could be found, there
existed some doubt. An ancient Arabic manuscript,
even if it were shredded and in a bad state of disrepair,
would be an invaluable addition to any museum and
would have been treasured and guarded.

And so, the argument, continued and on occasion
took on the tones of attempting to prove that the founding of the Shrine in the United States was centered
in either the Scottish or York Rites. It was not until
1927 that anything like a final statement was made,
and that came from Charles P. Fleming, one of the
doctor's two sons.

Melish had implied in an article printed in the New
York *Herald Tribune* that the origin of the Shrine was
still shrouded in mystery. Apparently he was mis-
quoted, but it came to Charles Fleming's attention and
he immediately issued a long statement which appeared in the Bridgeport, Connecticut *Star*. Fleming
also transmitted a clipping of his statement to Recorder

Donnatin at Mecca Temple. In his letter, Fleming said that "at the time the article by Brother Melish was published in the *Herald Tribune,* an old friend of mine in Bridgeport urged me to make a statement as to the true facts of the Shrine's origin. I demurred at first, but finally consented. My decision to do so was grounded on the fact that several times in his last years, my father said he regretted the necessity of so much mystery regarding the founding of the Order, but he deemed it essential at the time to gain the interest of the public, and it soon got out of hand, and the true facts were known but to a few. The statements I have given herewith in the article enclosed I heard my father make many times to old friends and associates, so there is naught contained therein that he would object to my making were he still with us. I have heard my father say that he could not recall more than two or three occasions that Florence even attended ceremonies of the Shrine. He did nothing whatever concerning it beyond lending the use of his name in connection therewith to his old friend, my father." He declared that in the Shrine there was never any Oriental connection whatever and that "the conception of the idea was my father's alone and that he received his greatest and most valuable aid from Bro. Charles Thompson McClenachan, who was considered an authority on all matters Masonic and who was conceded to be one of the best ritualists in the country." Young Fleming concluded:

My father frequently stated that without assistance of McClenachan in the construction of the Order, it would have been "Love's Labor Lost."

Wm. Jermyn Florence, 32° and the third factor in the Shrinal history whose name is more generally linked and known throughout the land in connection with it than any other had nothing whatever to do with the work of establishing the Order, beyond permitting the use of his popular name in abetting and getting the Mystic Shrine into the limelight of public attention and favor in the seventies and eighties.

At the inception of the Order, to give it emphasis and to add to its impressiveness it was said to have emanated from "The Order of the Crescent" under the "Throne of the Bektash." This however was purely a figment of Dr. Fleming's imagination. The announcement of a visit of Brother Florence to this Order in continental Europe, thereby imbibing the original idea, was purely garnishment for the purpose of propagating the new Order.

The Order was inaugurated in 1870 at the Knickerbocker Cottage, 28th St. and 6th Ave., later and more recently Moquin's restaurant. Its object, the exercise of charity, the improvement of the mind, and an ally of the Fraternity of Freemasonry of the United States.

I have the original charter, granting my father the authority to confer the Order throughout the United States and Western Hemisphere. It was supposed to come from Mecca, Arabia and is dated August 13, 1870. Actually it was conceived by my father, and drawn and made by Bro. Benjamin F. Brady, whose office at that time was in Barclay Street, just back of the old Astor House.

All the words and ceremonials were conceived and compiled by my father. The charge was taken from a poem by Francis Saltus, to be found in his book of poems published posthumously under the title of *Honey and Gall* and slightly altered to fit the requirements.

I possess a copy of this book. The costumes were designed under my father's suggestion, and in fact the entire onus of the early days fell upon his shoulders, with the above stated able assistance of Bro. McClenachan.

He was not made a 33rd until September 19, 1872, over two years later, so the yarn of Florence being but 32nd, turning over the promulgation of the idea to my father because of his being a 33rd is exploded.

The statement by Charles P. Fleming should have ended all of the discussion, but it didn't. As late as 1941 Louis Donnatin compiled massive data designed to prove that the records were essentially correct and that when Fleming and Paterson wrote their histories they must have known what they were talking about and were telling the truth.

Unfortunately, however, the facts as Fleming and

Florence related them do not stand up to the test of other facts. Arabic scholars have been consulted in the preparation of this book and they never heard of a Shrine or anything like it existing in all of the Middle East. The Bektash order of dervishes is Turkish, not Arabic; and the Bektash cannot trace their origin to the Caliph Ali (or Alee) as many of the dervish orders do. Weishaupt's Illuminati were barred many years before the advent of the Shrine, and according to the best historians never achieved a membership of more than two thousand in all of Europe.

But what difference? Fact, fancy, legend, myth. Perhaps all of these. But principally the Ancient Arabic Order Nobles of the Mystic Shrine is a fraternal romance. It is composed of almost one million boys grown tall, who maintain reverent minds and merry hearts; who contribute generously of their time and purse for the betterment of mankind.

5

In Death a Question

The name of William J. Florence is so intimately associated with the history of the Shrine that he cannot be ignored by the simple expedient of saying that he participated in the creation of a fiction, or that he did little more than permit the use of his name in promoting an infant fraternity. But it is possible that his death contributed more to the Order than his life.

There is no record that he ever attended an Imperial Session of the Order and on only a few occasions is he known to have attended meetings of individual temples. He apparently was present at the meeting of the original thirteen in 1871. He once attended a meeting of Lu Lu Temple in Philadelphia. He obligated Sam Briggs, who was to become the second Imperial Potentate, at a theater in Cleveland. And at least once he attended a meeting of Mecca Temple in New York. There are unconfirmed statements that he visited Moslem and Damascus temples. Frequently the Shriners appeared at a theater where he was playing, and always he greeted them as a Shriner.

Much has been made of Florence's visit to Mecca Temple by those who have supported the theory that Florence actually was the founder of the Order in America, but here again there are differing versions of the same story. The official minutes of the meeting on September 29, 1882, report that Ill. Wm. J. Florence was "announced and introduced by Ill. J. F. Collins in an eloquent speech that touched on all the noble qualities and high deeds of one who merited the title of 'Father of the Order' in America. The Grand Potentate [Fleming] cordially welcomed the illustrious Noble and tendered him the hospitalities of Mecca Temple. Illustrious Noble W. J. Florence accepted the welcome in a brief speech and said that when he assisted in introducing the Order in this country he never expected to behold the magnificence of ritual and ceremony which surrounded him, and the large numbers who took such unalloyed pleasure in pursuing the unwritten teachings, laws and ceremonies and participating in the celebrations observed by the order. At Algiers, Cairo and Marseilles he was very much impressed with the Arabian mysteries which he had then beheld for the first time and it resulted in bringing before those found worthy in the U.S. an order whose teachings were profitable. After the ceremonies of the evening, the Illustrious Noble expressed his unbounded delight at the beauty and magnificence with which Mecca Temple had imbued the weird Arabic ceremony and that he had never witnessed such an exemplification in all of his travels."

Those are the official minutes of the meeting, but McGee gives a slightly different version of Florence's appearance. He sets the date as December 19, 1884, on the occasion of the first ladies' night ever held by Mecca Temple. If that date is correct then he must have made two visits, for it is difficult to dispute the official minutes of a meeting: McGee records that Fleming learned that Florence was in the city unexpectedly and personally went to his quarters in the Fifth Avenue Hotel and "refusing to take 'no' for an answer personally escorted him to Masonic Hall at Twenty-third Street and Sixth Avenue."

McGee then recalls that Fleming greeted the actor with "one of his characteristic and inimitable 'welcomes' for which the doctor was long famous and concluded his reception with a presentation to Florence of a Fez and an expensively gold-mounted pair of tiger claws. The visiting Noble [Florence] accepted the same and after a hand-shake with all of the professional entertainers, preceded by a social bite and sip of the menu in evidence, the widely known author, dramatist, actor and bon vivant took his departure and in so doing remarked to this 'chronicler' that said visit was the very first time that he had ever been a participant in any sense at a Mystic Shrine function."

Strangely enough both dates and both visits may be correct. Certainly it must be assumed that the minutes of the meeting in 1882 are correct, and tending to confirm McGee's story is the jewel itself which was presented to Mecca Temple by Mrs. Florence after Billy's death. The jewel has this inscription on it:

Amir ul Umra
William J. Florence
August 1870
From Mecca Temple, Mystic Shrine N.Y.
Dec. 1884

This jewel and others belonging to Florence were given to the Shrine Rooms in the George Washington National Masonic Memorial and are now on display there. Among those jewels is also one that Florence gave to Mecca Temple. In a letter dated September 9, 1891, only a few weeks before his death, Florence wrote to Fleming: "Ills. Sir—Will you please accept for Mecca Temple the enclosed jewel—it is the first ever worn by a Christian. With it take the earnest wish that our beautiful work will spread from world to world till we are gathered to the sacred Shrine promised to the faithful by our Father Mamoud. Yours in the bonds of fire, William J. Florence."

It was the last communication Fleming was to receive from his friend. Billy was sixty years old and still as popular with audiences all over America as he was in the days when he romped across the boards with his wife Malvina. She had retired and was living in England, but Billy had formed an association with Joseph Jefferson, and they began a tour of the country from which Billy never returned.

In his death, there is one of the most unusual stories in American Masonic history.

Florence and Jefferson began their tour in Philadelphia in November of 1891, appearing in *Heir at Law*. During the week of November 9, Florence contracted a slight cold, but continued to perform each evening. On Friday, November 13, he was feverish and consulted a physician who advised him to remain indoors. But Florence insisted on continuing on Saturday, the 14th (the show must go on), and after the play that night gave a dinner for Mr. and Mrs. Kendal at the Continental Hotel, where he had his quarters. Florence, however, left the table before the conclusion of the supper and took to his bed. Sunday, the 15th, he was much worse and several consulting physicians were called in. According to the treatment in those days, Florence was "bled" to relieve his suffering, but he continued to grow worse and the newspapers report that he spent Tuesday and Wednesday "in a comatose condition."

The *Philadelphia Press* of Wednesday morning, November 18, reported that "the actor's life had been despaired of" and that Mrs. Florence "had been cabled for."

"Those inquiring persons," said the *Press*, "who slipped into the corridors of the Continental Hotel as late as one or two o'clock yesterday [Tuesday, November 17] morning learned that Mr. Florence's condition was just the same—'a trifle better than the day before.' But suddenly both the relatives and Dr. Dunnellen in Mr. Florence's apartment grew nervous and then hurriedly exchanged a few whispers. The great actor was breathing with great difficulty. The clock showed that it was within a few minutes of three o'clock. Father

Flannagan of St. Mary's church was sent for by Mrs. Williams. [Mrs. Williams was Mrs. Florence's sister and a devout Roman Catholic.] This, however, was without Mr. Florence's knowledge or, when he afterwards learned of it, without his consent as to the necessity of it. He did not at any time believe that he was in extremeness."

However, the *Press* reported that the clergyman must have had a different view and "apparently thought that the comedian was close to the shadow of death and he administered to him the last rites of religion." The *Press* also reported that Father Prat of New York "who was a warm friend of the distinguished actor assisted in the administration of the extreme unction."

On Wednesday, November 18, Florence slept most of the day under the influence of morphine which had been administered to relieve pains caused by sciatica, but the Philadelphia *Public Ledger* said that when he was awake, he chided his friends for their anxiety about him, that he had a pretty strong case of sickness, but that he would come out all right.

Peter Conlin, Florence's brother and a New York police inspector, was so cheered that he left Philadelphia to return to his work, but shortly after nine o'clock that night, November 19, 1891, Billy Florence took a sudden turn for the worse and died. His death occurred a comparatively few steps from where he had been made a Master Mason in 1853.

Shortly after his death, Mrs. Williams and Mrs. Norman Wiard, Florence's own sister, cabled Mrs. Florence in London: "Dearest Sister—With unutterable and profound grief we send you the terrible tidings that our beloved one suddenly became worse and at 8:30 this [Thursday] evening passed away quietly, peacefully and painlessly. His last thoughts and his constant words were in tenderness for you. Telegraph dearest whatever suggestion you wish to guide us. Everything has been done and all will be done as we feel you would have it to be."

Mrs. Florence replied in a long cablegram which was never made public, but which the newspapers reported requested that funeral services for the great actor be held in St. Agnes' Roman Catholic Church on Forty-third Street just off Lexington Avenue, in New York. The Philadelphia *Press* said that "the great actor has given a great deal of money to this church and helped materially to found it by a contribution of $15,000. Mr. Florence has been a very benevolent man to the church of his faith—the Roman Catholic—and has given thousands of dollars to charity."

The announcement that Florence's funeral would be held in a Roman Catholic church caused something of a furor in New York, where the newspapers raised the question of how a Master Mason could also be a member of the Roman Catholic church. The New York *Sun* reported in connection with the funeral arrangements: "For many years Mr. Florence had been a Freemason and it was thought that the Catholic authorities might object at having the funeral services at a Catholic church. The law of the Catholic church is that a man who has been a Mason and who dies without renouncing the Order cannot receive Catholic burial. Dr. Brant, pastor of St. Agnes' Church said yesterday that he had proved that Mr. Florence received the church's last sacrament and had, therefore, renounced Freemasonry."

"A few days before his death," Dr. Brant told a *Sun* reporter, "Father Prat of this city, one of the most eminent friends, went to Philadelphia to see him. Father Prat brought a priest from St. Mary's Church in Philadelphia [Father Flannagan] to Mr. Florence's bedside. He heard Mr. Florence's confession and gave him absolution. That proves that Mr. Florence renounced Freemasonry for he could not have obtained absolution if he had not. Mr. Florence was a good Catholic at heart.

He and his wife were among the best friends of St. Agnes' Church. He was intimately acquainted with my predecessor, the late Father McDowell. A few years ago he presented to the church a lamp that he obtained from the Shrine of St. Agnes in Rome. Other tokens of his esteem of Father McDowell, and his respect for the church, are in the place from which ever appropriately his funeral is to take place. He had many friends among the Catholic clergy. Once he told a priest that whenever he heard the gong on an ambulance, he always said a prayer for the unfortunate who had been killed or injured. Billy Florence was a noble man, and I am sure that when he became a Mason he did not do so with the idea of being contrary to his church."

Another New York newspaper inquired from Father Shean, an assistant priest at St. Agnes' Church, about the matter and was told that no attempt had been or would be made to inquire into the circumstances of Florence's receiving the last sacrament in Philadelphia.

"We are bound to believe," said Father Shean, "that the priest who administered the last sacrament to the dying man was convinced that Mr. Florence had renounced Freemasonry and was, therefore, entitled to the blessing. Of course, if we knew that Mr. Florence had not renounced Masonry before his death and had not repented, only one course would be open to us. The law of the church is perfectly clear and explicit. No member of any secret organization can be buried from a Catholic church or have the last rites administered to him. Our position in the matter is very simple. It is not necessary for us to go behind the action of the priest in Philadelphia, as we are bound to believe that he took all proper precautions."

At the same time, Edward M. L. Ehlers, Grand Secretary of the Masonic Lodges of New York, announced that Florence would receive no Masonic honors since he received the last sacraments of the Catholic church. And also at the same time Father Brant announced that no Masonic order would be admitted to the church for the service, but that Masons would be admitted as individuals if they appeared without uniforms. There is no evidence that any of them actually attended the services, but the New York *Times* reported that there were two floral pieces probably never seen in a Catholic church before. One was from the Actors' Order of Friendship and the other from the Mystic Shrine. Both contained the Masonic Square and Compass.

After the funeral, the body was taken to a mausoleum in Greenwood Cemetery in Brooklyn to await the arrival of Mrs. Florence; and when she arrived some days later, the mortal remains of Billy Florence were taken to a grave in the same cemetery, a burial plot that Florence himself had purchased, and over which was raised a monument declaring that he was one of the founders of the Shrine in North America.

There are some rather strange circumstances in connection with the Catholic burial of Billy Florence. First of all, and perhaps most important, is the question whether he ever was a member of the Roman Catholic Church. Records of St. Mary's Roman Catholic Church in Albany, which was the only Catholic church in that city at the time of Florence's birth, do not reveal his baptism. It is to be doubted that he was a member of that faith in 1853 when he received his Masonic degrees in Philadelphia or when he participated in the founding of the Shrine in 1871. He continued to pay his dues each year in all of the Masonic bodies until his death, excepting the two occasions when he was suspended prior to 1871.

There is no record of his marriage to Malvina Pray. Marriage licenses were not required in New York at that time; and while some of the clergy occasionally reported their weddings, Florence's was not one of them. Newspapers of January 1, 1851, made no mention of the wedding and subsequent biographies failed to mention where the wedding was held and by whom they were married. Mrs. Florence and Mrs. Williams, it is known, were devout Catholics, but when Mrs. Norman Wiard (Florence's sister) died in 1927 in Tacoma, Washington, her funeral was conducted by a Unitarian minister, her body was cremated, and the ashes were buried in the Conlin plot in Greenwood Cemetery. Catholic law does not permit cremation since it contravenes the Catholic teaching of the resurrection of the body. That portion of Greenwood Cemetery in which the Florence-Conlin burial plot is located is unconsecrated by the church. Furthermore, records in the archives in Washington show that when Peter Conlin, Florence's brother, was married, the wedding was held in a Methodist church.

So, strange indeed were the circumstances of Billy Florence's death and burial. Masons in general, and Shriners in particular, have never believed that he renounced Masonry on his deathbed; that when priests administered the last sacrament, it was done at the request of Mrs. Williams alone and that Florence, already in a coma, had no knowledge of what was taking place.

Sam Briggs of Al Koran Temple in Cleveland was the Imperial Potentate when Billy died and waxed eloquent in his eulogy.

Though the Catholic church and the Freemasons behaved with rare and admirable tact, now that Billy Florence's wholesome jovial body is under the turf and his great generous soul rests in perpetual peace which at last awaits well-doers of all creeds and no creed at all, the truth of the matter begins to break like a morning futilely hid by window blinds. William Conlin Florence, no matter what his fondness for the good priests he knew and for the beneficence and beauty of the creed they preached, was a Freemason who loved Freemasonry, who believed in its nobility, who practiced its charity, who was true to its obligations and who never, even on his deathbed, renounced it. He stood high up in its roll. He was proud of the honors it bestowed upon him and none of its craftsmen ever failed to receive at his hands the fullest exemplifications of its precepts. To impute against him that the last moment of his life would reverse the thoughts and beliefs of a lifetime is to asperse with insult the new grave in Greenwood.

Kings, statesmen, journalists, financiers all courted the genial Billy. Nobody was the worse for knowing him. And, ah, the good dinners he ate! The good wine he drank, and good stories he told and the good deeds he performed. Billy Florence was an accessory to the existence of this Order which will stand as a lasting monument, exemplary of his very life.

And Dr. Fleming also had a last word. He told a *New York Times* reporter that "of course Florence was a member of the Shrine at the time of his death. No secret was made of it at the time. I issued the proclamation of his death which was printed in the *Times* and other newspapers. The story that he renounced the Order on his deathbed is false. He was not accountable for anything he may have said to the Philadelphia priest. And of course we have no positive assurance that he did say anything like a renunciation."

Thus a question, a dilemma, and a mystery.

6

The Turning Point

If Dr. Fleming exuded a confidence not entirely justified by fact when he delivered his first annual address to the second meeting of the Imperial Council in 1877, he may be excused on the ground of his inherent enthusiasm and optimism and that indeed his words were prophetic. Only once since he wrote it had the Ritual been performed, and even that performance, like much of the early history of the Shrine, is shrouded in a certain amount of mystery, occasioned by lost or destroyed records and bad memories.

There seems to be little question that the first full initiatory ceremonial was given by Damascus Temple in Rochester, New York, but there are differing reports of the number of candidates and the date on which it was held.

One of the earliest members of the infant Order was George F. Loder of Rochester, and while there is no evidence that there had been a previous association between him and Dr. Fleming during the years the physician practiced in the upstate New York city, it must be considered likely. Loder, in later years, when the controversy over the origin of the Shrine was at its height, declared that he had been obligated by Florence in Dr. Fleming's office in June of 1872, but Loder was depending on his memory since his certificate had been destroyed by fire and Mecca Temple had not even been organized. Paterson in his recollection of those early years reported that Loder and seven other Rochester Masons had been obligated on January 4, 1875. And just to confuse the matter still further, a card was found in the records of Mecca Temple, signed by both Fleming and Paterson, dating Loder's certificate as June 26, 1875, but with the notation that "it ought to date from June 26, 1872." Oh, well! The boys cared little about records. What they wanted was fun.

Loder was a costumer with headquarters in Rochester, serving churches, lodges, military schools and theatrical societies, and after becoming a Shriner he returned to Rochester and organized Genesee Temple No. 2 of the Mystic Shrine. There was no charter, for there was no Imperial Council. But as a created Past Potentate, he had authority to organize and he had a copy of the Ritual. By 1875, he had obligated more than 135 members in Rochester, all of them with the advanced Masonic degrees as prerequisites. And because Fleming wanted it that way, Loder abandoned the Indian name of Genesee and established Damascus Temple, conforming to what was to become a standard practice of naming temples with some Moslem connotation. The Damascus charter actually is dated June 6, 1875, a full year before the establishment of the Imperial Council.

It was at about this time that Loder determined to perform the Ritual. From his extensive costume wardrobes, he outfitted the brethren and rehearsed them diligently and finally set the date of October 12, 1875. According to his own statement and the records of Damascus Temple, Billy Florence was playing in Rochester at the time and was present for the ceremonial. In addition, Loder invited Fleming and Paterson to attend, which they did, and watched for the first time the performance of the Ritual. There was one candidate—J. Clinton Hall, a stock actor and the manager of the Rochester opera house. He was the first Shrine initiate in North America.

To that point, Fleming and Mecca Temple had never

performed the Ritual, and it was to be many more years before Fleming would have the opportunity to preside as Potentate over the Ritual he had written.

Fleming explained to the Imperial Council in 1877 that his duties as Imperial Potentate had made it impossible for him to give time and attention to Mecca Temple and its ceremonials, but actually there is a suspicion that it was a lack of money which delayed activities in New York. After all, the nation had been through a severe financial panic, beginning in 1873, and though there had been some improvement in general economic conditions by 1876, the improvement was not sufficient to help many of the fraternal orders. Well-established lodges, Commanderies and Consistories were feeling the pinch as members failed to pay dues, and a new Order such as the Shrine was in a much worse condition. But, against almost insurmountable odds, Fleming and Paterson persevered even though at the start of 1878 it was touch and go whether the infant Order would survive. The formal session of the Imperial Council, scheduled for Albany in February of 1878, was called off, and an informal session was held in New York City. Fleming told the temples outside of New York City that there was so little to report that the formal session would not justify the expenses which would have to be borne by the individual delegates. It is likely that Fleming knew that delegates would not attend the Albany session and to avoid embarrassment to the new Order, he decided to call it off.

Nonetheless, about thirty of the boys in Mecca Temple got together in the New York Masonic Temple at eight o'clock on the evening of February 6, 1878, and went through the procedure of an annual Imperial Session, but it was brief and adjourned early. Fleming could report that he had granted a charter to Oriental Temple in Troy, New York, which he said was in a "flourishing condition." He also reported that he had

granted dispensations for the establishment of Mohammed Temple in New Haven, Connecticut, Pyramid
Temple in Bridgeport, Connecticut, Syria Temple in
Pittsburgh, and Ziyara Temple in Utica, New York. The
proceedings also record, as they did in 1877, that inquiries were being received and that "prospects are favorable for its prosperity."

This was not quite true. If there was any hope for
the new Order at all, it rested in the heart and soul
of Fleming and a few of his closest associates. The new
temples were supposed to send in some money to help
carry on the work, but they were remiss; and when
the annual session was held at Albany in February of
1879, Fleming declared that little had been accomplished even then "in our financial status or the perfection of the work."

"Still," the doctor said, "however embarrassed it may
now appear, we should not despair, as it is the universal
and inevitable result of the calamitous apathy of all
branches of business, even where men devote almost
their entire time to promote its prosperity and success.
The crisis of the almost paralyzed commerce of the
world, we trust, has passed . . . and we have every
reason to believe that the success and advancement
of the Order of the Shrine will be numbered among
the first to make rapid strides toward perfect position,
and there stand second to none in the country."

After all, Fleming could point to the fact that the
Shrine on December 31, 1878, had 425 members in
thirteen temples, the largest of which was Damascus
at Rochester. And true to his prediction, the business
panic was ending and the year 1879 saw a turn in the
fortunes of the new Order. Actually only thirteen (note
that mysterious figure again) new members were created during the year; but when the fifth annual session
was held in Albany on February 4, 1880, Fleming was
able to report that "although many of the subordinate
temples still remain inactive, and confer the three sec-

tions of the Order by communication, some, far more energetic and active than their sister temples, are fully and completely equipped with costumes, regalia, paraphernalia, and all the requisite mechanism for the full exemplification of the ceremonies in all of their details, and are conferring the Order in commendable and impressive form, which, with the appropriate music, impress all who have witnessed it most favorably, and the liveliest interest is manifested, and the roll of applications for membership comprises a list of such magnitude, as to palpably attest the favor with which it is received."

Fleming gave full credit in his report to Al Koran Temple of Cleveland for a fine new exemplification of the work, and he pointed to Sam Briggs in particular, the Potentate of Al Koran. The pat on the back eventually led to Briggs' election as Grand Assistant Rabban at the 1880 session, his first step toward his election six years later as the Imperial Potentate to succeed Fleming. Briggs was not even present at that meeting.

Actually, the work that Briggs and Al Koran Temple had done during the past year in creating a Ritualistic team and exemplifying the Ritual of the Shrine acted as a tonic to the entire Grand Council. Fleming could report that he and Mecca Temple also had followed the lead of Al Koran and that in January of 1880 had initiated more than a hundred candidates in full form. Furthermore, for the first time, Fleming felt confident enough of the future of the Shrine to suggest that it was time for the Grand Council to crack the whip over the temples and Nobles who were not complying with the rules and regulations.

As much as any words he ever uttered, Fleming's report to the 1880 session revealed the trials he had endured. He said:

I have personally assumed the duties of answering all inquiries, and transmitted to the apparently interested, copies of both the history and the Statutes and Regulations. And I have found it no trivial task to comply with all the demands made upon my time, and the individual assumption of many of the obligations incurred in behalf of the Institution; and with the exception of the personal aid of two or three of our members, accessible in the City of New York, who have kindly assisted me, as far as was possible for them to do, the duties, both mental and pecuniary, have devolved almost entirely on your humble servant. Still, I have not wearied or yielded to discouragement; but to the full measure of my ability, I have endeavored to surmount all obstacles, and striven for the success, prosperity, and advancement of the Order. I only ask in return the aid and support of my constituents, in any capacity which I may assume in the deliberations of the Council. I have no personal ambitions beyond the sincere interest in the welfare of the Order, to which I have devoted so much time and toil, and, I regret to say, not always encouraged by a like interest on the part of others. . . .

Fleming was wordy and his text occasionally became involved, but he nevertheless made his position quite clear. He thought if the boys wanted the Order at all, they ought to pitch in and help. By unanimous consent, he was reelected Imperial Potentate for another three-year term and, of course, he accepted. There was no one else with the zeal and determination not only to promote the Shrine but to hold it together. It had been ten years since Fleming created the Ritual, and perhaps he was growing a little tired despite his avowal that he had never yielded to discouragement. He would soon be forty-two years old, was growing a little paunchy from the rich food and wine that he could afford as a result of his growing medical practice. His interest also was developing in the treatment of mental disorders, particularly dipsomania, and he was becoming a bit disconcerted by the time, effort and money necessary to the development of the Shrine, especially if the boys weren't interested enough to help him.

It's a good thing Fleming didn't yield to discouragement and that he assumed the leadership for another three years, for 1880 was a crucial year. The annual meeting was changed, as Fleming suggested, from a winter session in conjunction with the Royal Arch grand session in Albany to a summer session in conjunction with Grand Lodge meeting in New York City. What Fleming called the Sixth Session of the Imperial Council was held just four months later on June 2, and it was this second session in the same year which led to some confusion among the nobility as to the exact age of the Shrine. The number of sessions is always one greater than the number of years the Shrine has been in existence.

There was little to report at the June session, but Fleming did, once again, bring up the matter of money, of which there was a continuing shortage.

A year later, at the 1881 session, Fleming was able to report a total membership of 587, a gain of 149 during the year, but once more also had to report that "expenditures exceed receipts." Apparently, however, Fleming was now getting some financial assistance from Florence. At least, at the meeting in 1882, he told the delegates that for eleven years the burden of expense "has fallen almost entirely on your presiding officer and no insignificant amount upon our Illustrious Noble and Deputy, and, I may say, instigator of the project, William J. Florence. A vote of thanks, therefore, is eminently due Noble Florence for his interest in, tenacity to and sacrifices for the Mystic Shrine, being first to bring it to available disposal."

Reacting to the recommendation for a vote of thanks, the Committee on Transactions of Grand Officers reported: "Your committee in considering the commendations contained in the address is applied to one whom we might almost deem the founder of the Order, at least in this country, Noble William J. Florence, join in great sincerity in wishing to pay just homage. Your

committee cannot but think, in the matter of the intro-
duction of this Order, Noble Florence built much better
than he knew."

That the Shrine was building, there could be no question. At the ninth annual session held in the Masonic
Temple in New York in June, 1883, Fleming boasted
that Mecca Temple, of which he was still the Potentate,
had nearly five hundred members. Seven temples—
Mecca, Cyprus, Damascus, Moslem, Oriental, Pyramid,
and Syrian—were represented when the session got
underway, the most since the organization of the Shrine
in 1876. Once again Fleming was reelected Imperial
Potentate for his fourth—and last—three-year term.
Loder, Ehlers and Briggs were again elected as Deputy
Potentate, Chief and Assistant Rabbans, but there was
one new officer who was destined to play a dominant
part in the affairs of the Shrine for the next forty years.
He was William B. Melish of Syrian Temple, Cincinnati,
who became the Second Ceremonial Master. It was
also at this session that Florence and A. L. Rawson were
elected emeritus members of the Imperial Council. The
election of Florence to this status is entirely understandable, but the election of Rawson, as much as anything else, indicates the power Fleming exercised over
the Imperial Council. Rawson is a rather fleeting character in the history of the Shrine. His position was never
exactly clear. On one occasion, Fleming described him
as an Arabic scholar. There were statements at one
time or another that he actually had made a pilgrimage
to the forbidden city of Mecca, but authoritative historians fail to include his name among the infidels who
have successfully traversed the sandy road to Mohammed's holy city. The New York City directories of the
time list Albert Leighton Rawson as an artist, and certainly he did do the pen-and-ink drawings for a work
on esoteric religions of the Mediterranean.

In retrospect, it is possible to say that the 1883 meeting was the real turning point in the life of the Shrine.

From that moment it appears to have found its place in the sun as evidenced by the activity of the nobility in their respective temples.

"The principal part of the laborious work which characterizes the inauguration of all newly formed institutions has been accomplished," Fleming reported in his annual address. "The Oriental Ritualistic work has been perfected; the dispensations, charters and diplomas are complete; the history and Statutes and Regulations are in your hands and eminently worthy of your praise and approbation. Our Proceedings have finally appeared, a compilation formidable but complete with authentic information concerning the Order, together with detailed recapitulation of the transactions of this Imperial Council since its organization. The exemplification of the Work has been brought to perfection and everything appertaining to the Order is now upon the high-road to an unprecedented success, and no obstacle now remains to a rapid advancement of strength, power and superiority."

Fleming would serve three more years, three years in which would be established some of the traditions that were to make the Shrine famous. Fleming may have completed, as he said, the laborious work of starting a new Order, but the craft was not to have smooth sailing. There were still stormy seas ahead. But this is traditional in the institution of and the early years of any new organization.

7

Shrine's Initial Major Charity and Fleming Says Farewell

On June 14, 1886, the triennial conclave of the Knights Templar was held in Cleveland and it was quite an event. For two weeks, the Cleveland newspapers had been filled with news of the impending session. The city was decorated as never before. The City Hall was bedecked with great festoons of red, white and blue cambric, and evergreens stretched across the front, weaving a great sign of welcome. The county buildings also had been made beautiful in anticipation of the great event, and on the day the Knights gave their big parade one newspaper required six full columns to recount the activities.

There were fifty-seven bands in the line of march, leading four thousand men, their white plumes waving in the breezes that swept in off Lake Erie. The *Plain Dealer* said that these magnificent parades are "pleasing to the eye and have their proper place and appropriate use, but there is something in the Order of Knights Templar more to be admired than gorgeous pageantry, something transcending in importance all mere physical display such as its noble efforts in the cause of benevolence. The fame of the Order is not measured by military display, nor by the number and grandeur of its temples; its usefulness is measured not by its age and wealth, nor the number and respectability of its members, but by the bread it has fed to the hungry, the clothing it has bestowed upon the poor, the destitute widows it has aided and supported and orphans it has maintained and educated, and the human wrecks it has rescued and restored to the sunlight of happiness."

Yes, all Cleveland paid its tribute to the Knights who enjoyed the hospitality of the city. But theirs was by no means the only Masonic event held in Cleveland on the same days. In a gaily bedecked hall on Superior Street, nearly opposite Bank Street, Al Koran Temple of the Ancient Arabic Order Nobles of the Mystic Shrine had made arrangements to entertain the twelfth annual session and the fourth triennial conclave of the Imperial Council, the last time the Shrine deliberately scheduled its annual affair with that of another Masonic body. The thousands of Knights in Cleveland couldn't possibly miss the place. Inside, a well of Zemzem had been set up and there was a bountiful supply of camel's milk, available to Shriners and to Knights who exhibited the slightest interest in the fun organization. Red-fezzed Shriners stood outside the hall, and let all know that there was still time for fun.

Reporting on the affair, the *Plain Dealer* said, "A business meeting of the Shriners was held in the Asylum of Holyrood Commandery and at 9 o'clock began the festivities of a banquet which were prolonged far toward sunrise. There was nothing mystical about the banquet, but the lack of mystery was fully compensated by the conviviality of the feast, washed down by good fellowship and the best of Mumm's extra-dry. Mr. Sam Briggs was toastmaster and the various features of the evening were intermingled with the songs of the Arion quartet and an overture of bells, given by a select band of the Nobles, was received with great enthusiasm and applause. . . ."

There had been other such affairs, but this was the first time that the public prints had been quite so plain in describing the conviviality of the Shriners and how they entertained themselves. There had been a rather large banquet in Detroit in March of 1882 when Fleming, Briggs and twenty-four other Nobles from Mecca and Al Koran Temples had exemplified the Ritual for a number of new candidates in Moslem Temple. And there had been pilgrimages, principally by Mecca Nobles, to Oriental Temple in Troy, New York, and to Pyramid Temple in Bridgeport, Connecticut. But there had never been anything like the party that Sam Briggs gave, even the one Mecca Temple had when "Tony" Pastor, the great theatrical producer, and a few others were initiated in due form at New York's Masonic Temple in a late night ceremonial.

Recorder William Paterson included that event in his history, written in 1893. "On November 30, 1883," Paterson wrote, "a midnight session, in addition to the regular one, was held for the benefit of Nobles G. B. Claflin, Gus Williams [famous actor] and 'Tony' Pastor, who were unable to receive the order at an early hour on account of their theatrical engagements. They were created Nobles in full form, and the temple was closed at one o'clock. The next morning the public and the fraternity were startled by the report that the top floor and roof had been burned out. This caused the loss of everything on that floor, costumes, paraphernalia, etc., valued at $2,750. . . . The fire always has been regarded as mysterious and the press throughout the country gave the Nobles many adverse comments. The fire marshal, however, reported the fire had been caused by a defective flue."

Then there had been a pleasurable pilgrimage to Medinah Temple in Chicago, April 16 to 21, 1884. Mecca's history records that "for the nonce the pilgrims became boys again with all kinds of old-time games and tricks. . . . The soul of mischief pervaded the party. At every stage, the platform was filled with spectators who quaintly inquired who these fez-bedecked Arabs were. . . ."

Oh, those were great times for the infant organization. Mecca even had a band, although it wasn't called a Shrine band. It was a private musical organization conducted by the famous cornet soloist Liberati, who was a member of Mecca. Liberati's band played at Troy, New York, Bridgeport and New Haven and on any other pilgrimage Mecca Temple happened to make. But the first real Shrine parade of which there is record, the first of thousands of parades all over North America, the first of the parades that were to become more gorgeous and resplendent with each passing year, the first of the parades that were later to make the Shrine the showcase of Masonry, even though it was not Masonic, was held in Baltimore on June 7, 1884. The occasion was the investiture of Boumi Temple by Lu Lu Temple of Philadelphia. The representative of the Imperial Council was James McGee.

Even though Lu Lu Temple itself was only four months old, it was intensely active and determined to make the Baltimore pilgrimage one to be remembered. Seventy-seven Nobles of Lu Lu and the St. Alban's Commandery band made the trip to Baltimore by special train and, escorted by the charter members of Boumi, marched from the station to the Carrollton Hotel. A newspaper report of the day said the Nobles "attracted much attention, not only on account of their fine appearance, but by the red fez that rested on their heads, giving them somewhat the appearance of Turks." After dinner at the hotel, headed by their band, the Lu Lu Nobles again paraded, this time to the Masonic Temple, where in "magnificent costumes and with gorgeous paraphernalia costing over fifteen hundred dollars which Lu Lu had brought with them," the Ritual of the Order was enacted.

And so it was with this background of fun and accomplishment that Fleming and his Imperial Divan arrived in Cleveland for the Imperial Session of 1886. In fifteen years he had come a long way with his Ancient Arabic

Order Nobles of the Mystic Shrine. From the original thirteen who had met at Masonic Hall in New York and agreed to organize a temple, the Order had grown to more than three thousand members. Already there were nineteen temples in operation and eight more were to be created at the Cleveland session.

It was destined to be the last but one Imperial Session Fleming ever attended. Whether he stepped down as Imperial Potentate from choice is not recorded in the Proceedings. They simply say that on ballot Sam Briggs of Al Koran Temple was elected Imperial Potentate for the ensuing three years. Fleming never explained why he lost interest in the Imperial Council. As Past Imperial Potentate he had full rights and voting privileges for life; and besides he continued to serve as Potentate of Mecca Temple for another two years. On occasion, he did send his regrets by mail, but mostly there was no response—from 1886 to 1913—when his name was called on the session floor. It is likely that

George J. Kossuth photos

DR. WALTER M. FLEMING   *WILLIAM J. FLORENCE*

From the original portraits hanging in the Shrine Rooms, George Washington National Masonic Memorial, Alexandria, Virginia

Fleming simply wanted to retire from the national picture to devote more of his time to Mecca Temple, which was growing with phenomenal speed and was engaging frequently in social functions and pilgrimages.

Fleming was forty-eight years old. He had spent vast sums of his own funds and perhaps too much time in cultivating the Shrine. He was having some difficulties at home, which eventually were to lead to divorce. But in his annual address in Cleveland there was no evidence of bitterness.

"And now, illustrious Nobles," he concluded, "after twelve years of official service and the many honors of which I have been the recipient at your hands, I am about to retire from the throne of the Imperial body of the Shrine and submit its destinies to the tender cares of others not less earnest and loyal than myself, others whose zeal and constancy entitle them to the recognition of your suffrage and your confidence. . . . Although I most willingly yield up the scepter and power, I cannot say it is without pain. No official, it matters not how arduous his duties nor how imperative the exactions on his time or attention may have been, can yield up his position without a realization of something like a throe of regret. . . ."

William Melish then moved that a committee draft resolutions expressive of the sentiments of the Imperial Council for the services of Walter Millard Fleming and providing that a suitable testimonial be procured for him. With that Dr. Fleming made his adieu. The infancy of the Shrine was over. For the present at least, it would follow a course set by Sam Briggs of Cleveland, and Briggs was a character who might have stepped out of the Arabian Nights.

As energetic as Fleming, he was at the same time more dynamic and more openly convivial with Shriners wherever he might find them. In his first annual address to the Imperial Council session in Indianapolis on June

20, 1887, Briggs told the temple representatives that "in your sessions, I desire that the cultivation of the social features be encouraged and that every effort be put forth to promote harmonious relations among the nobility else our title is a misnomer. Increased membership is of secondary import to the necessity of inculcating the intimate acquaintance and fellowship of those already in possession of the attributes of our Order, to the end that, with the opportunities afforded by our institution, it may exist in favorable contrast with other organizations, and that soon may be realized to the fullest extent the desire of the Prophet that—'Ye shall sit on seats facing one another; all grudges shall be taken away out of your hearts.' " Briggs served as Potentate of Al Koran Temple for 25 years.

A lot of the fun of being a Shriner in those years derived from the pilgrimages of one temple to another. The most extensive journeys were organized by Mecca Temple, no doubt instigated by Fleming, but managed by James McGee. Two of these pilgrimages stand out because important "firsts" were achieved.

In September of 1886, 145 Nobles from Mecca Temple chartered a train to take them to St. Louis, where they would participate in the activities incident to the creation of Moolah Temple. Actually, Medinah Temple of Chicago considered Moolah her baby and ran the show. After weeks of preparation, the Chicago nobility took their costumes and paraphernalia to St. Louis, rented a building and set up a headquarters, where refreshments were constantly available. Medinah's quartet sang at any time, and then on Wednesday evening there was a magnificent procession of two thousand Nobles, some in evening dress, others in costume. Among those in costume were twenty-four of Medinah's well-drilled Nobles who, according to a Mecca report, "carried scimitars and executed intricate movements en route, such as stars and crescents with bands of music interspersed." It made a very impressive sight and may well have been the first appearance of an Arab patrol.

On January 20, 1887, Mecca chartered another train and, joined by some Nobles from Lu Lu in Philadelphia and Boumi in Baltimore, visited Almas Temple in Washington. The Washington depot was alive with Nobles when the Mecca train arrived; and to furnish music for the occasion the United States Marine Band was present under the direction of John Philip Sousa, who was to become one of the most illustrious Nobles of Almas Temple. The entire nobility marched through the streets of Washington to Willard's Hotel and that night held a ceremonial. The following day, again led by Sousa and his Marine band, the Nobles paraded along Pennsylvania Avenue to the Treasury steps, where they had a picture taken. Again on the march, the Meccans paraded through the arch at the White House before going onto their train for another visit with Acca Temple at Richmond.

As much as anything else, these pilgrimages prompted members of the nobility who were not actually members of or representatives to the Imperial Council to attend the Imperial Sessions. The practice that was to build the Shrine conventions to mammoth size began June 20, 1887, when the Imperial Council was the guest of Murat Temple in Indianapolis.

Most of the Shriners were housed at the Dennison House, the leading hotel of that time in Indianapolis. After an informal reception the visiting delegates and other members of the nobility escorted Sam Briggs from the hotel to the Scottish Rite temple. They were togged out in full evening dress and wore their fezzes. It was more of a procession than a parade, but it attracted attention, particularly the banquet that followed the ceremonial during which fifteen initiates crossed the hot sands of the desert. James McGee described that banquet as "perfect and without flaw, performed as it was by one hundred Nubians (actual full count)." Murat Temple, he said, had forgotten nothing in an effort to set a pattern and incentive for other convention cities to live up to. Three hundred Nobles attended the banquet that the Indianapolis *News* said was the most elaborate ever laid in Indiana. Twenty toasts were drunk that night. And when the festivities were over, Sam Briggs could think back on his first year as Imperial Potentate and find it pleasing. He could report almost five thousand members in a total of thirty-seven temples. And there was money in the bank so that travel expenses of the temple representatives could be paid.

And so it went. With each successive year, there was some innovation. On June 25, 1888, the first Imperial Session outside the United States was held at Toronto, Ontario, where Rameses Temple was the host, and although the Canadian oasis was only a year old—having been chartered in Indianapolis—the Shriners there attempted to outdo the boys from Murat, and perhaps they did. For this convention, the ladies were invited, and they arrived in the Canadian city by the hundreds. Mecca Temple—and others—had chartered special trains, and Rameses Temple chartered the Lake steamer *Cibola* for a moonlight cruise on Lake Erie not only for Shriners but, significantly in the light of later developments, for their lady friends.

Equally important to the festivities of the Imperial Session in Toronto was the serious side of the meeting. Recorder Paterson reported that 3,299 Nobles had been created during the year and that the total in good standing at the start of the year was 7,210. There were forty-eight temples, thirty-two of them under charter and the remainder under dispensation, but in connection with the creation of new temples, Briggs was perturbed. Some of the newer temples, he said, had failed to evidence the prosperity hoped for, and because of their failure he had hesitated to grant dispensations for still more new temples. On the other hand, when applications were received, the enthusiasm was so great, he said, that he hesitated to deny the request. He therefore suggested that some guarantee be made to the Imperial Council that cities requiring new temples would be able to support them.

Briggs didn't always live up to his recommendations, and, as it developed, it was a good thing he didn't. A case in point is that of Morocco Temple of Jacksonville, Florida, which was chartered at the Toronto session. The granting of that charter had been a touch-and-go affair. In a letter still in the possession of Morocco Temple, Chief Rabban James H. Thompson of Chicago wrote to Henry S. Ely, one of the Jacksonville organizers, that he had better move swiftly. "Pardon me for not replying earlier, but Sam Briggs was over from Cleveland and I didn't get home until 5 A.M. He approves of your temple name and will give you Georgia and Alabama (in addition to Florida) but you must be expeditious as a person in Macon, Georgia, has been to New Orleans and received the degree preparatory to starting a temple there."

The dispensation was issued as promptly as Thompson had promised, but when the boys in Morocco got together for their first meeting, they found they had only six members, when seven were requried. A hurried message to Briggs brought a telegraphic response that they might include at their original ceremony Thad M. Chapman of Montpelier, Vermont, to join Morocco.

Six months later when the yellow fever epidemic laid Jacksonville waste, Morocco Temple and the Jacksonville Knights Templar were leaders in the fight against the plague, which struck a fourth of the city. Dr. Baldwin, the Recorder of Morocco, was himself a victim of the fever. Jacksonville was a city of 20,000 in August of 1888 when the epidemic struck. Almost five thousand persons were affected and 427 died before freezing weather reached the city in November and destroyed the virus. The city was panic-stricken after the eighth of August when the epidemic was announced. Trains and boats out of the city were loaded with those who sought to flee, but when they arrived at other ports and stations, they were turned back.

Among those who worked hardest against the fever was Dr. Joseph Y. Porter, later to become Florida's first state health officer, who carried card No. 17 in Morocco Temple. Altogether various temples, Commanderies and lodges of Masons contributed more than ten thousand dollars to assuage the suffering in Jacksonville; and when the Imperial Session of the Shrine met in Chicago on June 17, 1889, Briggs reported: "The tokened pestilence, where death is sure, has made sad inroads on the community where was located the youngest of our chartered temples, Morocco, at Jacksonville, Florida, and a history of the sad matter is the most doleful chronicle of the year 1888. . . . The officers and members of Morocco Temple, aided by associate Knights Templar, organized themselves into a relief corps, and full knightly with their armor on, displayed the beauties of fraternal love and affection to all the suffering, irrespective of race, creed or affiliation."

This was the first major charity ever undertaken by the Shrine. Only a few months later temples from all over the United States contributed thousands of dollars for the relief of victims of the Johnstown Flood of May 31, 1889. In the years that followed, every Imperial Potentate urged Shriners everywhere to carry on works of charity; and the record is replete with the results of these pleas, culminating in the glory of the Shriners' Hospitals for Crippled Children.

It was at the 1889 session of the Imperial Council that the last of the original thirteen members of the Shrine bade farewell to the national organization. William S. Paterson retired as Imperial Recorder and was succeeded by Frank M. Luce, who was to become one of the most controversial officials in all the history of the fraternity.

Briggs was reelected for another three-year term as Imperial Potentate, and William B. Melish of Cincinnati was advanced to the office of Chief Rabban.

King Kalakaua

Among the most active temples during the Gay Nineties was Islam in San Francisco, the first temple in the Far West, with jurisdiction over the entire area, including the Hawaiian Islands. The Kings had served as Lodge Masters, Grand Masters, received advanced degrees, and now on January 14, 1891, the last King of Hawaii was to become a Shriner. King Kalahaua had arranged a tour of California just after Christmas in 1890. Near Santa Barbara he suffered a slight paralysis, but recovered sufficiently to reach San Francisco on January 7. The King took to his bed on January 13 to prepare for his entrance into the Mystic Shrine the following night.

Urged by doctors not to go, the King replied: "I must go, and nothing shall prevent me from going. I must go to The Shrine."

And he did. He was initiated in full form, the first and only King on the rosters of the Shrine. He died January 20, 1891, in San Francisco.

8

Arabic Feasting

James McGee said the Shrine was formed as a "relax" where Masons might escape the cares of the day and the serious formality of Masonic fraternalism, yet meet together as brothers who had been tried in the Faith and found true. Certainly when Fleming wrote his original Ritual he had something of the sort in mind; for he divided it into three sections, the first and third containing moralistic teachings, couched in the terminology of the desert, the Islamic faith of Omar and the Oriental pageantry and splendor of the Arabic Nabob. But in the second section Fleming let his imagination run riot, creating—as it were—fun for both the novitiate and the obligated believer.

It was inevitable that under such circumstances, feasting should become as much a part of Shrine affairs as it was a part of tribal ceremonies in ancient Araby. Masons were famous for the banquets served on occasion.

It is possible and even probable that Fleming himself introduced the custom. Certainly he had participated happily in the feast prepared in his honor when he left Rochester. It is even possible that his whole idea of the Shrine developed from his reading of the second version of FitzGerald's second translation of the *Rubáiyát* of Omar Khayyám, which was published in 1868, just two years before Fleming wrote his ritual. The *Rubáiyát* is indeed filled with terminologies that have found their way into the Shrine. The word *divan*, name of the officer group in the Shrine, has three Oriental meanings—a book of philosophical poems, the ruling power, and the room or banquet hall from which the power emanates. Frequently Omar mentions the Sultani, the Temple, the Alchemist, Naishapur and Babylon, Mahi, Mahmud—but all through his writings, Omar refers most to the grape, and thus it is quite possible that Fleming should instill some of Omar's philosophy (and his own) into the activities incident to ceremonial feasts.

A committee was assigned to look into the various practices and came back with a resolution, which was adopted. It said that the "Imperial Council emphatically condemns all immoral and vulgar practices and declares that repetition of such proceedings shall be sufficient cause for the revocation of the charter of any such temple." The resolution further held the Potentate of each temple responsible for stopping the offenses on the penalty of expulsion.

> Imperial Potentate Melish stated that he was not one of those who decry the use of wine. I believe in the creed with which I closed my annual address to you in 1893: "Pleasure without intemperance, hospitality without rudeness and jollity without coarseness should here prevail among all of the true Faith."

As a result of some complaints, the Imperial Council again prepared and adopted a resolution which prohibited all coarse and obscene literature in the Shrine and gave the Imperial Potentate the power to decide whether the literature might be in violation and suspend any and all who might have prepared it.

Augustus Peters, Potentate of Mecca Temple, was quoted in 1897 by the Detroit *News*. He said, "Of course we have business to transact. This is a great organization. This talk about no prosperity is bosh. If there is no prosperity there would be no Shriners. If there were no Shriners, life would be one long hollow blank. We are going to adopt resolutions at the convention that will show this conclusively and all the citizens of the country will believe it.

Strangely enough, the elimination of spirits as an integral part of Shrine functions didn't come about as the result of either Imperial or Masonic edicts. Rather, with the advent and development of the Shriners' Hospitals for Crippled Children as one of the world's great charities, the Shrine and the Shriners suddenly grew up. Whatever drinking was done, was for the most part in the privacy of hotel rooms. They spent money, time and effort to create fun for themselves and for the public; and in the process they created exactly what Fleming and Briggs had sought—a fraternal order of the highest merit, composed of gentlemen of quality. With that development, the Shrine grew beyond the wildest dreams of its founders.

9

Reaching Maturity

When Sam Briggs retired in 1892 after six years as the Imperial Potentate, he could boast of considerable accomplishment. He had created thirty new temples and the membership had jumped from three thousand to more than twenty-two thousand Nobles. Yet Briggs had done more than just develop the Order in size. He also had established important precedents and changes. He had brought about one revision of the Ritual and had set the stage for still another one. But more than anything else, he had created a continental atmosphere in the Shrine. It was no longer dominated by Mecca Temple and its Orient was no longer New York. Beginning with the Imperial Session in Cleveland in 1886, the representatives had held successive sessions in Indianapolis, Toronto, Chicago, Pittsburgh, and Niagara Falls; and now, in 1892, at the western cow town of Omaha, Nebraska, the Shriners held their first national parade.

During Briggs' six-year tenure as Imperial Potentate, he had encouraged the attendance at the Imperial Sessions of the rank and file of the nobility, but not until 1892 did the attendance reach such proportions that the Shrine could command certain dispensations from the cities where it might choose to hold its conventions. Many ladies had attended the Imperial Session in Toronto in 1888, and even more had appeared at the scenic wonder of Niagara Falls in 1891, but there appeared to be a mass of them in Omaha.

The Omaha *World-Herald* reported (possibly with

tongue in cheek) the arrival of the Shriners at the Paxton Hotel on August 15. It was hot, of course, but the only dampening of the spirits of the Shriners was internal. More than 850 Shriners had registered at the tents of the Paxtonite tribe by that Sunday evening. The Nobles of Tangier Temple (Omaha) were the hosts and they had prepared well. The next day, the *World-Herald* said in its leading story that there was a concert in the Paxton Tent "and skillful men played upon instruments of silver and brass and the music they made was most pleasing to the ear for it was like the soft sighing of the winds as they sway the branches of the palm trees in a green oasis and it fell upon the ears of the pilgrims that heard it as welcome as the sound of the lapping waters to the thirsty Sons of the Desert. The music was by a band called the 3rd Infantry from a place called Fort Snelling in the land of Minnesota and they were brought here by the tribe of Zuhrah from that same place and there was also with the Tem-

Shrine Arabs on Parade

ple of Zuhrah a quartet of sweet singers who filled the whole air with their harmony and lo, they did go out from the tents of the Arabs and even into the tents of the Philistines, which is across the street, even into the tents of the *World-Herald* and they did most sweetly sing to the staff. And now when it came time that Allah (may His name be ever adored) had set aside for his children to rest, they retired to their tents and all was silent in Arabia."

After the big night parade, the Omaha *World-Herald* was forced to abandon its Oriental style in writing of the Shriners and their exploits. It was too big, too startling—too everything—to be couched in the flowing melodic wordiness of Omar and Hafiz. The Omaha reporters switched, rather, to the breezy, descriptive style of the West:

Noise! Shriners! Fezzes! Shriners! Dress suits! Noise! Red Fire! Shriners! Sky rockets! Camels! Elephants! More noise! More dress suits! More Fezzes! And that was the grand parade of the Nobles of the Mystic Shrine last evening and it was one of the most unique sights that has been seen in Omaha in years. There were 1,600 Shriners in the line, marching twelve abreast and they made a fine display in their dress suits and red fezzes. . . .

Chief of Police Seavey headed the parade with a squad of policemen. Following this was the 2nd Infantry band and behind this was the Thurston Zouave drum corps. Noble France, chief of parade, and his aides, Nobles Potter, Williams, Anderson, Smith and Horton on prancing steeds of Arabia, headed the first division of the Shriners. There were forty platoons, twelve Shriners to a platoon. The 3rd Infantry band headed the second division of Shriners, numbering 26 platoons. Then came 22 more platoons. Then came the elephant of which so much has been written and so many tall stories told. It was not a very big elephant, but it was a work of genius. The elephant was of mechanical construction and was made for Moslem Temple in Detroit. It was about four feet high and a perfect imitation of the two-tailed beast. And when his trunk is gently pulled, he trumpets "Shriner Welcome." . . .

The elephant was mounted on a wagon drawn by six

horses and had a coal-black slave at his side to make him talk, and at the cry of "play ball" from the faithful followers behind him, he would scream most loudly. Then came 70 Nobles of Moslem dressed in tunic, Zouave trousers and fezzes. They were a sight for the gods and attracted a great deal of attention.

Then at last came the camels that have been talked of so much. There was no imitation about them. They breathed and wobbled their frightened riders about like a school in a Kansas cyclone. To Tangier had been given the honor of guarding the camels. They were preceded by 60 of the Nobles on foot, and on each side of them walked ten Nobles dressed in wild, weird costumes of blue trousers and blouses and each was armed with a big wood saber about six sizes too big for him. . . .

From start to finish, the parade was one glittering pageant. Red and blue fire lighted up the scene with a spectral glare and skyrockets and Roman candles added their showers of fire to the general combustion. Imperial Potentate Sam Briggs reviewed the parade from the veranda of the Paxton Hotel and as each temple passed, they raised aloft their voices in their Shrine yells and waved their handkerchiefs and made sure they were seen.

Moslem Temple made the great hit here as they came before the reviewing stand. They deployed right and left and executed several intricate maneuvers that brought out considerable enthusiasm from the spectators. The teams drawing the Michigan elephant were frightened at 16th Street and Capital Avenue and turned out of the parade and into the crowd. Detective Vizzard grabbed the leaders by the bit and stopped them. His bravery and presence of mind averted a panic and also loss of life. Moslem had the Great Western Band of Detroit with them and the Detroit Commandery gave several fine drills while marching.

And such was the impartial report of the first big parade the Shrine ever held at an Imperial Session. Here was the first pageantry with the mechanical elephant and the camels. Here were the first costumes. Here were the red fire and the fireworks, and perhaps even the first patrol, although it was unofficial and was not called a patrol. Still, the boys from Moslem did march and execute intricate steps.

The first official Shrine patrol is clamed by Zuhrah Temple of Minneapolis and did not make its appearance in an Imperial parade until two years later in Denver. There they were dressed in white trousers and blue coats and wore a sort of yachting cap, and emanated, as most Masonic marching units did in those days, from the Commandery. The first official Zouave patrol dressed in Arabic costume is claimed by Medinah Temple of Chicago and appeared at an Imperial Session sometime later, although it had made an appearance in St. Louis when Moolah was instituted in 1886.

But who arranged for such a parade as that in Omaha? The boys from Tangier Temple? Certainly they had made elaborate preparations for holding the finest Imperial Session since the organization of the Shrine twenty years before, and they proved to be fine hosts. Briggs? Or perhaps William B. Melish, who succeeded him? Details are buried somewhere in the musty, dust-covered archives.

And no matter, except that the Shriners did have a good time in Omaha. "The Shriners have a right royal style of enjoying themselves," said the *World-Herald.* "Good fellowship reigns supreme. Every Shriner is a good fellow and so is his neighbor. The hotel rotundas are filled with the music of bands, cheering the Nobles on to renewed attacks upon the punch bowl. Then at intervals, all the merrymakers at one headquarters form a line and, led by the band, will march through the streets to other headquarters and there they are royally entertained. Then they go on to pay their respects to other temples. Good feeling is everywhere and there is nothing else."

There was sorrow, however, in the official session of the representatives held in the Masonic Hall. There Briggs announced the death of Billy Florence and eulogized him, and he also announced the death of David

Kalakaua, King of the Hawaiian Islands, 33°, and a member of Islam Temple of San Francisco.

It was under these conditions that Briggs passed from the Imperial picture. He had been a colorful, romantic, dashing figure—the exact fellow for the job in the six years he held it. But, as thousands of names were added to the rolls, there had been resentment that one man should hold the power for so long. In 1890, a resolution had been adopted, and it had been confirmed in 1891, abolishing the triennial term of office, effective with the end of the second Briggs term.

As Briggs delivered his annual address, he saw a great future ahead: "The Shrine is now so well founded and in addition to the mere social features, so much real dignity pervades the whole, it looks as though the Shrine has come to stay, and we trust it will, for it certainly fills a department in the cabinet of secret organizations long desired and yearned for. So hail to the Shrine. May it ride on in power, in glory and usefulness and prove a refreshing Oasis as we wander over the weary desert of life. May all the Shriners guard it with jealous care and permit none to join its caravan or to become influential in its courts who through thoughtlessness or viciousness pervert its beautiful work and thereby bring it into contempt."

With these words of caution for the future, Sam Briggs was succeeded by William Bromwell Melish, of Cincinnati, one of the most controversial and one of the most powerful figures in the long history of the Shrine. From the day of his election as Imperial Potentate in 1892 until his death in 1927, it could well be said that he was Mr. Shriner. Both Fleming and Briggs served longer officially as Imperial Potentate, but neither of them could match the vast power Melish wielded for so long.

Melish was a big man both physically and mentally, and—what is perhaps more important—he was an indefatigable worker in business, in civic life and in Masonry. From the time he entered the Bromwell Brush and Wire Goods Company, in 1871, he was a natural leader and a born salesman. He organized the Convention League of Cincinnati and later merged it with the Cincinnati Chamber of Commerce, of which he became president. He headed the Knights Templar Masonic Mutual Aid Association, and during the first World War he headed the Masonic War Relief Association. From 1896 to 1900 he served as senior aide-de-camp on the staff of Governor Asa G. Bushnell of Ohio and from 1897 to 1908 was an active member of the Cincinnati Waterworks Commission.

Melish first became a member of the Imperial Divan in 1883 when he was elected Imperial Second Ceremonial Master under Walter Fleming, and he held various posts in the Shrine under Briggs. He should have been aware of the internal politics of the organization, but Melish was never one to play politics. To him, right was right and wrong was wrong and there was no middle ground. The result was that his first year as Imperial Potentate was not a particularly happy one; and when the Imperial Council assembled June 13, 1893, in Cincinnati, he faced defeat on three major decisions he had made during the year. Eventually the defeat was to be engineered by Imperial Recorder Frank M. Luce, who had been suspended by Melish, and by a group from Mecca Temple, headed by McClenachan and Millar, who were upset by Melish's refusal to pay a small bill for advertising in a New York Arabic newspaper. The incidents were entirely unrelated and were reflected only in the political opportunism necessary to bring about Melish's defeat.

Syrian Temple and the city of Cincinnati had outdone itself in preparations for the Imperial Session. Eleven thousand tricolored gaslights had been installed on each side of Fourth Street, down which the parade was to pass. The Cincinnati *Enquirer* records that "it was a sight worthy of the noble Order whose festivities

transformed the city into a Mecca for the nobility."
Just as the parade was about to get under way to escort
the Imperial Potentate from the Grand Hotel to the
Scottish Rite Cathedral, there was a burst of fireworks
and red light was touched off along the entire line of
march, making the greatest display ever witnessed in
the Queen City by the Ohio. The parade itself lasted
only a half-hour, but it included four bands, an elephant, two camels and a corps of bicycle couriers,
dressed in Arabic costume.

But the gaudy glamour of lights and the garlands
of Shrine banners that hung from the buildings could
not forestall the unhappy session of the Imperial Council in store for Imperial Potentate Melish. Repercussions from it were to be heard until the 1894 session
in Denver, in fact.

The trouble was that Melish failed to fit into the mold
that had been created for the Imperial Potentate by
both Fleming and Briggs. When Melish assumed office
in Omaha, there were already rumblings of the financial depression and panic that was to follow in 1893.
Farmers were unhappy with the Silver Purchase Act
of the government. Railroads were beginning to feel
the pinch that was to bankrupt many of them, and
the Shrine's financial condition was not good, even
though more temples were being created and the
membership had risen to more than 27,000 Nobles.

Melish had inherited as his Imperial Recorder Frank
M. Luce of Medinah Temple in Chicago, who, like
Briggs, was a railroad man, and who had first taken
over the office in 1889 when Paterson retired. Briggs
had left all of the business affairs of the Shrine to Luce.
He couldn't be bothered with detail. Because of his
business sense, Melish began to have trouble with Luce
shortly after taking office. He discovered, he said, that
Luce was not paying over promptly to the Imperial
Treasurer the monies which he received from the several temples.

Melish didn't approve of such and there were other financial affairs that also violated his sense of good business. He thought the appropriation in Omaha for a $2,500 gift for Sam Briggs was all wrong and that the annual payment of $500 a year to John Worthington for his services as representative of the Shrine in the East was all nonsense and that he wouldn't pay it.

"Under our Constitution and in its government of the Order as at present established," Melish told the Imperial Council in his annual address, "there is no authority for the creation of foreign representatives, or 'Representative to Temples in the East,' etc., etc. . . . While I do not question the antiquity of the Arabic Orders from which we inherit our mystic rites, and do not decry the lessons, symbols, rites and customs held in such high esteem by those who practiced them centuries ago, yet in the conduct of the business of this Imperial Council for North America, we certainly ought to make alliances only with our own and await overtures from them, or else ask for recognition at their hands through recognized channels of communication."

The fact is that Briggs and Luce had built a rather powerful political machine in the Shrine, which they didn't intend to have disturbed.

Melish had bided his time, even though the controversy continued. Then, in January, when Luce had printed what Melish considered to be an incorrect list of temple officials, Melish advised all Potentates and Recorders not to use the Luce list if received, and he specifically forbade Luce to issue it. Luce ignored Melish, and at this point Melish issued an order suspending him. He appointed William H. Mayo of St. Louis as Acting Imperial Recorder until the meeting of the Imperial Council in Cincinnati.

Of course, the entire dispute had to go before the Imperial Council when it met in Cincinnati in 1893. In his annual address, Melish, as we have seen, detailed what had happened and gave his reasons for the action he had taken. When Luce was called on for a report, he submitted what facts and figures were necessary and then said that his defense to the charges that had been brought against him would be given by a committee. Actually, his defense was never submitted because of a parliamentary maneuver inside the Imperial Council.

Following established custom, the actions of the Imperial Potentate were turned over to various committees, which then would report back to the Imperial Council with recommendations for approval or disapproval. The action regarding the Imperial Recorder went to the Jurisprudence and Laws Committee, composed of J. L. Dobbin, Harrison Dingman, Bun F. Price, George H. Burnham and Lawrence M. Knepfly. After holding hearings, the committee reported to the Imperial Council:

> That they have carefully examined the law and the facts pertaining to said case, and, after duly considering the same, believe that the Imperial Potentate was fully justified by law and precedent in the course adopted by him. Your committee are of the unanimous opinion that during the interim of the sessions of the Imperial Council, the Imperial Potentate is by the constitution of this body endowed with the same powers as those of the Council itself. If this be not true, then there is no authority whatever in the Order except when the Imperial Council is in session.
>
> Upon careful investigation, we find it to be the universal law in all Grand Secret Society bodies, Masonic and otherwise, that the presiding officer of the Grand Body is the absolute and only authority when the Grand Body is not itself in session, and when the Constitution of a Body fails to clearly express the authority of a presiding officer, precedent, custom and usage must govern in determining the extent of his authority.
>
> If it be granted that the Imperial Potentate has the same powers that the Imperial Council has during the interim between sessions, except when they are specially limited by the Constitution itself, then the matter is clear. The

Constitution, Sec. 3, gives the Imperial Council the right to try, discipline, suspend, or expel its members for violation and disobedience of its Constitution, regulations and edicts.

Your committee believes the Imperial Potentate has the same right, subject of course to an appeal to the Imperial Council.

If no such power is inherent in the office of Imperial Potentate during the interim of sessions of the Imperial Council, then an officer occupying a position of trust and confidence could deliberately rob the body, squander its funds, obstruct and set at defiance its laws, and for a period of three hundred and sixty-five days in the year, say to the presiding officer, "What are you going to do about it?" Common sense must certainly dictate that the presiding officer has some power in the premises to protect the interest of the Order over which he presides and whose interest he is to protect. . . .

Your committee are of the opinion that if an Imperial Potentate can suspend the work of a chartered temple, he can certainly suspend an officer from office for cause, even if he be elective. A charter for life is certainly as important as the election to an office for one year; both are subject to good behavior and can be corrected by competent authority. Potentate Briggs . . . quoted Sec. 4, Art. 5 which reads: "During the recess of the Imperial Council, he (the Imperial Potentate) is invested with a general supervision of the Order throughout the jurisdiction."

Your committee are of the opinion that this clause of the Constitution gives the Imperial Potentate the power to supervise, correct, and remove any officer if the good of the Order demands it. The Imperial Council endorsed the acts of Imperial Potentate Briggs in the fullest sense.

The committee then called attention to an order issued by Grand Master Dean of the Grand Encampment of Knights Templar, specifically ordering Grand Recorder Parvin not to distribute a number of circulars which were held to be calculated to bring disrespect and disgrace on the Grand Encampment, and pointed out that the actions of the Grand Master had been upheld by the Grand Encampment.

In conclusion, your committee desire to state that they are of the unanimous opinion that the act of the Imperial Potentate in suspending Noble Frank Luce from the office of Imperial Recorder is in accordance with the law and should be approved.

The logic was sound, of course, and eventually would be enacted into Shrine law, but such questions are not always decided by logic, either in secret societies or in any other human endeavor. Melish's opponents had prepared well for the eventual showdown.

After his suspension, Luce had contacted the officials of Mecca Temple, who by that time had become bitterly opposed to Melish and his policies. With the added power of Briggs behind them, Mecca Temple and Luce had formed a committee to fight the reelection of Melish in Cincinnati and to bring about the restoration of Luce to power.

When the nobility began to arrive in Cincinnati for the Imperial Session, they were greeted at the station with invitations to attend a meeting on Monday evening to confer on matters that were to be presented to the Council session. The invitations were signed by George W. Millar, Charles L. Field, Frank Locke, Walter M. Fleming, Joseph S. Wright, William A. Stiles, A. B. McGaffey, H. H. McGaffey, Sam Briggs, E. F. Allen and Charles W. Cushman. Of those who signed the call, three were officers in the Imperial line and two were former Imperial Potentates.

The meeting was held, Briggs was present with all his charm. So was Walter Fleming, but he apparently played a lesser part. It is easy enough to form a picture of the event. The Imperial Potentate was painted as a high-handed dictator who wanted to make the Shrine into a Sunday School picnic, who wanted to destroy the traditions so laboriously built since 1872, and who had been so manifestly unfair to Recorder Luce, who had served faithfully under dear old Sam Briggs.

All of this had reached the Cincinnati press and the

anticipated debate was watched with interest by the citizenry. It was under these conditions that the debate began on the resolution presented by the Jurisprudence and Laws Committee supporting and approving the action of the Imperial Potentate in removing the Imperial Recorder from office.

Lawrence M. Knepfly of Hella Temple in Dallas and Noble Allen Andrews of Hamilton, Ohio, a member of Syrian Temple, spoke on behalf of the resolution. Opposed to the resolution were John W. Smith of Medinah Temple in Chicago and Curtis H. Winsor of El Riad Temple of Sioux Falls, South Dakota. John W. Smith, it developed, was the only Noble ever officially listed as a guest of John W. Worthington at Malta. He had been traveling in the Mediterranean and incurred an illness which required his sojourn on the island over a period of weeks. Since Worthington was the American consul, it was not only natural, but obligatory, that he be contacted. That both men were Shriners only added to their association. But, as it was later pointed out, Smith was well able to pay his own way at Malta, and did, which was one of the reasons why Melish declined to pay Worthington the five hundred dollars he had been voted.

Smith was present by specific arrangement with Medinah Temple and obviously to defend Luce. Shortly before the convening of the Imperial Council, Representative John A. May had resigned, and at a special election, Smith had been named to replace him as one of the four Medinah representatives.

Far from being heartless, Melish actually had written Luce: "It is with the deepest regret that I learn of the sad affliction to yourself and wife in the death of your little girl. I hope that Mrs. Luce may have a rapid recovery of health, and that the burden of sorrow may be lifted as speedily as human hearts can heal, although it takes a long time."

At one point in his debate, Smith argued that there

is no authority for a presiding officer to suspend an elected officer in any secret society, but again the Jurisprudence and Laws Committee was ready with a defense. They pointed out that Smith had served as Grand Master of the Grand Commandery of the State of Illinois and that in its Constitution, it was expressly provided that the Grand Master "may suspend from the functions of his office any officer of the Grand or subordinate Commanderies or arrest the charter or dispensation of a Commandery."

As it turned out, the debate had little real effect on the outcome of the issue. That had been decided at the caucus on Monday evening. Furthermore, the delegates who had pledged themselves were put on the spot when Sam Briggs moved, when the debate was concluded, that a roll-call vote be taken on the issue. The final vote was seventy-five to forty-seven, with ten representatives not voting. Fifteen were absent. Neither Luce nor Mecca Temple had presented one iota of evidence, but they had won.

Melish declared that, as a result of the vote, Luce was entitled to all books and papers of the Imperial Council, and Imperial Recorder Mayo immediately handed them over. But the drama was not ended. Melish was to suffer three more defeats in his home city. The Council, by virtually the same vote recorded in the principal issue, ordered the $500 paid to Worthington, and the $213 advertising bill for the Arabic paper *Kawkab* also was approved. But the severest blow of all came at the election of officers when, again by almost the same vote, Melish was defeated for reelection as Imperial Potentate and in his place went Thomas J. Hudson of Syria Temple in Pittsburgh.

Perhaps the crowning insult so far as Melish was concerned came later when the official proceedings were printed and distributed. In these proceedings, at the proper point, Luce had inserted above his own signature this statement: "The presentation of the differences between the Imperial Potentate and the Imperial Recorder by Noble J. W. Smith and Noble Curtis H. Winsor, being so fair, and the vote of the Nobles of the Imperial Council such a complete vindication of the Imperial Recorder, all letters and papers that might have been here inserted are withheld as no further defense is necessary."

It was the position of Syrian Temple that neither Luce nor his representatives had made such a statement in the Council session and that, therefore, the statement could not properly be recorded in the official proceedings. Perhaps they were right. In any event, Melish, who was still the Potentate of Syrian Temple, resolved to play the game differently when the Imperial Council assembled in Denver in 1894.

From June of 1893 to July 24 of 1894, the economy of the country grew progressively worse. Railroads, banks, retail and manufacturing businesses failed. Farmers were in despair through failure of the corn crop. The government itself resorted to borrowing, principally from the House of Morgan, and then borrowing again to pay off the first loan. Labor disputes were rife. Just after the Cincinnati session, the famous Homestead, Colorado, steel and iron strike and its pitched battle occurred; and, just before the Denver convention of 1894, Eugene V. Debs led the Pullman strike in Chicago, which was broken when federal troops were ordered out by President Cleveland. On the very day the Shriners arrived in Denver the Chinese-Japanese war broke out. But all of these things were secondary to Melish and Syrian Temple.

During the year, Syrian Temple had prepared an open letter to Shriners everywhere detailing the Melish-Luce affair. This had been mailed in advance to all of the representatives, and when the remainder of the nobility arrived in Denver they were handed copies of the pamphlet. Melish's fight to vindicate his actions and his administration was common knowledge and was reported prominently in all of the Denver papers. Syrian Temple brought a delegation of ninety-four Nobles, and though Mecca Temple continued to display animosity toward Melish, it was mostly verbal. There was no organized opposition, and when Luce presented his annual report, he announced that for personal reasons he would not accept reelection under any circumstances. One report in a Denver paper said that he had been forbidden to run by Medinah Temple. Luce told the nobility: "You will pardon me if in closing this report I repeat what I said one year ago, 'that owing to other and important duties, I would not for any consideration be a candidate for reelection.' "

At the election of officers, Melish defeated Charles L. Field of Islam Temple, San Francisco, to resume his office as Imperial Potentate and the long bitter feud was ended. Melish and Syrian Temple felt they had been vindicated at last, and for the more than thirty years that followed, Melish was ever to be a power in the Order.

Because of the financial condition of the country, only about one thousand Nobles were present in Denver, but they made a good showing in the parade, appearing in full dress with their red fezzes. And they had a good time. Zemzem wells were set up in all of the hotels by various temples and there was a great deal of marching back and forth to drink freely of the cooling waters. Sixty weary Sons of the Desert were initiated at a ceremonial function. The ladies gazed in awe at Mt. Evans and the Denver citizenry enjoyed the pranks, especially the appearance of James A. Fox, Potentate of Aleppo Temple of Boston, who looked like President Grover Cleveland and was frequently introduced as such.

There were four bands in the parade, and the Zuhrah patrol from Zuhrah Temple of Minneapolis created quite a sensation. Forty Nobles had been organized into a marching unit. They wore white flannel trousers, white shirts, blue coats, brilliant flowing red neckties and yachting caps. Their intricate maneuvers while marching attracted the attention of everyone. This was the patrol under Captain John Shuey that is claimed to be the first in Shrine history.

Denverites laughed at the appearance of ex-mayor Wolfson astride a camel, and they laughed even louder when it was announced that the wild Arabian asses that had been kept in one of the Denver parks would not be able to participate in the parade. The asses had grown so fat they couldn't get into the cars provided for their transportation.

Officially the Denver session was important beyond the vindication of Melish. A resolution was presented officially delineating the power of the Imperial Potentate to suspend in any year until the next meeting of the Imperial Council any officer of that Council. But there was one matter of perhaps even more importance.

Imperial Potentate Hudson in his annual address reported: "Doubtless many, if not all of you, are aware of the fact that there exists in the states of Ohio, Illinois, Missouri, Texas and perhaps other western states, organizations composed of our colored fellow citizens, who have pirated our title almost verbatim, and for this and other various reasons, after conference with a number of the officers of this Council, it was deemed advisable to have our body duly incorporated not only that we might hold our present style and title exclusively, but that should it become necessary to own property, we would be able to hold same as a Body with a legal status."

Corporate entity actually had been obtained from the state of New York, but the matter had been referred to a committee for one year, and the action of the Imperial Potentate in initiating the program was not approved.

The right to full title in the name of the Order and

its emblems was to plague the Imperial Council for more than a score of years to come.

Also at the Denver Session, the Committee for the revision of the Ritual that had been working at its task for several years made its report, and the new Ritual was adopted unanimously.

Now, Melish assumed again the office of Imperial Potentate, and the Imperial Recorder's office was placed in the hands of Ben Rowell of Boston, who was to serve in that capacity for many years. And when they began to examine the books, they made the startling discovery that the Imperial Council was broke. Melish used the word "bankrupt" to describe the condition of the treasury when he reported to the next session of the Imperial Council, held at Nantasket Beach, a summer resort near Boston.

In some respects the meeting of 1895 was unique. For the first time the Imperial Potentate, Imperial Recorder and Imperial Treasurer were housed in the same hotel, which incidentally provided "room and eats on the good old American plan for $3.50 a day." And for the first time the Imperial Council began operation on the basis of a fiscal year in an attempt to clear up deficits and live within its income. Thus, reports of all descriptions from the various temples were based for that one year on a span of time beginning January 1, 1894, and ending on April 30, 1895.

In his annual report, Melish declared that because of the bankrupt condition of the treasury following the meeting in Denver, he had ordained that expenses be held to a minimum. As a result, he said, he had made only two visitations during the entire year. One was to Aladdin Temple in Columbus, Ohio, which was near his home in Cincinnati, and the other was to Louisville, where Kosair Temple became the first to portray the new and revised Ritual that had been approved at Denver. Melish had also presided both as Potentate of Syrian and as the Imperial Potentate at a ceremonial in his own temple on February 22, 1895, when 219 candidates received the Mystic Rites, the largest class to that time in the history of the Shrine. And the Shrine was growing rapidly. More than 7,000 new members were initiated by all of the various temples from January 1, 1894, to January 1, 1895, making a total of 37,348. The estimated worth of the seventy-one temples in forty-three states was placed at $348,928.85, a sizable amount for a fraternal organization that was not yet twenty-five years old.

Aleppo Temple of Boston had become the largest in Shrinedom. It boasted 2,573 members. Mecca was still second with 2,378, Lu Lu of Philadelphia was third with 2,315, Medinah of Chicago was fourth with 2,107, and Syrian was fifth with 1,255. By and large they were a happy group of men, but once again in 1895 as he had in 1893, Melish realized that jollity, camaraderie and hospitality were not enough.

During his first term as Imperial Potentate, Melish had challenged the various temples to develop some local charity. Some had responded and others had not, but during his second term he put the pressure on the temple Potentates in a letter to each of them, urging them in some manner to undertake a philanthropic enterprise. This time most of the temples responded. Some collected money from the members which was turned into baskets of groceries and clothing at Christmastime for the unfortunates, whether they were Shriners (even Masons) or not. Most of the charity was showered on non-Shriners, of course, since most Shriners didn't need it. But there were a few who had found themselves in straitened circumstances, and for them Mecca Temple set up its own employment agency to help the Shriners help themselves. Over the years these charitable enterprises were to grow until eventually there would be created what has been called the "world's greatest philanthropy," the Shriners' Hospitals for Crippled Children.

Also at this session, Melish won his point with respect to the power of the Imperial Potentate. A resolution was adopted which said: "The Imperial Potentate is the executive officer of the Order within the Jurisdiction of this Imperial Council. He may suspend until the next session of the Imperial Council, or for a less time, any official of the Imperial Council, or any temple or officer thereof, for violation or disobedience of the Constitution, Regulations, or Edicts of the Imperial Council."

Melish was largely instrumental also in having the Imperial Council officially decline the Charter which had been obtained by Hudson and Luce in the previous year from the state of New York. Incorporation, the Council said, is "neither desirable nor necessary."

So, Melish left office, the last Imperial Potentate ever to serve more than one year. For him, it had been a triumphant year, for he had managed to institute some reforms that were necessary if the Shrine was to continue. Principal among these was a more businesslike way of conducting the fraternity's affairs. There was still much to be desired, for Rowell as the Imperial Recorder and the various temple Recorders didn't care too much about records. Nevertheless there were signs that the Shrine was reaching maturity; and even if he were not in authority, Melish was to make it a point to be around to challenge constantly the Imperial Council to do better. Under his whiplash, they did so in the years ahead.

So things were improving.

10

Era Ends—Charity Begins

"O spirits gay and kindly heart!
Precious the blessings ye impart!
JOANNA BAILLIE

In 1886, when the Shrine had held its convention in Cleveland, it could boast of 3,039 members. Ten years later, when the Imperial Session again was held in Cleveland with Al Koran Temple as the host, the Shrine had grown to 41,502 members. It was almost unbelievable, even to the Imperial officials. But there it was in official figures, and it became plain to harassed Officers that with growth there naturally would be problems. It was for this reason that in Cleveland, the Imperial Council declined to change the annual meetings of the Imperial Session to triennial affairs, the plan followed by the Knights Templar.

"Our Order is young," said the Jurisprudence and Laws Committee in declining to sanction the change, "and some of its features, not to say principles, are evolutionary, and some of the measures adopted for its government are still experimental. . . . [But] as we understand it, the only argument made against the position we maintain grows out of financial considerations."

Actually the panic of 1893 was over and there was prosperity on every hand. And if the world generally was in a turmoil, it didn't appear to affect either the Shrine or the United States. The Ethiopians had slaughtered 4,600 Italian troops and 3,000 natives under Italian command in a surprise attack at Adowa on February

28, but it meant little or nothing to the Shriners. Nor, for that matter, did the slaughter of 5,000 Armenians in Constantinople by the Turks in late August, just a month after the Cleveland meeting. Three weeks before the session convened on June 23, Britain had granted a wireless patent to Marconi, but the Shriners had never heard of it, and it was to be many years before a parade would be broadcast. H. A. Becquerel discovered in that year the radioactivity of uranium, but it would be a half-century before its destructive force would be utilized by man.

What bothered the Shriners in those days was the Shrine. It simply was too good a thing to let slip. One of the more controversial issues before the Cleveland meeting was that of prerequisite membership in other Masonic bodies. What happened when for one reason or another a Shriner failed to continue his membership in either the Scottish Rite or the Knights Templar? The 1896 convention attempted to answer the question.

The Imperial Council approved the following statement, with respect to the problem, by the Jurisprudence and Laws Committee:

Since good standing in Templar or Scottish Rite Masonry is the basis of membership in this Order, it is fair that suspension or expulsion by either, as held by the Imperial Potentate, should disqualify one for membership in this organization. It is true an applicant, in order to enter here, need not belong to both the other societies, but having rendered himself unworthy of affiliation in either he ought not to find shelter here on the ground that the other took no notice of his shortcomings. This we regard as correct interpretation of the spirit of our Order, for by this rule we hold up the highest standard of manhood, and preserve on the highest plane the friendly and fraternal relations between the Arabic Order and Templar and Scottish Rite Masonry.

But at the same time it should be set forth as a true statement of our law, that there is nothing in its provision that in any way disqualifies a Noble for continuous membership in the Temple or in any way subjects him to discipline, if, having been a member of either or both the prerequisite orders, he voluntarily and honorably withdraws from either or both of them and lives without offense against their laws.

But though the Imperial Council approved that statement in 1896, it was by no means a permanent interpretation of Shrine law. It just couldn't work. If advanced Masonic degrees were to be a prerequisite, they must be a permanent prerequisite. Otherwise those Masons who wanted to be Shriners and nothing else could go through the motions of becoming 32° Masons or Knights Templar and then drop them as soon as they had experienced the Shrine. A similar program also might be evolved with respect to basic Masonry itself.

In later years as disagreements developed within several of the Masonic jurisdictions, there was a movement (which died aborning) to make the Shrine entirely independent of the Masons. But the spiritual thread and the moral teachings of Masonry, the Rites and the Shrine were too closely interwoven to be raveled by those who had been rebuked for violations of the law. As a matter of fact (as will be seen) the real trend was exactly the opposite as one Imperial Potentate after another, in various forms, adopted as the theme of his year in office a closer association with Masonry and the Rites.

One other change was made in Cleveland which also was to be temporary. Following the lead of other fraternal organizations, the Imperial Council ordained that of the thirteen officers in the Imperial Divan, the last five should be appointed by the Imperial Potentate. The trial-and-error method of government in the Shrine was still in operation and would be for years to come.

During the years that followed, the new Imperial Potentate, Harrison Dingman of Almas Temple in

Washington, experimented a bit. There were no dissensions or problems, he reported to the twenty-third annual session held in Detroit, beginning June 8, 1897, but he did report that he had taken the first steps toward the possible establishment of Shrine temples outside of North America. Noble J. Lew Rake, a member of Rajah Temple in Reading, Pennsylvania, planned a business trip to England and reported to Dingman that there had been reports that a number of Masons in York, England, had expressed a desire to organize a temple there. Accordingly, Rake was appointed a special deputy of the Imperial Potentate and authorized to investigate. But the whole affair ended right there. The British Masons simply were not interested in the breezy program of the American fun-loving Shriners.

Several thousand Shriners arrived in Dallas, Texas, June 12, 1898, to be the guests of Hella Temple, but the Shrine did not make the front page of the local papers until two days later. The nation was at war. The *Maine* had been sunk in Santiago Harbor on February 15. Admiral Dewey had destroyed the Spanish fleet in Manila Bay on May 1. Just as the Shriners arrived, the Marines landed outside Santiago. Thirty transports with 27,000 American soldiers were afloat somewhere off Tampa, Florida, under the command of Admiral Sampson. But the Shriners were determined to have fun anyway. The Order was still growing despite the war and most of the Shriners were too old for military service anyway.

The Dallas *News* reported on Monday morning, June 13, that "the advance guard of the Shriners hit Dallas yesterday afternoon. They hit it hard and the jolt was felt for blocks around. In fact, ever since their arrival, they have kept up a succession of jolts that kept the church bells ringing and awoke the chickens."

"The only event of importance today [Monday, June 13]," reported the *News*, "is the opening of the Hella cistern at the Oriental Hotel. This cistern is reported to contain nothing but Adams Ale. Every devout Shriner is requested to come and bring his fellow along." But that was only the beginning. If Detroit had been gay, Dallas was gayer, as the Hella Shriners had promised, even with a war in full swing.

The Dallas *News* sent its cartoonists (it was before the day of newspaper photography) to depict for the readers what the Shriners were doing. One cartoon showed the fez-topped gentlemen gathered around the Hella cistern. And the writer telling the people of Dallas of the profusion of red fezzes said, "The Shriners made the town look like it had a bad case of measles and it sounded like it was in the center of an attack on Guantánamo. . . . The average Shriner never ventures out of doors without his fez for fear of catching cold and the only thing that can surpass his voice in volume and density is a well-trained fog horn, skillfully handled. The Shriners are a unique class. They are made up almost exclusively of businessmen and yet during their sessions of the Imperial Council they throw all of this to the winds. They are usually dignified, but on such occasions as this they relegate their dignity to the ashbarrel, give a whoop and turn things loose. They do not violate any of the laws of decency or decorum. Long experience has taught them how to have a good time without any violation."

By the time the official escort parade was ready to start on Tuesday morning, June 14, the Dallas newspapers could no longer keep their story on the inside pages, war or no war. After all, one railroad president from Columbus, Ohio, had brought the boys from Aladdin Temple to Dallas in his own private car. Another group of railroaders from Palestine, Texas, sent their band to march in the parade, and a professional band from Dallas also participated. There was a long line of carriages, drawn by matched black and white horses, containing all of the representatives to the Imperial Council. In the last vehicle was Imperial Potentate Albert B. McGaffey of El Jebel Temple in Denver. His equipage was drawn by two black and two white horses, each of them led by what appeared to be a Nubian slave.

There were several reasons for the selection of Buffalo as the meeting place for the 1899 Imperial Session. Most important, perhaps, was the fact that members of Ismailia Temple wanted to entertain the Imperial dignitaries and had campaigned in Dallas for the meeting, wearing special signs on their shirts saying, "Put me off at Buffalo." Furthermore, they elected their George L. Brown as the new Oriental Guide, the lowest elective office in those days, and he wanted to show off his town and his temple. But perhaps equally important was the fact that Ismailia Temple had been in the forefront of charitable activities, which now had reached important proportions.

As early as 1890, three years after receiving its charter, Ismailia Temple had introduced a charitable enterprise which in the years to come and in various forms was to be one of the foundations of the Order. On April 9 of that year Ismailia had given a Grand Ball, attended by the elite of the city, and followed it on July 18 with an outing by the shores of Lake Erie. The press reported at the time that the Nobles appeared in gorgeous regalia, the talk of which brings memories to all who attended. From the two events, Ismailia Temple raised more than $1,800, all of which was applied to the Newsboys' and Bootblacks' Home. This perhaps was the first instance of a Shrine temple's raising funds through public enterprise.

Other temples raised their charitable funds through gifts of Shriners, and Imperial Potentate Ethelbert F. Allen of Ararat Temple in Kansas City, Missouri, reported in Dallas that seventy-one of the seventy-eight temples had that year engaged in some form of charity. For most of them, it was contributions of money or food at Christmastime. Others sent their charitable gifts to Masonic Homes in their respective states, but there was no doubt that charity, just for the sake of sweet charity, was pretty well established by the end of the century as a prime tenet of Shrine policy, although it was not yet a part of Shrine law.

Then, too, Buffalo was perhaps chosen because of its nearness to Niagara Falls, which was just coming into its own as the great haven for honeymooners and sightseers from everywhere. The convention held at the resort city in 1891 had attracted a fair crowd, but it was before the day of Imperial parades, and it rated only passing mention in the press. Now things were different. The parade was important, and Buffalo's extensive German population loved a parade.

Actually, when the parade was finally held on June 14, 1899, it was a rather mixed-up affair. The event had been planned, all right, except for one thing: the parade was bigger than the Nobles of Ismailia had anticipated. Month by month, new units were being formed in the temples, and it seemed that most of them arrived in Buffalo unheralded and unsung. It was too late to change the line of march, which had been arranged toward its end in a sort of circular movement. When the head of the parade reached the point where it should normally cross its own line of march, the end of the parade was still passing that corner. The front of the parade had to wait. And jammed behind the head, of course, were all the rest.

The only really important report in the entire official session was negative rather than positive. The Imperial Potentate reported he didn't think it necessary to encumber any special committee or take up the time of the Imperial Council with a program to establish temples in England, Mexico or the Sandwich Islands. He didn't even mention the Philippines, for which there had been agitation for a new temple because of the American civilian and military personnel established there following the Spanish-American War.

Thus ended the prime effort to establish temples outside of North America. Mexico and, of course, Hawaii eventually were to have temples of their own, but under later interpretation. Hawaii was then considered to be a part of North America because it was a territorial possession of the United States.

And so ended the era of the Gay Nineties. The Shriners had shown all America that they could be the gayest of the gay, and if their parades had not yet reached the size and gorgeous military splendor of the Knights Templar, certainly there was evidence on which to predict the future.

On January 1, 1900, the Shrine had 55,455 members. Patrols and bands of various types were forming so fast that regalia manufacturers were hard-pressed to keep up with them, especially to make each design different from the next. The Shriners had more fun than anybody.

Truly, it had been a glorious decade for the infant fraternity, but even then no one could really foresee the future or imagine its growth in the half-century that was to follow. Nor could they foresee the trend or the extent of the Shrine charity that was to come.

For the moment, they looked forward only to the next year and the next Imperial Session, which was to be held in Washington, D.C., where at least some of them were to meet William McKinley, a Mason but not a Shriner, who was the President of the United States. To meet him would be a thrilling experience.

11

Presidential Participation

There have been many Shrine parades larger and more gorgeous in their panoply than that of 1900, but somehow that Imperial Session in Washington, D.C., has carved for itself a place not to be usurped by bigness and splendor alone. It was perhaps like the comparatively small battles of Trenton and Princeton at the Yuletide season of 1776. As battles go, they were pretty small, but they represented a turning point in the Revolution and convinced Washington that his tatterdemalion army could win independence for colonial America.

So it was with the event in Washington, which was already celebrating the victory over Spain and was in the mood for any jollity the Shriners could provide.

There were seventy-nine temples under charter all across the land, and three more were under dispensation. It seemed that every member who could raise the funds wanted to attend the Imperial Session in Washington. After all, it was the capital of the nation. They would have a chance to see and perhaps shake hands with the popular William McKinley. They could see the beautiful buildings and even the Smithsonian Institution.

No records were ever kept of just how many Shriners and their families arrived in Washington for the three days of fun and, of course, the more serious business of the Imperial Council Session. But there were enough. The Washington *Post* reported on May 22 that the "city is in possession of the Nobles of the Mystic

Shrine." Never before had Washington been decorated for an event as it was for the nobility. One of the committees from Almas Temple had offered prizes for the best decorations in downtown Washington, and the merchants and realtors had responded. The red, green and yellow colors were everywhere. Some merchants had even erected miniature mosques across the fronts of buildings and in store windows. Jewelers were offering souvenir silver spoons commemorating the occasion.

When Imperial Potentate John H. Atwood of Leavenworth, Kansas, arrived, he was greeted by a section of the Marine Band, dressed in Arabic costume for the occasion. They marched him to his headquarters in the Riggs House and then proceeded to play for hours in

Sphinx Temple Band, Hartford, Conn.
Photographed in Washington, D.C., 1900

the lobby of the hotel, establishing the custom of band-playing in the hotels at Imperial Sessions which has never been abandoned.

Then came the morning of May 23. The newspapers had prepared their readers for the great event when Atwood would be escorted from the Riggs House to the Columbia Theater, where the Imperial Session was to be held. Column after column in the *Post* had detailed the line of march, the temples that would participate, the bands (most of them hired) that were to lead each section. And the people responded. The sides of Pennsylvania Avenue were filled with spectators when the mounted Washington police began to move at exactly 9:00 A.M.

Behind the police came the Arabic-costumed Marine Band, the Colors and then what was to remain in the

President McKinley Reviews the Shriners, Washington, 1900

memory of Washingtonians for years—an Arabic horse patrol of one hundred members of Almas Temple. They had scoured the Virginia and Maryland countryside for the finest horses to be found; and while they did not ride with the precision that was to be achieved in the years ahead by many Shrine horse patrols, they were decidedly the hit of the parade. Cheers went up everywhere as they passed.

After them came the patrols of various temples, headed by bands and, of course, the straggling evening-suited Nobles. Down Pennsylvania Avenue they moved. With cheers ringing on every hand, the parade reached the Treasury Turn and then moved into the White House grounds, where they were greeted by President McKinley, who stood on the South Portico and reviewed the full three thousand who were in the line of march, every band playing "Hail to the Chief," and every Shriner shouting a greeting to him.

Imperial Potentate Atwood was the last in the parade. He sat in a gorgeous barouche, drawn by six prancing black horses in shining harness; and as he passed the President, he stood and salaamed in fitting manner.

"It was impressive," the *Post* said, "to see the President of the United States stand to receive and to respond to the salutation of his brothers in the Mason's craft. It was impressive to see the long line that stretched in varicolored hue from one end of Pennsylvania Avenue to the other, and it was impressive to think that all these men, so fantastic and strange, with 50,000 others, are bound together by the most solemn vows to stand for all that man could hold most dear, all that makes a nation great, all that goes to improve mankind at large."

But with this parade, reviewed by the President, the festivities were only just beginning. Atwood was a great orator of the flowery persuasion. He had traveled untold thousands of miles, visiting temples, creating new ones and spellbinding the nobility. His speech at the opening of the Imperial Session was a masterpiece.

After receiving the welcome of Noble John W. Ross, Commissioner of the District of Columbia, and of Past Imperial Potentate Harrison Dingman on behalf of the other Masonic bodies, Atwood responded in part:

"By the shore of the Gulf of California; where the green waters of the St. Lawrence lave the shores of the Thousand Isles; amid the mighty forests where rolls the Oregon; and where the tireless tide of the Atlantic forever frets the Narragansett coast; in the pineland of the north and the palm lands of the south and in the measureless pastures of the boundless west, the black tents of our many tribes cast their shadows in the setting sun; from every clime and from every corner of the continent, we, the representatives of all these many tribes, have come as Moslems to their Mecca, and as citizens and guests to the city that capitals the mightiest empire seen by the sun, or washed by the waves of any sea. There are among us who, as subjects and citizens, owe allegiance to a different power than here is seated in incomparable splendor by the banks of the Potomac; but they will join with us, whose nation this is, in paying tribute to you, the denizens of our capital city, and they would not stay my tongue when I say that here stands the metropolis of a realm, matchless indeed—an empire above whose tropic islands of the sea flashes the Southern Cross, and over whose continental provinces the pale polestar stands as a steadfast sentinel. . . .

"May the walls of your homes and palaces of your great municipality prove to be made of stones from the quarries of Estherphane, and may they lift their heads high as the topless towers of Ilium, to stand forever as a symbol of liberty, as a token of freedom, until in the rush and roll of the coming years, time shall have become eternity, and earth be remanded to chaos again."

But even with this tribute to Washington and the patriotism he inspired among the nobility, Atwood was by no means finished. There was still his tribute to the Shrine itself. In his flowery words, he set a pattern that the Shrine was to follow in the years ahead.

"The Shriner," he said, "proclaims the doctrine of joy—teaches the lesson that such joy as enters unto man's life is a boon and a blessing, sent to alleviate the darker hours that must come to all. . . .

"Let us remember, too, that a smile adds beauty to the plainest countenance, while a frown can but mar the features of the most beautiful; that the light of pleasantness and peace in the eyes of man or woman, makes dark places bright, while scowls are centurions in the cohorts of darkness. . . .

"These lessons man is coming fast to learn, as is made manifest by the growth of our noble Order. For in the years of its life upon this continent, it has waxed exceedingly and grown to proportions that are magnificent indeed. From sea to sea and from Montreal to Mexico, our temples lift aloft their heads to flash back the splendors of the rising sun."

Judged by the oratorical standards of a half-century later, Atwood's remarks would have been a bit too verbose. But in 1900 the standards had been set by the then reigning prince of oratory, William Jennings Bryan, and the Imperial Potentate was wildly cheered by the nobility.

The principal work of the session was the adoption of a resolution which as much as anything else spiked the efforts of a renegade group which had claimed exclusive jurisdiction for the Scottish Rite in the United States. Walter M. Fleming, among others, had participated in the effort to establish once and forever the supreme jurisdiction of the Northern and Southern Supreme Councils as the only authoritative voice of the Scottish Rite. This had been a sore rankling in the Masonic bodies for some time. And the action of the Shrine in Washington, confining its membership to Knights Templar and members of the two American Scottish Rite jurisdictions, as much as any other one event, eliminated the efforts of the renegades.

Otherwise, the representatives and the Imperial Divan hurried through the work they had to do in order to participate in the great night parade; and if the people of Washington had been astounded by the morning parade, they were to be dumbfounded by the night affair, even the worldly-wise reporters for the capital newspapers.

"They passed, it seemed, in unending myriads," said the Washington *Post.* "The music of the bands was continuous. The order was perfect. The whole scene was wonderful. Then the lights sprung up and the whole city was flooded with illumination that far surpassed anything that had ever been thought possible. The scenes were spectacular to a degree. They were in no regard below the standard the most fertile imagination could possibly have conceived. Nothing equalling their demonstration of strength upon the most historic thoroughfare in the nation's capital will ever be seen again in the history of Shrinedom until the Nobles again make their pilgrimage to this oasis. The Shriners gave Washington such a spectacle as even the capital of the nation does not often have an opportunity to see. Perhaps never before did three thousand men march down Pennsylvania Avenue, attired in evening dress to the music of a dozen bands, and lighted on their way by fires of every color."

And if the Almas horse patrol and the precision marching of the Al Koran foot patrol had stolen the show in the morning, then the red-fezzed gentlemen from Oriental Temple in Troy, New York, stole the night parade. Attached to the lapels of their evening suits, the Troy men had attached large red artificial roses, in the center of which was a tiny electric bulb, and on the proper order, they would stop and suddenly the lights would gleam, powered by dry batteries, which was something of an innovation in those days.

The parade ended in Monument Park, where the greatest fireworks display in history was held, or at least that's what the Washington reporters said. The first fiery piece was a giant Shrine pin in red, green and yellow fire, and the last, of course, was a giant flag, which sprang to life as the Marine Band played "The Star-Spangled Banner."

The parade and the fireworks lasted so long that it was almost eleven o'clock before the representatives

Nobles Call on the President

sat down for the Imperial banquet, held in the grand ballroom of the Riggs House. The decorations were on the most lavish scale ever devised in Washington, according to the *Post*. The entire ballroom was like a conservatory, filled with pink, red and white tropical foliage.

But the crowning event of the entire three days was the reception given by the President and Mrs. McKinley, members of the Cabinet and their wives at the White House for the nobility. Like the Riggs House, the Blue and East Rooms had been decorated profusely. Two bands, including the President's own Marines, played constantly, and five thousand persons were greeted by Mr. McKinley in a space of two hours. It was McKinley's most lavish reception during his tenure in the White House. He was a devout Mason and Knight Templar, but never became a Shriner.

Following in normal line, Lou Winsor, a member of Saladin Temple in Grand Rapids, Michigan, was elected Imperial Potentate, and he was destined to make a great contribution to the traditions of the Order. At the next session in Kansas City, the Imperial Council would celebrate its silver anniversary and, like the next several sessions to come, it was to be bigger and better than ever.

The Shrine was becoming of age.

12

With Charity for All

There was and is nothing so dear to the heart of a Shriner as a pilgrimage. Ever since the day of the Mecca prilgrimage through the great West, Nobles from every temple have moved from place to place, just to visit with their fraternal associates and to see the wonders of the world. There was—and is—no significance other than the fun they have. In playing at Moslems and infidels, they have no thought for the hot sands that must be traversed to touch the Kaaba in the holy city of Mecca by the true pilgrims of the Islamic faith. But they do have itchy feet, and for those who can afford it, there is a pilgrimage somewhere almost anytime.

Lou B. Winsor and his retinue made the great pilgrimage to Hawaii. It was the crowning event of his administration.

In the course of the nineteenth century, Hawaii had become a crossroads of the Pacific, with ships of many lands stopping there. Yet geographically, if not ethnically, the islands—lying some two thousand miles off San Francisco—were closer to the United States than to any other nation, and trade had been building up between the two countries. More Americans, attracted by the climate of the islands, were migrating there. The result was that the people of Hawaii, a republic since 1893, when Queen Liliuokalani was overthrown, voted to be annexed to the United States. Congress passed the necessary legislation, and the islands became a territory in 1900.

Meanwhile, Masonry in Hawaii was growing. Also,

a number of Masons of the higher degrees had become members of Islam Temple in San Francisco and, on their visits to the mainland, would enjoy themselves within the shelter of that Oasis. It was by no means surprising, then, that at the meeting in Washington the nobility of Honolulu asked for and received—with the blessings of Mother Islam—a dispensation to open a new temple in Hawaii to be known as Aloha. (If the name lacked Arabic meaning, it was sufficiently foreign to the English tongue to be used).

Shortly after he assumed office, Imperial Potentate Winsor expressed the thought that he would enjoy constituting Aloha Temple himself, and his own Saladin Temple, of which he was still the Potentate, undertook the work of organizing the pilgrimage. Accordingly, on February 25, 1901, the Imperial special train steamed out of the Grand Rapids station, bound for Medinah Temple in Chicago, where the traveling nobility would be entertained. In Chicago, the train grew in size, and it continued to grow until, when the caravan reached San Francisco, there were 114 Nobles and 58 ladies aboard. They visited temples all across the land and on March 14, after a long sea voyage, Aloha Temple was instituted under designation. The charter would not be granted until the 1901 Imperial Session in Kansas City.

This was the first of many pilgrimages made to Hawaii, until now each succeeding Imperial Potentate makes the Imperial cruise to the islands. Altogether Winsor and his party traveled 7,346 miles by land and 4,000 miles by sea. And perhaps equally important to the pilgrimage itself is the fact that it was on the first cruise to the islands that Winsor and twelve of his closest associates gathered together and formed the Jesters, the first of the organizations within the Shrine.

Including the pilgrimage, Winsor was able to report to the 1901 session of the Imperial Council that he had spent nearly half his time during the past year at Shrine affairs. The Shrine, indeed, was becoming a major organization. Within a few years it would be almost compulsory for an Imperial Potentate to devote his entire time to the job of administering the affairs of the fraternity.

When the Shriners arrived in Kansas City for their meeting on June 11, 1901, the Nobles of Ararat Temple had done everything they could do to make the event a joyful one. They had to try to live up to the session held in Washington, and that was to be difficult, principally because the city administration had made no arrangements for handling the crowds. But if the parade in Kansas City fell a bit short of the desired results, the parade in San Francisco in June of 1902 made up for it, even though there were travel difficulties involving Philip Shaffer, the Imperial Potentate from Lu Lu Temple in Philadelphia.

The affair began well enough and attracted considerable public attention. Special trains were popular in those days, and Shaffer and a group of Nobles from Lu Lu and Boumi in Baltimore chartered one for the joyous trip across the nation. At the same time, James McGee arranged another special train from New York in association with temples in the New England area, and before the trains reached Chicago something of a race had developed. Actually, the New York train was so long that it had to be divided into two sections. McGee said it was because the railroads didn't have water hoses long enough at some of the way stations to water the entire train. But others along the line said that was silly because the Shriners didn't need water anyway.

The Mecca trains were well ahead when they reached Denver, and Shaffer suffered a great indignity there when railroad officials put a slow train on the tracks ahead of his special. Still further along in Colorado, the engine pulling the Imperial Potentate's train broke a drive shaft. When Shaffer and his party finally arrived in San Francisco, it was just barely in time for him to participate in the parade.

He arrived to gaze upon a fairyland. The *Examiner* reported: "The big, sometimes prosaic city was transformed into a fairy region of beautifully blended hues. So brilliant was the night that a crescent moon which hung in the western sky, vainly tried to win recognition among the glowing crescents that in honor of the Mystic Shriners adorned the town." Electric lights were just coming into their own and San Francisco made the most of them. The Ferry Building was a beautiful sight. And spelled out in electric letters five feet high over the City Hall, was "Es Selamu Aleikum," the traditional welcome greeting of the Shriners. There was the parade, the like of which the West had never seen before. Three giant searchlights played their beams on the multicolored marching columns. Colored fire burned from a dozen stands along the line of march. Skyrockets and Roman candles were fired by the marchers at every opportunity. And the big hit of the parade was a float entered by the Masons of San Francisco. It was a giant prairie schooner, pulled by thirty oxen and containing a number of pioneer Masons of the city. The wagon was surrounded by cowboys and followed by a screeching band of Indians making periodic attacks on the wagon. Behind this group was another float representing an army camp; naturally the blue-clad soldiers invariably saved the occupants of the schooner.

The Imperial Session itself took some notable actions that were to have a profound effect upon the Shrine and its future. In the field of fraternal government, there had been some difficulty within the Imperial Divan when temples failed to reelect as representatives those who aspired to become Imperial Potentate. Under the Shrine code it is necessary to be a member of the Imperial Council to be elected to the Imperial Divan, but no provision had been made to keep such a member in the Council. A temple could reelect or reject anyone as a representative, and this had been done. It was even possible that a man who was about to be elected Imperial Potentate could be rejected by his temple, in which event he could not hold the high office.

This didn't seem quite cricket and the representatives proceeded to amend the law. As adopted, it read: "An Imperial Potentate does not become a Past Imperial Potentate until his successor in office is elected and installed. His temple should elect him as a representative to the session of the Imperial Council over which he is to preside as Imperial Potentate, but failure to re-elect him does not deprive him of any of his official rights or prerogatives as Imperial Potentate."

Meanwhile the development of Shrine charity had become ever more dear to the heart of each succeeding Imperial Potentate. After the Galveston, Texas, hurricane and tidal wave which caused six thousand deaths, in September of 1900, Imperial Potentate Winsor had sent a contribution from the Shrine emergency fund. Both Winsor and Imperial Potentate Shaffer in the following year called on the temples all over the land to send as much as they could and they responded heartily. But, in addition, Shaffer once again called for Christmas charity contributions.

As they had in the past, the nobility responded with thousands of dollars that were expended for Christmas baskets for the poor of their communities. In addition, there were toys for the children and extra donations for the various Masonic homes. By and large, none of the charity was expended on Shriners or their families; but with the growth of the Shrine there was talk of a Shrine home, patterned, on a national basis, after many of the jurisdictional Masonic homes, and it was at the 1902 session of the Imperial Council that the subject came before the nobility officially.

Morocco Temple of Jacksonville, Florida, made the proposal to establish a national permanent home for indigent Shriners, and a school where the children of such Shriners and the dependent orphans of Shriners might be educated, and where the dependent widows of deceased Shriners might find employment and homes.

But the Committee on Jurisprudence and Laws could see no need for such charity. It reported to the session that "we can see no necessity at this time for such action on the part of the Imperial Council. Under the blessings which Allah the Great has bestowed on the oases in which we have erected our temples, each member of the nobility has opportunity afforded him to care for himself and those dependent upon him. Besides, the spirit of charity, especially to those of the household of faith, is so thoroughly inculcated in the hearts of the nobility that indigence is almost unknown amongst Shriners, and, if known, it can find relief in each temple. The many homes for orphans and widows which have been established by the bodies, membership in which is prerequisite for admission to the Ancient Arabic Order, and of which homes we are advocates and supporters, precludes the necessity of establishing an eleemosynary institution under the auspices or control of the Imperial Council. We therefore recommend that the communication of Morocco Temple be printed in our proceedings and that no further consideration be given to the suggestions offered at this time."

The Imperial Representatives went along with the recommendation, but there was talk among the Nobles that perhaps some national charity, instead of local effort by individual temples, might be desirable. The recommendation by Morocco Temple and the rejection of it by the Jurisprudence and Laws Committee both may well have been prophetic. With the passing of time, it became apparent to the Shrine leaders that some international charity was not only desirable but almost a necessity, though the charity was not to be for Shriners.

13

The New Century

The astonishing growth of the Ancient Arabic Order
Nobles of the Mystic Shrine in the first decade of the
twentieth century brought its problems, among which
was the question of where the Imperial Council sessions
should be held. Ever since Al Koran Temple had invited the Imperial Council to hold its session in Cleveland, it had become customary for the Imperial officers
to await an invitation before deciding on the next meeting place, and during the following years this had been
a most satisfactory arrangement. But, beginning with
the 1900 session in Washington, the expense to the
local temple of entertaining the Imperial Session was
so great as to become embarrassing.

Almost from the time the 1900 parade marched under the White House portico and cheered President
McKinley, there were two distinct divisions of the Imperial Session. There was the official meeting of the
representatives and the Imperial Divan, where official
business was transacted and laws enacted or amended;
and there was also the business of pageantry and parade. With each passing year, as we have seen, the
pageantry and parades were growing bigger and more
gorgeous. Decorations were more extensive and more
costly, and someone had to pay the bill. Still, it could
not be denied that, if the membership wanted to parade, it certainly had a right to do so. Reports from
various temples indicated that the units were the very
lifeblood of the organization. With each passing year,

more temples added patrols. As early as 1889, Lu Lu
Temple in Philadelphia had appropriated money to buy
instruments and uniforms for an all-Shrine band. Almas,
Lu Lu and Al Chymia Temples had horse patrols, and
still the Shrine was growing and more and more members wanted to participate in these activities.

From the 55,455 members on January 1, 1900, the
Shrine grew to 149,157 members on January 1, 1910,
and it was during this period that the problem of a
meeting place became important. There were no invitations from cities with temples in 1902, and the session
in 1903 was held at the summer resort village of Saratoga Springs, New York. In 1904, it was held at the
seashore resort of Atlantic City, New Jersey, and it was
there that the Imperial Council decided to take some
official action with respect to a meeting place.

The Committee on Time and Place reported that
the Imperial Council is a distinctive body in itself, apart
from the rank and file of the great Order that creates
it, and should not depend on an invitation from a subordinate temple in order to be guided for the selection
of a place to meet. Therefore, for future meetings it
was the committee's opinion that the Imperial Council
would be wise in selecting a place (summer resort pre-
ferred) where there was no temple.

The report was adopted by the Imperial Council,
and the 1905 session was held in Niagara Falls, New
York, but there were difficulties. The boys liked to dress
up in their Arabic costumes and play Moslems and infidels. They liked the weekly rehearsals of band and patrol. But what was the use of parading if there was
no one to watch and cheer? The fact was that when
the Shrine took over a summer resort, there was no
one about except the Shriners and they all wanted to
be in the parade.

The result was that by 1906 the Shrine conventions
were back in the cities again; and except for Atlantic
City and Miami, both of which offer parade crowds,

the sessions since invariably have been held in cities. After the Second World War, the Imperial Council contributed at the rate of ten cents a member to the temple which entertained the Imperial Sessions.

The first city to win an Imperial Session after the ukase of 1904 was Los Angeles. The Time and Place Committee, meeting in Niagara Falls in 1905 evidently had learned from the uniformed units that summer resorts might not be as desirable as had been expected. Henry A. Collins of Rameses Temple in Toronto, the first Imperial Potentate from a temple outside the United States, had been elected to that exalted office at Niagara Falls, and he put his stamp of approval on the invitation from Al Malaikah Temple. But the session never reached Los Angeles. Instead, by an edict of the Imperial Potentate, it was changed almost at the last minute to Chicago, because on April 18, 1906, San Francisco was almost destroyed by an earthquake and fire:

> We are meeting today in the city of Chicago instead of in that beautiful city of Southern California. This is owing to the dreadful catastrophe that overtook San Francisco, and I will, in as few sentences as possible, give you my reasons for postponing the meeting in Los Angeles and the convening of it in Chicago.
>
> When the dreadful news was flashed around the world that San Francisco, the beautiful, had been almost entirely obliterated, and that want, suffering and misery had predominated, the question arose in my mind—what about the meeting of the Imperial Council? . . .
>
> I had considerable difficulty making up my mind as to the postponement of that meeting. I was fully cognizant of the fact that the Nobles of Los Angeles had gone to considerable trouble and expense to make the Assembly of the Imperial Council what it would have been—a pronounced success. . . . On the other hand I had to give considerable thought as to the effect our making the pilgrimage to Los Angeles would have on the Shrine body, and on the Masonic fraternity in general. I knew we would be open to the charge of heartlessness and want of proper

consideration for the sufferings of others, so that in the cause of common humanity, I felt it my duty to call off the meeting in Los Angeles and assemble in the city of Chicago. . . .

And as for the Imperial Council's assistance to fire-ravaged San Francisco, Collins reported:

I telegraphed the Imperial Treasurer to send the sum of $25,000 from our funds to Past Imperial Potentate Field, fully realizing the fact in so doing that the man who gives quickly gives twice. Whether I had the authority to so dispose of your funds is for you to say. However, I did so, and I take the full responsibility for the same. Correspondence with Noble Field will demonstrate to you how timely that assistance was, and I am delighted to say that many Temples have promptly come forward and by their donations have shown that they were in sympathy with the sufferings of the Nobles of Islam Temple.

Of course, the action of the Imperial Potentate was approved. Though the loss of life at San Francisco was placed at 452 (as nothing compared to the 6,000 lives lost in the Galveston hurricane and tidal wave in 1900) the property damage of $350,000,000 was appalling. And just to show that the nobility realized the inconvenience done to Al Malaikah Temple, Los Angeles was chosen by acclamation for the 1907 session of the Imperial Council.

The San Francisco disaster occurred less than two months before the Imperial Council was due to assemble. The result was that only the barest of preparations could be made for the session in Chicago, but there was no complaint of consequence. In fact, the charity extended to their fellow Nobles made the Shriners feel good. The representatives adopted a resolution which said:

The organic law of our body being inadequate to cover in time the exigency that then arose, he [Collins] wisely looked to the spirit of the law, and his conclusion already has received your official approbation, and in all the glorious history of the Shrine, no pages more splendid can be found than that which proclaims the prompt action of our Imperial Potentate and the wide-reaching charity of our Order; not so much in the dollars as in the fact that the timely gift was a tangible and material expression of the heartfelt sympathy and devotion felt for the stricken brethren of the nobility from every corner of our continent and from the far off islands of the sea; by his prompt and happy action, Noble Collins made proclamation to the world that in the minds and eyes of all Shriners the greatest of all things under the sun is Charity.

And so, once more—and in quite forceful fashion— the sweet name of charity resounded in the figurative tents of the American sons of Araby. The Shriners wanted to be charitable. It was all well and good to have their fun and spend fabulous sums on themselves in the process, but they wanted—even though the want might be subconscious—something more tangible. Fun without sharing could pall in time and the leaders were wise enough to know it.

By the close of the annual session of 1910, held in New Orleans, there were 120 temples, most of them with at least one parade unit and many of them with several. While most of the Nobles who wanted to participate in the unit activities probably could afford to finance themselves, there were many who could not. It soon became apparent to the temple administrations, therefore, that sending their units to all of the Shrine sessions was impossible, since frequently this represented trips all the way across the nation. Railroad fares, hotel accommodations, and meals, even at reduced rates, represented a strain on the temple finances that at times became impossible. Since it was unfair to tax the entire membership for the benefit of a few, some of the temples began to raise money for these purposes from outside activities. A number of temples resorted to raffles; others, to entertainments of one kind or another, principal among which was an indoor Shrine

Circus, apparently originated in Detroit in 1906. So successful have the circuses become that there were more than one hundred Shrine Circuses each year. Some of them are used to support the units, others to raise money for the Shrine Hospitals, but it is almost certain that the Shrine has been responsible, more than any other organization, for preserving the circus as a part of the American way of life. In 1910, there were scores of circuses all over the United States, performing under tents in large towns and small. There were big circuses such as Barnum and Bailey, Ringling Brothers, Sells-Floto, Hagenbeck and Wallace, and there were dozens of small ones. Some traveled by railroad and some in wagons and later in trucks. But by the end of the Second World War, there were only a handful, and were it not for the Shrine Circuses, the man on the flying trapeze and the wild animal acts would be almost extinct.

Some of the temples were becoming well-to-do, if not wealthy, and there were demands from the nobility that the Shriners own their own buildings and not be dependent on the various Masonic bodies for housing space. As early as 1908, some temples erected their own mosques and built them in the fairyland designs of ancient Arabia, replete with minarets and stately domes and decorated with mosaic and murals.

New uniformed units had also been created, among them the first Oriental Band in Shrinedom. Like many other Shrine organizations, it was happenstance rather than design that brought it about.

During Chicago's great world's fair in 1893 to celebrate the city's recovery from the disastrous fire caused by Mrs. O'Leary's cow, there were any number of Turkish exhibits and shows, including the beautiful and justly famed Oriental dancers. To ballyhoo the shows, including the one which starred "Little Egypt," there appeared on outdoor platforms the spieler and two performers, one playing a reed horn and the other a tomtom. Whether it was the horn and tomtom or the dancers that lingered in the memory of the Medinah nobles is not recorded, but in 1899 the redoubtable Frank Roundy, Potentate of Medinah and organizer of the first Arab Patrol in the Shrine, suggested that Medinah needed a band. He commissioned George J. Kurzenknabe, the temple organist, to form that band, and its initial membership was composed of the organist and the four members of the temple quartet.

No such instruments as were used at the World's Fair could be found in Chicago, and a German instrument maker was commissioned to design one. But when it was finally completed, it cost twenty dollars. Medinah's treasury in those days couldn't afford twenty dollars for one horn and besides it just didn't sound right. Inquiry continued, however, and in 1900 Kurzenknabe found a similar horn, which sounded just right, at the establishment of Sing Fat and Company in San Francisco. Best of all, the horn sold for one dollar.

With the arrival of the horns and tomtoms, a silver triangle and a Chinese gong, the band began rehearsals. There was just one tune, which for want of a better name was called "The Midway." Thousands of Shriners will remember some of the words that were sung to it:

"Mind what your mama says, and mind what your papa says,
  And don't go near that hootchie kootchie dance."

The band made its first public appearance at the April ceremonial of Medinah in 1900. By the time the September ceremonial was held, there were several more members of the band, but still just one tune, and the nobility was a bit tired of it, no matter how sensuous it might be. Word reached the band that unless new tunes were to be found, ripe tomatoes, seltzer bottles and whatnots would be brought into play. Kurzenknabe hastily dashed off some music that would fit the strange reed instruments and saved the band.

The Medinah Oriental Band made its first parade appearance at the 1901 session of the Imperial Council, but the rough cobbled streets of Kansas City made it difficult to play and the Medinah Patrol, which had been marching to the strange cadences, complained. And rightly so. But two more years of rehearsal improved the technique; and when the Orientalists marched at Saratoga Springs they were such a success that they went high hat and looked down on ordinary brass bands. The fact was that as they played "The Midway" at Saratoga, many of the watchers were transformed into muscle dancers and pseudo-contortionists. Since then, the Oriental Band has become a standard uniformed unit of almost every temple.

On June 12, 1906 at the Imperial Council session held at Medinah Temple in Chicago, Alvah "Pet" Clayton of Moila Temple in St. Joseph, Missouri, became the Imperial Potentate, and it was to be quite a year, even among all the other flamboyant conventions the Shrine had held since the first one in 1876, for Clayton was a consummate showman. Millar had learned this when he visited St. Joseph in 1905.

Clayton liked to travel, and he liked to have Shriners travel with him, and visiting one temple in the United States was not much different from visiting another. But, on November 12, 1906, Clayton received in the mail a request for a new temple in Mexico City, and while records are incomplete, the request undoubtedly sparked an idea—perhaps a caravan to the ancient city.

Clayton reported to the Imperial Council session in Los Angeles on May 7, 1907 that he had given considerable thought to the request from south of the border, and granted a dispensation to eleven Nobles who had signed the petition to form Anezeh Temple. Furthermore, because Shrine laws, rules and regulations were not as strict as they were to become in later years, Clayton began organizing his caravan without waiting for official action by the Imperial Council, and selected his own Moila Temple to become the mother temple for the new one.

On January 15, 1907 the "Shriners Special to Mexico City," with six sleeping cars, two diners and a baggage car pulled out of St. Joseph with 200 Nobles and their ladies aboard from Moila, Mecca, Za-Ga-Zig, El Kahir, Tangier and Sesostris Temples. Other special trains from the east and middle west joined the original sponsors of the new temple, and all arrived in Mexico City on the evening of January 19, where they were met by all the other American Shriners who had transferred their residence to the Mexican capital.

Altogether, Clayton reported to the Imperial Council that there were some 700 pilgrims present, including the ladies, and all were received in a special audience on Sunday morning at the Imperial Palace by President Porfirio Diaz, resplendent in full dress uniform. Noble David E. Thompson, the American Ambassador, was present to introduce the Imperial Potentate and his aides.

All in all, Clayton was impressed and decided he had made no mistake in granting a dispensation for the new temple to the nobility, and decided that the quality of the Shriners in Mexico City was high enough to institute the temple immediately. Clayton himself served as potentate on the evening of Monday, January 21. The degrees were conferred on eighty novices that evening, among them Diaz, who was the first of four presidents of Mexico to become a member of the order. Others in later years were Don Pascual Ortiz Rubio, General Don Abelardo Rodriguez and Licenciado Miguel Aleman Valdes.

Paintings of the four Mexican Presidents, four American Presidents and a Canadian Prime Minister hang in the Shrine rooms of the George Washington National Masonic Memorial in Alexandria, Virginia.

Clayton had had a hectic year, which began when

Heads of Government

Warren G. Harding

Franklin D. Roosevelt

Harry S. Truman

Gerald R. Ford

John Diefenbaker

Four Presidents of the United States and the Prime Minister of Canada, prominent members of the Shrine of North America.

Porfirio Diaz

Pascual Ortiz Rubio

Abelardo L. Rodriquez

Miguel Aleman Valdes

King Kalakaua

Mexican Presidents and King Kalakaua of Hawaii, who were Shriners.

New Mexico City Orthopedic Hospital

the San Francisco earthquake and fire forced the convention of 1906 to Chicago, but at long last, the time came for Al Malaikah Temple to entertain the Imperial Session of 1907 in Los Angeles; but it was an ill-starred meeting from the first. First of all, the postponement because of the San Francisco disaster had produced some hurt feelings in Al Malaikah and had caused some financial loss to the temple. Also, before the session even opened, the special train in which Lu Lu Temple of Philadelphia had traveled across the nation was wrecked just before it reached Los Angeles. There were no serious injuries, but more than 250 of the Nobles and their ladies had to be removed from the wreckage and placed on open flatcars to complete their journey. Much of the baggage was left at the scene, totally unusable.

Then, two days after the closing of the Imperial Session, occurred the worst disaster in the long history of the Shrine. On that Saturday of May 11, there were a score or more of special trains carrying the Nobles and their ladies on sightseeing tours of California. Some were from a single temple; others were from a group of temples which had special cars made up into a single train. Stops were being made at various points throughout the state. Among these special trains was one carrying members of Rajah Temple of Reading, Pennsylvania, Ismailia Temple of Buffalo, Al Koran Temple of Cleveland and Kalurah Temple of Binghamton, New York. The train had left Los Angeles the preceding afternoon, May 10; and after an overnight stop in Santa Barbara, it moved northward over the Southern Pacific tracks toward San Francisco, taking the shore route so that the nobility might see the wonders of the Pacific coast. Suddenly, near the town of Honda, sixty-three miles north of Santa Barbara, on a little peninsula that juts into the ocean beyond the town of Lompoc, the engine crashed into a defective switch.

One wheel of the engine was broken, so that it jumped the track and plowed into the sandy terrain at fifty miles an hour. The baggage car buckled, fell on top of the engine, then half-buried itself in the sand. The dining car, which followed the baggage car in the train, buckled and became little more than splinters. A sleeping car also jumped the track, but was less damaged. The remaining two sleepers remained upright— and fortunately, for the Nobles in those cars formed the only rescue force for hours after the accident. Altogether, thirty-one Nobles or their ladies were killed in the wreck, most of them from Rajah Temple. They had been in the dining car having a late lunch. Twenty other Nobles were injured and they were removed to San Luis Obispo by special trains provided by the railroad. When the trains arrived at the station, they were met by a group of Masons in the town who had been hastily organized into a relief corps that moved the injured to hospitals and into private homes until arrangements could be made for their further travel.

It was a horrible affair, but as usual the Masons and the Shrine rose to the occasion to give what relief they could. The newly elected Imperial Potentate, Frank C. Roundy of Chicago, was immediately notified, and he made arrangements with banks in Santa Barbara and San Luis Obispo to place unlimited credit at the disposal of Past Imperial Potentate George L. Brown of Ismailia Temple for the aid of the dead and injured. And he was authorized to call on all the resources of the Imperial Council as well as the resources of Al Malaikah and Islam Temples for what might be needed.

Yet, though the Los Angeles session had an unfortunate beginning and ending, the pageant itself was magnificent, coordinated as it was with the city's own Fiesta of Light, an outstanding parade of dozens of floats, displaying thousands of multicolored roses and carrying beautiful girls just as in the Rose Parades of later years. Millions of lights decorated the streets of the city. As the papers of the day said, the scene beggared description. In fact, it was, by far, the outstanding pageant in the history of the Shrine to that time.

After Los Angeles and its "Fiesta of Light," St. Paul and Louisville entertained the continental reunion of the Shriners; and if those cities lacked the facilities for a rose parade, they certainly did everything else to make the Shriners welcome. Each succeeding Imperial Session was becoming larger and gaudier than the last. When George L. Street of Acca Temple delivered his annual address in New Orleans in 1910, he commented that most Shriners thought nothing could ever exceed the decorations in Louisville, but that New Orleans had really outdone itself.

Still, all was not sweetness and light. With the tremendous growth of the fraternity, new problems constantly were being called to the attention of the Imperial Potentates. Frank C. Roundy, who had been one of the most popular of all the high executive officers of the Shrine, realized that growth itself was a problem because many thoughtless Shriners could be hidden in the multitude and many of their misdeeds, according to Shrine law, never brought to light. But his program was to uplift by policy and example rather than by use of the whip. In his annual address in St. Paul in 1908 he had declared, "We stand, it seems to me, for the finer spirit of Christianity; for the spirit that says 'I am my brother's keeper. What comes to him comes to me. Where he goes, there I go.' This being our spirit, the soul of this common country, the faith of all the faiths that constitute our nation, we should as Nobles strive to spread it ever wider and wider over this broad land."

It might be said that from the time he discovered the Shrine, Roundy's whole life had been given to it. It was he, it will be recalled, who instituted Arabian dress for the Medinah patrol. He served as director of Medinah and for many years as its Potentate.

But one of the knottiest and most controversial problems in the first decade of the new century was yet to be faced. Some of the Shrine leadership had seen it coming, but it was not until Louisville that it had reached such proportions that something had to be done about it. Perhaps it had really begun in Toronto in 1888, when many of the representatives took their wives with them and enjoyed the boat ride on the lake. With each passing year, more and more women attended the Imperial Sessions. Then in Los Angeles in 1907 the "Fiesta of Light" parade included girls riding on the floats. The fact that the "Fiesta of Light" parade was held jointly with the Shrine parade in no wise made them a part of the Shrine pageant, but everyone didn't know that.

In any event, the result was that in 1909 in Louisville, women actually participated in the Shrine parade itself. There were marching units and leaders of the band. Some Shriners took their wives right onto the street with them. It might well be that they enhanced the parade and made it lovelier than it really had a right to be, but the fact was that such activity was strictly against Shrine law; and when he issued the call for the 1910 meeting in New Orleans, Imperial Potentate

Street issued strict orders that no women were to appear in the parade under any circumstances whatever.

Actually, the parading was only a part of the problem. In Pittsburgh, for example, wives, daughters, sisters and even mothers of Shriners had organized a Ladies' Oriental Shrine, applied to Syria Temple for the privilege of purchasing old equipment, and demanded space in the mosque for meetings, recognition by the temple and the privilege of parading at the annual sessions. And when the some 31,000 Shriners and their wives arrived in New Orleans, it was noticeable that there were hundreds of white fezzes being worn by the women, some of them with the name of the Shrine temple of their home city on the fez. In the Far West, there had sprung up almost simultaneously another women's organization composed of relatives of Shriners called the "Daughters of Isis."

To correct the situation, Imperial Potentate Street in his official order on the female organizations cautioned temples and their officers against giving "any encouragement or support to any organization of women or men, purporting to be an Oriental Shrine, composed of the female members of the families of Nobles of our Order and I hereby forbid any Temple of Nobles of the Mystic Shrine, its officers or members, recognizing any such order of women."

What had happened, of course, was that the women had begun to see just how much fun the men were having as a result of their Shrine membership, and they wanted in on the act. It was not to be.

The Shrine meeting in New Orleans is still remembered by those who attended. It was by far the largest session ever held up to that time. One hundred and twenty-one temples were represented, most of them, it seemed, by uniformed units. Canal Street was a mass of light at night, but Bourbon Street was dim—as many of the Shriners wanted it. Jerusalem Temple had worked for a year for the great event, and the great contribution of the city was the reproduction of the great Mardi Gras parade, with all of the many carnival clubs participating. Newspapers of the city devoted page after page to the great event, decorating their pages with half-column cartoons of the Shriners in their baggy pantaloons, many of them smoking Turkish pipes.

Alee Temple of Savannah, Georgia, won considerable fame by publicizing its famous Chatham Artillery Punch, which the members claimed was made outside of Savannah only on the rarest and most important occasions. Only a few members were supposed to know the secret recipe dating to 1786, but astute reporters for the New Orleans papers found one Noble who gave the ingredients. He said: "Take the witchery of a southern belle, the magic of southern moonlight, the melody of the mockingbird and mingle them with the dew and you have it." It was notable that the Noble did not even mention "mountain dew."

The newspapers also were impressed by the fact that the Shriners almost invariably doffed their fezzes when they entered the myriad bars of the famous city. "It is because the Shriners are sworn never to wear a fez where they would not take their wife, mother, daughter or sweetheart," the paper said.

One of the most famous Shriners at the New Orleans meeting was Simon Michale of El Maida Temple of El Paso. He was the only Shriner present who had ever made the real pilgrimage to Mecca. He wore the same costume he had worn on that famous trip, and recalled that it was the hottest trip he ever made. "I stood against the sacred stone—that is the Kaaba—and the sun was so hot it scorched my forehead and my lips when I pressed them against the stone."

In between the parades and other social activities, the representatives took official action on three of the mandates laid down by Imperial Potentate Street, all of which are still a part of the Shrine law. The Imperial

Council forbade any temple or the membership of any temple to participate in any activity which might lead to the development of a female organization based on Shriner relationship, and it forbade the appearance of any but members of the Order, uniformed bands or male servants in the parade. But there was one more request Street had made, based on a standing resolution submitted at the 1909 session in Louisville. This concerned so-called temple headquarters being established at Imperial Sessions for the dispensation of hospitality.

Over the years it had become customary for various temples to have special suites of rooms at the hotels, where special gifts were handed out. At New Orleans, for example, Islam Temple of San Francisco gave out packages of raisins, sips of grape juice and even wines, including champagne. Medinah Temple of Chicago gave away thousands of roses to the ladies. As a result of all these activities, all too often some representatives had been delayed in their attendance at official council sessions. This was frowned upon and the 1910 session put a stop to it.

Furthermore, it was decided that liquor in any form would be prohibited in the various temple headquarters at Imperial Sessions, in effect sounding the death knell of the old custom of having hospitality headquarters maintained by the various temples. With each succeeding year, there were fewer of these oases, until they virtually disappeared. There were other and better places to go, particularly to the private suites of Potentates and other temple officials and to the headquarters of various uniformed units.

The temperance movement was gaining ground rapidly, particularly in various segments of the Protestant church, and most Shriners were members of the Protestant churches. Prohibition was being discussed openly, and in fact was only a few years away. But, equally important, the Shrine was becoming more complex. The very size of it made it so. With so many men, scattered over such a tremendous area, with sectional, regional and even national influences, there were bound to be differences of opinion and even jealousies (despite the universal Masonic background). These could be resolved only by law. The Imperial Council was the lawgiver, and its membership harkened to its task.

If the first decade of the new century had been one of growth, the second decade would be even more so; but the second decade would be also one of startling change, even though that change would be so subtle in its development that it would pass almost unnoticed until it burst resoundingly upon the scene in Portland, Oregon.

New faces were appearing at the Imperial Sessions and reaching the Imperial Divan, among them W. Freeland Kendrick of Lu Lu Temple, whose flamboyant showmanship and almost unbelievable popularity with Shriners everywhere were to make him one of the most powerful Potentates in the history of the Shrine. He was elected Imperial Outer Guard at the 1910 session of the Imperial Council.

14

To Faraway Places

The decade that began in 1910 at New Orleans and ended June 24, 1920, in Portland, Oregon, included what might be called the "glory years" in the history of the Shrine. They were years of fun and frolic, years of pilgrimage to far points of the world, years of growth more astounding than even the first decade of the new century, years of problems created by that growth, and, perhaps most important, years in which the Shrine was to be affected by the events of history itself.

Fred A. Hines of Al Malaikah (Los Angeles) was elected Imperial Potentate at New Orleans. At the very least, he was one of the hardest-working executives the Shrine ever had. He served for fifteen months, one of the longest tenures, occasioned by the fact that he had been elected in April and the 1911 session in Rochester, New York, was not held until July. During that period, he visited seventy-one cities in North America and the Hawaiian Islands. He was actually on the road in behalf of the Shrine for twelve full months and submitted a bill for expenses at the end of his term for $6,500, which was paid. It was an innovation and a portent of things to come, for the job of Imperial Potentate had reached such proportions that it was a full-time task. It meant a year in which the Imperial Potentate would have no time for his regular business, no matter what it might be.

Out of the welter of knowledge, Hines had gained in his service to the Shrine, he developed some rather novel ideas, and he proceeded to submit them to the representatives at the Rochester meeting. He was a forceful writer and a forceful speaker. He minced no words in his annual address. The Shrine, he said, must face the fact that few cities in North America could properly handle the annual sessions of the Imperial Council. They had become too big. There was not enough hotel space. He suggested that perhaps North America should be divided into four or five jurisdictions, each headed by a deputy Imperial Potentate, each holding an annual session which could be attended by the Imperial Potentate, Imperial Recorder and Imperial Treasurer. He also suggested that the Shrine might buy five thousand or more acres of land in the upper Middle West as a national headquarters. Hotels could be built there. He would build a convention hall and sports fields, including a golf course.

"Give to each Shrine temple," he said, "ten acres of ground on which to erect its own headquarters as long as the temple obeys Shrine law. The temples could vie with one another for the beauty of their respective places. Give to each Shriner an acre of ground on condition that he build and maintain a one thousand dollar bungalow."

It was Hines' thought that the settlement could be used on a year-round basis for recreational purposes, but too, he said, "It would permit us to get away from the hoodlums that are in every city, who take advantage of the occasion to make all kinds of disturbances, and for which we, as an organization, get the credit."

"The more we increase in numbers," Hines told the Rochester session, "the more necessary it is that when appearing before the public, as Shriners, we should not only collectively but individually maintain our proud title of gentlemen, and the time must come when the wearing of the Shrine jewel will have only that meaning. . . .

"The men who originated the Shrine in this country

had little idea that the few who were called together were to be the nucleus of such an institution as the Mystic Shrine is proving today; if they had they would have commenced with more stringent laws and probably would not have made the success of it that they did. Be that as it may, the condition now confronts us of possessing a wonderful power, a power that can be grasped with ease now, but which allowed to go on in its pursuit of pleasure only, will dash itself against the rocks of purposeless existence and go to pieces."

In the light of subsequent events, it may well be that Hines had a prophetic vision, for the purpose he sought and pleaded for was to develop a goal or a program, even though his hope for a permanent Mecca was to be dashed by the committee he appointed to investigate the prospects. The committee reported back to the 1912 session of the Imperial Council and its report was printed in the proceedings without debate. Nothing more was ever heard of the idea until 1958, when the Imperial Council authorized a permanent headquarters building in Chicago. After looking at many pieces of property, a committee signed papers for the purchase of an entire building at 323 Michigan Boulevard, to be occupied within a year after extensive remodeling. It is notable that the entire operation—purchasing and remodeling—was within the budget of $800,000 approved by the Imperial Council.

The Shriners had a good time in Rochester despite the inadequacy of housing, and they seemed not to have a care or thought outside their own pleasure, despite the warnings from Imperial Potentate Hines. But there were rumblings of things to come. All over the world there was discontent. China had thrown over the Manchu dynasty and Sun Yat-sen had established a republic. There was revolution in Mexico. The Balkans were seething with unrest, and Russia and Germany were taking sides in that controversy. Even in the United States, liberalism was gaining. Unionism was on the march and riots were by no means unique. Teddy Roosevelt was returning to the political wars because he disagreed with the conservatism of William Howard Taft. A new kind of life was in the making all over the world—even for the Shriners although most of them didn't know it.

The Shriners returned to Los Angeles for their 1912 Imperial Council session and, true to the reputation established in 1907 when the great rose parade was held, the committee from Al Malaikah created another great pageant, but it was subdued. It pictured the long-dead era of the Spanish Missions, many of which were even then decaying in picturesque ruin. It was more than a sight for the Shriners and other visitors to Los Angeles to behold. It was an historical event, a journey, as the Los Angeles *Herald* put it, into the land of yesterday. There was no fanfare of trumpets. There were no splashes of color to make the parade gaudy; no lively melodies to set the feet of spectators in motion. There was only the meaningful black, the virginal white, the devotional purple, the hopeful gray, and at the end of the long column as though a guard of honor, there was a single Arab patrol, marching with precision but without ostentation.

The Shriners, of course, held their own parade which was as bright and brilliant as the mission parade was somber, and the Shriners themselves were as gay as ever.

The greatest sensation of the entire session, however, was the escape from captivity of two black snakes that had been brought to Los Angeles by Ballut Abyad Temple of Albuquerque, New Mexico, for use in an Indian snake dance. A. M. Fitz and J. J. Sheridan were the custodians of the reptiles, and Fitz admitted later that it was he who had smuggled them into his hotel room, where he had them lodged in a box. The trouble was that he forgot to lock the box, or someone else unlocked it, for two of the snakes escaped and slithered across some of the adjoining roofs. Reporters and photographers arrived and the papers were filled with the episode, but after a good deal of scurrying around chimneys and other rooftop impedimenta, the snakes were finally captured and returned to their dens.

All in all, despite the subdued atmosphere of the pageant, the second visit of the Imperial Session to Los Angeles was full of fun and went unmarred by the disasters of 1907. There was important activity in the august chamber of representatives, too, activity that was to have a profound effect on important events of the future.

Imperial Potentate John F. Treat of El Zagal Temple in Fargo, North Dakota, reported at length in his annual message on his refusal to grant a dispensation to Islam, Osman or Jerusalem temples to hold a ceremonial in the newly created locks of the Panama Canal before water was turned into them, and his refusal was sustained by the Imperial Council. His argument was that Imperial law prescribes that dispensation for visiting ceremonials could be granted only in those states and territories where no Shrine temple existed. Taking the literal meaning of the law, he said the Panama Canal Zone was neither a state nor a territory. It did not fall into the same category as dispensations granted to hold ceremonials in the Territory of Alaska.

The Alaskan ceremonials had been held with great success, beginning in 1909, by Nile Temple of Seattle, the travelingest of all temples. Including the 1909 ceremonial, Nile has visited Alaska thirty-five times, creating Nobles in one or more cities while there. But in addition, Nile has made fifteen pilgrimages to the Orient, creating almost two thousand Nobles (including General Douglas MacArthur) in Manila, Shanghai, Tokyo, Yokohama, Hong Kong, Okinawa and Taipei. Most of the nobility created in the Orient have been in some manner in government service, either as military or civilian personnel. (In addition to Nile, Aahmes Temple of Oakland, California; Afifi of Tacoma, Washington; Al Malaikah of Los Angeles; Aloha of Honolulu; and Moslah Temple of Fort Worth, Texas, have made pilgrimages to Europe, performing ceemonials—principally for the military—in Paris, Heidelberg and Frankfurt.)

With this example before them, there was dismay among the members of Islam, Osman and Jerusalem temples at the action of the Imperial Council in refusing the dispensation for the Panama Canal ceremonial; and there was further dismay in the months that followed, for William J. Cunningham of Boumi Temple in Baltimore, who was elected Imperial Potentate in Los Angeles, also refused the dispensation on the same grounds followed by Imperial Potentate Treat. He so reported to the Imperial Council when it met in Dallas, Texas, May 13, 1913, and again the action was upheld. Yet, within a month after his election, Cunningham had granted another dispensation for a ceremonial in Alaska

The Dallas session is still one that is talked about by those who were there. The city had grown from the western cow town of 40,000 persons that had entertained the Imperial Session in 1898 to a metropolitan city of more than 100,000. But the Shrine had grown too. From the 79 temples and 50,000 members of 1898, the Shrine had grown to 133 temples with almost 200,000 members, and it seemed that most of them were in Dallas. Members of Hella Temple set up a hospital and a special corps of physicians in Fair Park to handle the huge throng, estimated at between 55,000 and 60,000, more than half the total population of the city.

Special trains began arriving on Sunday, May 11, and for the Shriners who arrived early, there was the excitement caused by the destruction by fire of the Nieman-Marcus store, one of the biggest in the city. But it was not until Monday that the real crowds began to arrive, taxing the facilities of the railroad yards. Among the early arrivals were the members of Al Chymia Temple of Memphis, Tennessee, who wanted the 1914 session in their city. They all wore placards which called Memphis the "largest dry city in the United States and the wettest dry city in the world." But the Imperial Council was unimpressed. It selected Atlanta, Georgia, for the next meeting.

The Dallas *News* reported that all day long the camels and elephants were coming. The downtown streets rocked to the rhythm of the marching bands, and the pomp and splendor and merrymaking went on until midnight in the streets, then continued much longer at dances that were held throughout the city. The illumination was such as Arabia had never known, and the Shriners also got their first taste of Texas life.

At one of the entertainments given for band and patrol members, there was suddenly a shot from a six-shooter held in the hands of a cowboy-attired Texan. A Negro boy let out a wild shout. There was another shot and a wilder yell from a flying black form that overturned a table and sent dishes crashing. The Shriners fell back in amazement. Some dodged behind posts. Some ducked under tables, and others simply threw themselves to the ground. Even some of the Dallas hosts were awed when the pistol was pointed at them. But it was all a put-up job of entertainment. Still, one Shriner from Mecca Temple said they might as well have been shot as scared to death.

The parade on Tuesday night, May 13, brought together the largest crowd ever assembled in Texas. The Shriners paraded for an hour and a half in Oriental finery that transformed Dallas into a new Baghdad. And after it was over, the Shriners were served with a mammoth barbecue, the biggest, the Nobles of Hella Temple said, in the history of the world. It included five hundred beeves, served on six thousand feet of table, with gallons of pickles.

The festivities were by no means dimmed by the reports to the Imperial Council of Shrine activities in disasters that had affected the nation during the past year. A series of storms had brought tornadoes and floods that had created havoc through much of the Middle West. On March 23, a tornado struck Omaha, Nebraska, killing 140 persons and injuring 350. Six hundred and forty-two houses were destroyed and more than a thousand damaged. More than two thousand were homeless. Tangier Temple of Omaha with the help of other temples contributed to the relief of the stricken city, and the Tangier Temple patrol voted to give up their trip to Dallas and put that money into the relief fund.

But it was in the Ohio valley that the greatest disasters occurred. On March 23 the streams were so swollen that fear was expressed that the levees would not hold. Already there was distress up and down the Ohio from Parkersburg, West Virginia, to the Mississippi and in most of the tributaries. A Masonic Relief Committee was formed even then, but the greatest disaster was yet to come. Sometime after 5:30 on the morning of March 25, the dam on the Miami River above Dayton burst. By ten o'clock that morning, Dayton was flooded and to a large extent destroyed. As the waters poured down on Hamilton, Ohio, and the other towns and villages near at hand, they also were affected.

As soon as word reached Cincinnati, Past Imperial Potentate William B. Melish communicated with Imperial Potentate Cunningham, who immediately authorized ten thousand dollars for relief from the Imperial treasury. The Potentate of Syrian Temple called a committee together within an hour after the news was received and the committee reached Dayton before nightfall. They found indescribable horror and called for help. Within twenty-four hours, four carloads of foodstuffs and medical supplies were on their way, sent by Syrian Temple. Thousands of cans of food were included. And later, motorboats to distribute the food were sent from Cincinnati by motor truck. Other cities up and down the Ohio and its tributaries where there were Shrine temples—Parkersburg, Columbus, Indianapolis, Terre Haute, Evansville and Louisville—all reported they would handle their own relief. Imperial Potentate Cunningham issued an official distress call to temples everywhere and they responded willingly with money to ease the suffering.

It was these and other events in the history of the Shrine that prompted the Dallas *News* to report in 1913 that the Shrine object is "to aid the distressed, comfort the afflicted, protect the innocent, harmonize rank and station, obliterate intolerance and perpetuate the welfare of mankind." It was a noble object, and nearer to material fruition than the Shriners of 1913 dreamed.

Elected as Imperial Potentate at the Dallas session was William W. Irwin of Osiris Temple in Wheeling, West Virginia, and he brought a new sparkle to the task, aided and perhaps urged forward to some extent by Dr. O. W. Burdats, a Past Potentate of Osiris, who was to gain a reputation during his life as the most fun-loving Shriner in the realm. It was Irwin who made possible three great pilgrimages in 1913 and 1914— Osman and Jerusalem Temples to the Panama Canal Zone and Nile Temple to the Philippine Islands. As much as anything else, the pilgrimages reflected the expansion of the United States into a world power, the dispersion of Americans to the four corners of the earth and their insistence that their Masonic affiliations should be maintained and their Masonic life nurtured even in the strange nations they inhabited.

As early as 1911, Shriners in the Canal Zone, members of several temples in the United States, had organized themselves into a Shriners' club; and because they always seemed to have fun, other Masons with the prerequisite degrees sought affiliation. Imperial Potentates

Treat and Cunningham had declined dispensation for ceremonials in the Canal Zone because, technically, these men had no Masonic residence; the Canal Zone not being included in any jurisdiction of either the Knights Templar or Scottish Rite. In 1912, however, Grand Commander William B. Melish of the Knights Templar issued a dispensation for the establishment of a Commandery in the Canal Zone and, later the same year, the Consistory of Louisiana announced it had adopted the Canal Zone into its jurisdiction.

With these obstacles removed, Imperial Potentate Irwin granted the dispensation for a ceremonial in the Canal Zone, to be held on Labor Day, September 1, 1913. That Osman Temple was chosen for the pilgrimage was largely due to the tireless efforts of J. Harry Lewis, Osman Potentate and editor and publisher of *The Crescent,* a national magazine for Shriners, and W. O. Washburn, the Chief Rabban of Osman.

There is a story told that, when the question of making the pilgrimage first went before the Osman Divan, Lewis had wired the chairs electrically in advance so that, when he asked for a rising vote and slyly pressed a button, the entire membership of the Divan immediately arose to its feet.

St. Paul made a great holiday of the departure of the Osman party. There were ceremonies at City Hall and at the State Capitol, with messages from the mayor and the governor for other mayors and governors who would be met on the trip. As the special train, carrying 165 Nobles and their ladies, including the Osman band and patrol, steamed out of the station on the night of August 19, 1913, factory whistles in the city let loose with a cacophony of "good speed."

The ceremonial in the Canal Zone was held on a stage erected on the floor of Miraflores Lock in the Canal. Afterwards a plaque was erected atop the lock above the exact spot where on September 1, 1913, the only ceremonial ever held in the Panama Canal was enacted and 170 weary Sons of the Desert were created Nobles of the Mystic Shrine.

The pilgrimage of Jerusalem Temple to the Canal Zone followed a convocation of the Scottish Rite, where additional Masons received the prerequisite degrees. It was held on a new pier at Colón on the night of March 28, 1914.

The Pilgrimage of Nile Temple to the Philippines was far longer, and was less impressive only because it could be repeated at some future date. Three thousand Nobles of Nile Temple cheered the Shrine ship *Minnesota* as it sailed from Seattle at high noon on December 30, 1913. After tourist stops in Japan, the ship arrived in Manila on January 30; and on the night of January 31, 140 additional Sons of the Desert were rewarded for their efforts by becoming members of the Shrine. The ship then visited China and returned to Seattle on March 12, having covered 14,000 miles. Two hundred Nobles and ladies, representing twenty-nine temples, were represented on the pilgrimage.

Those were indeed halcyon days, all too soon to be shattered by the turn of world events. And if only a few Shriners and only a few temples could make the world-wide pilgrimages, other temples could and did make lesser pilgrimages. To extinct volcanic craters, to deep caverns, to the California desert, and just to towns within their jurisdictions, the Shriners moved in their effort to have more fun themselves and to make more men Shriners so that they, too, could join in the fun.

Over the years, Shrine travelling has increased tenfold with several Imperial Pilgrimages annually and most temples take long jaunts each year.

15

A World Full of Sorrow

It was during the year that William W. Irwin served as Imperial Potentate that the last two of the original "13" who formed the Shrine passed the veil into the valley from which there is no return. Dr. Walter M. Fleming died at the home of his son in Mount Vernon, New York, on September 9, 1913, and George W. Millar died in New York March 28, 1914, forty-two years after the founding of the fraternity.

On January 1, 1914, the Imperial Recorder would report, the Shrine had passed the 200,000 mark in membership. It had been forty-two years of fun, frolic and service to their fellowmen; forty-two years during which the Shriners had become known everywhere as "high-up Masons" and during which they had replaced the Knights Templar as the foremost parading organization in the world.

At the Imperial Session, which began May 12, 1914, in Atlanta, Georgia, army recruiting stations reported that they had had a flood of applications from the young men of Georgia, who were impressed by the war scares in Mexico and Europe and by the Shrine uniforms. The young men combined the two and decided that army life must indeed be wonderful.

And it was quite a show that the members of Yaarab Temple of Atlanta, the people of Atlanta, and the Shriners put on. The Atlanta *Journal* (with perhaps exaggerated but pardonable pride) called the session the biggest convention in the history of the world and declared the city's decorations were the most stupendous ever known. There were 30,000 flags and 100,000 yards of bunting, all of which cost $30,000. Four thousand Shriners were housed in railroad trains in a railroad section that had been named Shrine Park. Streets were roped off for dances that began at eleven o'clock in the evening and continued until the bands went to sleep. For the first time in Georgia Tech history, the students were given an extra day off to watch the great parade. All the clubs in the city kept open house for the Shriners. One Shriner in a wornout police uniform arrested half the people on Peachtree Street, and directed traffic for an hour. One group of twenty Shriners made up a Kazoo band and toured the city playing the "Hootchie-Kootchie Dance."

When it was over, the Atlanta *Journal* editorially declared it to have been the merriest and most enchanting week in the life of Atlanta. "The Shriners have proved themselves to be royal guests. Every hour of their sojourn has been glorious with color and music and brimming over with good fellowship. They came in caravans of joy, rich-hearted pilgrims from every section of the western world and this oasis bloomed a thousand times more brightly . . . ."

But behind the pageantry and the fun, there was more serious business, too. With Mexico torn by revolution and the Marines already in Vera Cruz, a resolution was offered to the Imperial Council calling on all temples to render every possible service to refugee Nobles who might be expelled from Mexico and permitting the temples to call on the Imperial Council for a refund in any monies expended in behalf of the refugees. The Imperial Council never got around to acting on the proffered resolution, but there was talk about it and it was tacitly admitted that the Imperial Potentate would so act.

Then there was the resolution by David B. G. Rose of Kosair Temple in Louisville, which in essence was development of the 1902 resolution by Morocco Temple of Jacksonville, Florida, calling for the establishment of a Shrine tubercular sanitarium. Rose's resolution called for the Imperial Potentate to appoint a committee of five to investigate the possibility of the establishment of a benevolent institution for dependent Shriners and their families "in the name of, by, and through the influence and support of the A.A.O.N.M.S." It was another step in the movement of the Shrine toward the development of a Shrine project. However, though the resolution was adopted and the committee of five appointed by the new Imperial Potentate, Frederick R. Smith of Damascus Temple of Rochester, New York, the idea failed to muster much support. The committee reported to the Imperial Council in 1915 at Seattle, Washington, that the development of such an institution would be a benevolence worthy of the Order, but that at the present time it would be inadvisable and impracticable. The cost, the committee said, would be unwarranted; besides the Masonic Order maintained charitable and benevolent institutions in almost every jurisdiction, and since all Shriners were Masons, these institutions could be used. The extensive territorial jurisdiction of the Shrine, the location of such an institution and the selection of its guests made the whole thing almost impossible. The special committee moved to abandon the project and the Imperial Council unanimously agreed.

When the Shriners left Atlanta, they did so with merry hearts and reverent minds, but just six weeks later Gavrillo Prinzip, a Bosnian Serb terrorist, shot and killed Archduke Ferdinand, heir to the Austrian throne, an event that in itself attracted comparatively little interest among Americans but one which would precipitate other events leading to war, which officially was declared July 28 by Austria against Serbia. Events moved swiftly in Europe and as the winter holidays approached, all Europe was in flames. In the United

States, there was interest, particularly because Canadians had answered the call of King and Empire, but there was little thought that the United States would ever be drawn into the conflict: Among Masons, however, there was a realization that fraternal brothers at some time or other might need help, and on November 28, William B. Melish organized the Masonic War Relief Association of the United States, Arthur McArthur, Grand Master of the Grand Encampment of Knights Templar, was elected president, and Bernard G. Witt, General Grand High Priest of the Royal Arch Masons, and Imperial Potentate Frederick R. Smith served as vice president; but it was Melish, as chairman of the executive committee, who really operated the association.

Smith sent an appeal for funds to all Shrine temples. The object of the association, he said, was to aid the sufferers from the European war, and "as Masonry is universal, so too will this charity embrace the people of all the nations at war. . . ." By the time the Shrine assembled in Seattle on July 13, 1915, nearly ten thousand dollars had been raised by the temples alone for the Masonic charity. In the years that followed, the Shrine contributed thousands upon thousands more from the Imperial treasury. Individual temples and individual Shriners contributed still thousands more. Most of the money was used for the maintenance of two orphan asylums—one in Paris, the other near London—where the destitute victims of the conflict were treated with great understanding without regard for race, creed or national origin.

But this was only the beginning of the Shrine's part in the war. Even as the Imperial Council assembled in Seattle, the Shriners and for that matter most Americans had begun to realize that the war in Europe was no small Balkan squabble. There was horror at the starvation of the Belgians. There was even greater horror at the senseless sinking of the *Lusitania* in May of 1915 with a loss of American lives. Of course the Shriners paraded in Seattle as if there were no war. Times were good. American farmers were feeding the Allies. American industry was supplying much of the material of war. Still, there was an undercurrent of tension that went beyond regular Shrine affairs. Some American boys already had joined the Lafayette Escadrille. Others had joined up with Canadian forces. During the Imperial Session itself, the Liberty Bell passed through Seattle on its way to the San Francisco Exposition, and the Imperial officers and representatives went in a body to see it.

Officially, about the most important event of the three-day meeting in Seattle was the decision to have a special ceremonial presented in 1916 in Buffalo to show various temple officers how to execute it. The proposal for such a ceremonial came from Charles Symmes of El Riad Temple in Sioux Falls, South Dakota, who had gained something of a reputation as a ceremonial director. As so frequently happens, since he made the proposal, he could do the work. He was named chairman of the committee and when the ceremonial was presented in Buffalo, it was quite an affair.

New York designers and decorators had prepared special stage scenery; and from all over the continent the best patrols, ceremonial producers, singers, dancers and musicians participated in the great ceremonial. The officers were chosen for their individual talents, but it was to Symmes, who directed the entire affair, that the Nobles gave their applause.

At almost the same time that the Shriners were meeting in Buffalo, the Republicans and Democrats were nominating Charles Evans Hughes and Woodrow Wilson for President, and for the three months of the campaign the people would hear "He kept us out of war." But it was a foolish hope and was not to be. Many of the Shriners knew it, for already they were being called upon for work that sometimes verged on "cloak and

dagger" stuff. Henry F. Niedringhaus, Jr., of Moolah
Temple was elected Imperial Potentate at Buffalo; and
while he continued to make his regular visitations, even
after the United States entered the war near the end
of his tenure, he also devoted much time to war work.

Hardly had the convention in Buffalo closed when
a bomb exploded in a Los Angeles Preparedness Day
parade, resulting in the conviction and long court fight
of Tom Mooney. And on July 30, there was the famous
Black Tom explosion at munitions loading docks in Jersey City, New Jersey. The bloody battles of the Somme,
which were being fought even as the Shriners met,
continued on into August.

For three months, the nation listened to the oratory
of the politicians and finally reelected Wilson, even
though Hughes went to bed election night convinced
he had won. But even during the stirring times, there
was a noticeable trend toward patriotism. Parades were
held designed to raise funds for the Red Cross and
other patriotic organizations, and whenever asked, the
Shriners paraded too. After all, the Shriners were not
only the best parade group in every city, but were
by far the most colorful.

Day be day the tension grew. Unlimited submarine
warfare was declared by the Germans, and finally on
February 2, 1917, the United States severed diplomatic
relations with the Germans. Active preparations for
American entry into the war were stepped up. American merchant ships were armed, and on April 6, the
government declared a state of war existed with Germany.

Temples, as if they had planned it, swung into high
gear. All available funds were invested in Liberty
Bonds. Special Libery Loan auctions were held. The
Imperial Potentate was called in by Food Administrator
Herbert C. Hoover, and the Shrine curtailed its banquet operations. For the temple units, it was parade,
parade, parade, And parade they did. Comparatively

few of the Shriners were called into the armed services, for most of them were too old to carry a gun; but scores of them served as officers, and thousands upon thousands of Shriners watched their sons march away.

The 1917 session of the Imperial Council had been awarded to Minneapolis, and Zuhrah Temple went to considerable effort to prepare for it. But with the advent of war, there were complications. Railroad travel was difficult, and after long consultation with Charles E. Ovenshire of Zuhrah, who was to become the next Imperial Potentate, Niedringhaus told the temples not to send bands, patrols or other units. Hilarity would be out of place and the Minneapolis session would be devoted exclusively to the business of the fraternity. Many temple units which had raised funds for the trip to Minneapolis turned them over to various war relief societies.

Under the circumstances, the Minneapolis meeting was rather dull. No banquets. No parades. Just business. The representatives got it over with as quickly as possible and decided to meet in Atlantic City in 1918, when the war might be over. But it wasn't over "over there" and in fact the Germans were just at that time bringing the war almost to the beaches of New Jersey and New England. The Imperial officers and representatives began to arrive at the coastal resort on Sunday, June 2, 1918, and that evening, just at dusk, the German submarine U 37 stopped the passenger steamer *Carolina* 150 miles southeast of Atlantic City, ordered all hands and passengers into small boats and then sank the craft with gunfire. Some of the four hundred passengers reached Lewes, Delaware, and some were picked up by a coastwise trawler and taken to New York, but one small boat with twenty-nine passengers and sailors aboard reached the beach at Atlantic city on the morning of June 4. Shriners, some of them in "full regalia," as the New York *Times* put it, joined townspeople in wading into the surf to pull the craft ashore. The Lu

Lu Temple band that happened to be parading near the point where the lifeboat landed struck up "The Star-Spangled Banner," and everyone sang.

By the morning of June 5, the Shriners had contributed more than a thousand dollars for the relief of the destitute victims of the *Carolina* and this was formally handed to Noble Harry Bacharach, the mayor of Atlantic City, who responded with a patriotic speech. In fact, much of the Atlantic City Imperial session was flavored with patriotic fervor, and naturally so.

"In a world so full of sorrow," Imperial Potentate Charles E. Ovenshire reported, "the Mystic Shrine has added a touch of happiness with its ceremonials and afforded an opportunity of touching elbows with friends and giving to one another the moral support so much needed when civilization itself seems to be tottering, while at the same time it has cooperated with every branch of the government in every way."

Ovenshire also praised the temples that had organized units of women in their families to help with the war effort. It may have been a technical violation of the rules which prohibited any organization of women in the Shrine, but no one thought about such rules in the stress of conflict. "Their [the ladies] work," Ovenshire said, "may well be an inspiration to us, their spirit one to emulate, and their accomplishments a spur to renewed effort on our part to give the boys at the front every substantial evidence that we are behind them with every dollar, all our time, all our effort and all our sincerest wishes for their speedy and successful culmination of this crime of the ages."

And so it went. There were reports of temple funds that had been invested in Liberty Bonds, of the thousand of dollars given to the Red Cross, the Y.M.C.A., the Salvation Army and other organizations that contributed to the war. Ovenshire also reported that the membership in the Shrine had passed the quarter of a million mark with 259,113 Nobles, 11,649 of them in the service. Nearly 2,800 Nobles had been created while they were in uniform. Temple service flags had become dotted here and there with gold stars, and for them Ovenshire pronounced his benediction, "May Allah bless and protect them."

Among the stunts adopted by Shriners in the war effort was one created by Salaam Temple of Newark, New Jersey, that offered a sack of flour to be auctioned to the highest bidders for Liberty Bonds. Actually the sack of flour crossed the continent several times and resulted in the purchase of more than $80,000 in bonds.

The Shrine, too, had been active in its own charitable way. When a munitions ship exploded in the harbor of Halifax, Nova Scotia, on December 6, 1917, Ovenshire had sent one thousand dollars to the Potentate of little Philae Temple in that city and offered more as it was needed. A third of the city had been destroyed, and as many as 1,600 persons killed.

Except for the overtones of war, the Atlantic City session was devoted exclusively to the business of the Shrine. There were always minute details relating to jurisdictional lines and interpretations of Shrine law that had to be dealt with, but largely it was an harmonious session. It was the last of the war meetings.

Es Salumu Aleikum.

16

Playground Returns

The end of the war and the advent of prohibition both presented major problems to Elias J. Jacoby of Murat Temple, who was elected Imperial Potentate at the Atlantic City session. He had selected his home city of Indianapolis for the 1919 session of the Imperial Council, but because the war did not end until November 11, 1918, he could not anticipate with any degree of reality that bands, patrols and other units could be invited. As far as he could foresee by the first of the year, the Indianapolis meeting would again be strictly a business session.

On the date the Armistice was signed, Jacoby was in New Orleans. He was awakened early by the shrieking of whistles and the ringing of bells, proclaiming peace. By midday he had arrived at Hattiesburg, Mississippi, on his way to Meridian for an official visitation. Hattiesburg was one of the great war training centers; and all morning long there had been speeches, parades and joyous celebration at the news that the war was over. Of course the Imperial Potentate also was asked to speak from a platform at the railroad station. Again that evening, he spoke to the children in the Mississippi Masonic home in Meridian, hoping they might be spared in the future the ravages of conflict.

As quickly as possible, Jacoby got in touch with his committees in Indianapolis and made arrangements to expand the convention into a full-blown, prewar affair, but it was not until February 1, 1919, that he issued a special order to all of the temples, advising them that the patrols and bands would be invited to participate. It was short notice, but they responded. They had waited three years—since Buffalo in 1916—for a chance to parade. Furthermore, the Eighteenth Amendment had been approved. The Volstead Act was less than a year away and it was obvious that the wells of Zemzem were running dry.

The great heavyweight boxing champion, Medinah Temple Noble Jack Dempsey, with his Imperial Potentate's Aide fez, accompanied by the then Chief Deputy Imperial Marshal Edward E. Buckley of Kena Temple.

Noble Jack Dempsey had become the World's Heavyweight Boxing Champion and "The Georgia Peach," Noble Ty Cobb, was running wild on the bases and at bat for the Detroit Tigers.

The units and the Imperial officers and representatives began to arrive in Indianapolis on Monday, June 9, 1919, and they were greeted by as gaudy a sight as Shriners had ever witnessed. The Murat Shriners had gone all out to entertain their fraternal brothers. By Monday evening, there appeared to be a band concert on every corner and in every hotel lobby. And every temple had tried to think up something new by which they could have a good time.

J. H. Dickey of Moslah Temple in Fort Worth, Texas, brought along a lariat with a cowbell on it, and he threw it at pedestrians in true Western style. And when they were caught and well tied. Dickey demanded a contribution for the Salvation Army. He got it, too. The boys of El Mina Temple in Galveston, Texas, paraded around in horrible bathing suits. Jerusalem Temple of New Orleans brought along five colored women who were advertised as the champion praline makers of the world, and they displayed their art on the street. New Orleans also brought along a red-hot Black jazz band from Lower Basin Street that entertained throughout the convention. Al Malaikah Temple had enough California fruit to invite the whole city of Indianapolis to visit their headquarters.

The great night parade, the Indianapolis *News* said, would forever be known as *"The* parade." And perhaps to that time it was the greatest of all Shrine spectacles. There were five thousand Shriners in costume and another two thousand who marched in full evening dress.

After the session was over, the *News* said editorially: "There are conventions and conventions—but only one Shriners' convention. It is unique, unsurpassed and unsurpassable, inimitable, incomparable, sovereign, unparalleled, supreme. Indianapolis knows. Weeks will be required for recuperation. The streets will seem temporarily a morgue."

Indeed it was true. From that memorable week forward, the Shriners were to be known as the great conventioneers, the finest paraders, the most fun-loving

A photograph of the Ty Cobb plaque in the Baseball Hall of Fame and Museum at Cooperstown, New York. He was a long-term member of Moslem Temple, Detroit, having joined in 1912. His Blue Lodge was Royston No. 426, Georgia. He was born in 1886 and died July 17, 1961.

and fun-provoking organization in all the Americas. On January 1 of 1919, there were 288,697 of them, and a year later there were 363,744, and year by year more and more wanted to attend the Imperial Session and participate in the fun.

Despite all the hilarity, the Imperial Council itself engaged in important activities.

From time to time over the years since 1876, there

Ty Cobb, a Moslem Temple, Detroit, Noble, has been termed by many sports experts as "The Greatest All-Round Baseball player of the ages." Here, he is shown in his Detroit Tiger uniform during his heyday.

had been demands for the revision of the Ritual, and some few had been made as skeptical Nobles raised questions which as often as not were subject to the cliché that "a little knowledge is a dangerous thing." There were those who couldn't find the meaning of certain words. There were those who said the Ritual as it stood didn't make much sense and still others who demanded that the Ritual must be historically correct and factually impregnable. Jacoby had finally appointed a committee to consider the complaints. It is to Jacoby's credit that he named Past Imperial Potentate Ovenshire as the chairman of that committee, which had met in Indianapolis in November of 1918 and prepared

Phillip D. Gordon, Karnak Temple, Montreal

a report to be submitted to the Indianapolis session of the Imperial Council. The committee wrote:

> In our study of the original Ritual, written by our beloved, departed Illustrious Noble friend, Walter M. Fleming, and of the later Ritual adopted by the Imperial Council July 24, 1894, many glaring errors were discovered, particularly in the titles, terms and usages prevalent in the language of the Ritual. From an academic standpoint, our Shrine and our Ritual would be held up to ridicule by the savant, or even the progressive student of Arabic learning. Scarcely any of the alledged Arabic supports of the Ritual could stand the test of analytical examination without falling down completely. From such knowledge, your committee is led to the conclusion that Noble Fleming and his alleged twelve co-humorists perpetrated a huge and most successful canard in the origin of the Ritual of

the Mystic Shrine and to the dear old doctor's eternal credit be it said that he builded far better than he even suspected through his joke, which has become the merry and substantial foundation of the greatest, most liberal and most potent organization of friendly fellowship in the world today.

To revise the Ritual of the Shrine academically, to make it conform to Arabic nomenclature, customs, practices and ideals would be to drastically reconstruct the entire work of its ingenuous and humorous author and to deprive it of all that has made it so attractively amusing to its many thousands of admiring followers. The Ritual as it was has held its own with little or no criticism or objection for nearly forty years; on its foundation an organization of nobility numbering 300,000 has been erected. In the opinion of your committee any drastic attack on the established foundation of our organization would be a grievous mistake.

"The Mason's Playground" is a place of kindly, wholesome humor. Noble Fleming gave the Shrine such harmless humor in his conception of the Ritual. We would not mar his work through cold conformation to Arabic—or any other—customs.

There never again was to be an attempt directed toward a major revision of the Ritual. The committee's report was received and unanimously adopted, but it did not end the controversy over the background of the Shrine itself. That was to continue for years to come, even though it was academic. The Shriners who fashioned the fraternity had entered into an unseen temple, and the records they left behind for the millions who followed were fragmentary. The Shriners who investigated could not change the facts and, even if they could, would not have been permitted to do so by the hundreds of thousands of Shriners who enjoyed things as they had found them. Besides, there were more important things ahead.

Elected at Indianapolis in 1919 to succeed Elias Jacoby as Imperial Potentate was W. Freeland Kendrick, the Potentate of Lu Lu Temple in Philadelphia, and his election set off a chain reaction that was to give

the Shrine a soul—a soul so big that it passeth understanding, a soul so big that in the light of thirty years
of service it transformed a playground for "high-up
Masons" into a fraternity of love. It is likely that in
the whole history of humankind there never has been
an undertaking by any group of men that was created
so suddenly or developed and perfected so quickly as
the soul of the Shriners—their Hospitals for Crippled
Children, Temples of Mercy.

17

The "Bubbles" Speech

The atomic bomb was undreamed of, except by perhaps a few scientists, when Freeland Kendrick became Imperial Potentate in 1919, and the application of the words "chain reaction" to other than science was thirty years away. But the development of the Shriner's Hospital for Crippled Children was just that—a combination of factors, events, desires, needs and hopes, extending over a half-century of time, all pointing toward the same unnamed and perhaps unknown goal and triggered finally by a Philadelphia civic leader into an explosion of philanthropic love that would erase (or almost erase) crippled children from American streets. The concept of the Shriners' Hospitals was to have an even more far-reaching effect in the years to come, for in less than thirty years other organizations and even units of government would enter into active competition with the Shriners' Hospitals for the privilege of treating and helping those who could not—and cannot—help themselves.

To Masons in general and Shriners in particular, charity is a desirable human trait, but one that is strictly personal and not an intangible thing that can be imposed. Ever since the advent of Masonry into the New World, the lodges had practiced charity of some kind; but it was done without ostentation certainly, and more often than not in complete secrecy. Masonic fraternalism does not permit the glorification of the fortunate at the expense of the unfortunate. For most of the years of their fraternal existence, as we have seen, the Shriners had practiced charity of some kind. From the example of the first Christmas basket delivered by the members of Mecca Temple to some unnamed and now unknown family of New York back in the early eighties, the idea had spread. Eventually every temple of the Shrine had helped wherever, whenever and however it could.

Thus the idea of Shrine charity was by no means unknown when Freeland Kendrick became the Imperial Potentate. But the time had not been right or the idea hadn't quite suited when other attempts had been made to develop a goal for the Shrine beyond "the mere pursuit of pleasure." Perhaps the difference, as much as anything else, was Kendrick himself, for Kendrick—Philadelphia tax receiver in 1919; later, mayor of the city—was a consummate politician, a masterful showman, a devout Shriner and egocentric enough to believe that he could and should leave a lasting memorial to himself within the fraternity. Perhaps most important of all he was a softie when in the presence of an orphaned, destitute or crippled child.

There are hundreds of stories about Freeland Kendrick during the many years he served as Illustrious Potentate of Lu Lu Temple. There is no question that he held the temple in the palm of his hand or that he cracked the whip over the membership when it suited his purpose to do so. He was lovable and successful. He built Lu Lu into one of the top temples of Shrinedom. He gave the membership of Lu Lu something to remember as long as they lived in the ceremonials and shows he put on for them. Seldom would he walk into a temple when he could ride a charging white prancer, a camel or an elephant, and the boys loved it and him. But there are those, too, who will tell you that he also almost ruined Lu Lu Temple by failing to provide adequate trained leadership for those years when he would not serve as the undisputed leader.

Mrs. Freeland Kendrick doesn't remember the exact date when her husband first became interested in orphaned, destitute and crippled children, but it must have been shortly after he was elected Imperial Outer Guard at New Orleans in 1910, perhaps even a year or two later. In any case, Kendrick himself remembered the event. He had gone, he said, to the Home

Forrest Adair, Yaarab Temple, Atlanta

for Incurables at Forty-eighth Street and Woodland Avenue in Philadelphia for the purpose of taking three or four of the little patients of that institution for an automobile ride. It is likely that Mrs. Kendrick enticed him there, for she was active in charitable work in Philadelphia at the time. In any event, as he recalled it later, "What I saw there, what I heard there and what I sensed there made such a profound impression on me that for days and weeks I could not drive the sad scene from before me. This visit to the incurable institution prompted the birth of the idea to inaugurate a movement among the Shriners of North America for rehabilitating orphaned, friendless and crippled children."

Thus, when Kendrick went to Indianapolis, knowing he was to become the Imperial Potentate, he had a well-thought-out plan. He had enlisted the aid of Philip D. Gordon of Karnak Temple (Montreal), who had served for many years as chairman of the Jurisprudence and Laws Committee, and was one of the most powerful men in the Order. Privately, he had discussed his idea with other leaders of the Shrine, and found differing opinions. Being a great politician Kendrick could shrug off—as if they were unimportant—those who disagreed with him. But as a result of the differing opinions, he determined to tie his idea for the establishment of an institution for children to the patriotic fervor of the Shriners. The war was just over. Peace would lie ahead, and his institution could easily become a peace memorial.

Being a great showman, Kendrick had an unerring sense of timing, and so it was that his great proposal was held until the very last minute of the last day of the 1919 session of the Imperial Council. It was hot in Indianapolis. The Representatives were tired and wanted to get away. And it was at this precisely chosen moment that Gordon arose to offer a resolution. It read:

Whereas it is the opinion of this Imperial Council, in this year wherein the peace of the world has been established, it would be fitting that some lasting and tangible memorial be established showing to the world at large that we as a body of loyal and patriotic citizens from the various sections of the great North American continent and from which thousands of our membership have enlisted and scores have paid the supreme sacrifice in the cause of justice, liberty and democracy, for all of which our beloved order has stood so prominently,

And whereas, W. Freeland Kendrick, the Imperial Potentate-elect, has already intimated to this Imperial Council his wish that such a memorial, if possible, take the form of a home for friendless, orphaned and crippled children, in which charitable work he has already taken such a keen interest in his home state of Pennsylvania, now be it

Resolved, that this Imperial Council place itself on record as favoring such a proposition, the memorial to be styled "The Mystic Shriners' Peace Memorial for Friendless, Orphaned and Crippled Children," and that a committee be appointed by the incoming Imperial Potentate, with a view of purchasing a suitable site for this purpose and making all other arrangements necessary, and be it further

Resolved, that a special assessment of one dollar be made on each member of the Order, to be collected by the subordinate temples, in December next, from their membership in addition to the annual dues for 1920, and remitted to the Imperial Recorder when making their annual returns for the year 1919.

Thus Kendrick's name was attached to the hospital program from the very start, if the Imperial Council would just adopt it. But it was not to be—at least not in Indianapolis. The resolution never came to a vote and wasn't even debated. But it did permit Kendrick to discuss his proposal wherever he went during the year he served as Imperial Potentate.

At almost the same time Kendrick visited the hospital for incurables in Philadelphia, another event of far-reaching importance in the future of the Shriners' Hospitals was taking place in Atlanta, Georgia.

Wesley Memorial Hospital (now Emory University Hospital) had allotted two beds to little cripples who received free surgical treatment from Dr. Michael Hoke. The demand for the beds was great, but even greater was the need for a convalescent home where the children might be cared for after surgery, thus making the two hospital beds available for other cripples. Dr. Hoke was an inspired doctor and surgeon and, perhaps more important, a man with a vision. Everywhere he went he sought aid for his projects—not for himself but to provide more beds for more crippled children. But the kind of help Dr. Hoke needed was not easy to find, until, by coincidence, it developed from two sources at almost the same time.

Coincidence? Well, perhaps it was the inscrutable workings of the Master Architect of the Universe.

A railroad worker in Atlanta had been injured in falling from a train. It was an unusual injury, which failed to respond to normal treatment. Weeks dragged into months. The worker's funds were exhausted. His family was destitute. At that point, an appeal was made to Forrest Adair, head of the Scottish Rite bodies of Atlanta, where the worker was a member. Adair engaged Dr. Hoke to care for the worker, and in the many weeks that followed before he eventually returned to his job, Adair and Hoke met frequently. Hoke told his story of the needs of crippled children to Adair as he did to anyone else who would listen.

Simultaneously, a group of Atlanta women under the leadership of Mrs. William Clarke Wardlaw, began selling pencils on the streets of the city to equip a convalescent home—an event which also impressed Adair. The women raised $1,100 in their project, and Adair obtained $5,000 more from the Scottish Rite bodies. With this money, the combined group of women and Masons rented two cottages in the suburbs of Atlanta which on September 1, 1915, opened for patients with Dr. Hoke as chief surgeon and Miss Lillian Carter as superintendent. The hospital had twenty beds.

In the years that followed, this hospital became known as the Scottish Rite Hospital for Crippled Children. It treated thousands of crippled children from all of Georgia and even the surrounding states. New buildings were built. Nurses' homes were erected. Thousands of dollars were expended, but most important of all to the future of the Shriners' Hospitals for

Crippled Children—which were still seven years away—were the rules and regulations drawn up by Dr. Hoke and Adair. They were simple, but definite. No patient might pay. If the patient could pay, he should be in some other hospital. The patient must be under fourteen years of age and, in the opinion of the doctors, have a reasonable chance of being helped. The hospital was for orthopedic cases only. It was not to become a home for orphaned children. It was open to all in need, no matter what their color, their religion or their nationality. The rules have never been changed. They are exactly the same rules eventually adopted for the government of the Shriners' Hospitals, and it is quite possible that without the development of the Scottish Rite Hospital in Atlanta, the Shriners' Hospitals would never have been brought into being.

During the year he served as Imperial Potentate, Freeland Kendrick traveled more than 150,000 miles and managed to visit most of the temples in North America. It was a popular administration, for Kendrick was a popular man. The committee of the Imperial Council that went over his report of the year declared him to be a "pleasing and forceful speaker. His big heart has reached four hundred thousand of our nobility. He has made good to the full satisfaction and benefit of all." And everywhere he went the Imperial Potentate discussed his project which would give the Shriners a goal. Thus when he arrived in Portland, Oregon, for the forty-seventh session of the Imperial Council, he felt certain enough of the success of his report to go considerably farther than the original solution offered in Indianapolis. He recommended that the Imperial Council authorize a tax of five dollars (instead of one dollar) on every Shriner, effective immediately, to establish a Shriners' Home for Friendless, Orphan and Crippled Children and that a committee of seven be appointed by the incoming Imperial Potentate to select a site and arrange for immediate action in the construction of the Home.

When the committee to pass on the recommendation came in with its report, however, it went only so far as to open the matter for discussion on the floor. After discussion, the committee suggested that the project be returned to the local temples for a vote. The committee said its members believed in the idea, hoped it would be enacted, but that it felt that a matter so important should be passed on by the local temples. This report reached the Imperial Council on the morning of Wednesday, June 23, 1920.

When the report was read, there was a noticeable murmur in the meeting room, a sort of stir that Kendrick could sense. He hurriedly talked with some of his associates, including Gordon. There were further discussions during the luncheon hour, with the result that when the program was called up for discussion in the afternoon of that fateful Wednesday, Kendrick had a substitute resolution to offer. With Deputy Imperial Potentate Ellis Garretson of Al Kader Temple (Portland) in the chair, Kendrick took the floor.

"Imperial Sir," he said, "I have changed the original recommendation somewhat, as I believe it will come nearer to meeting with your approval in the present form and will bring about the object desired. I recommend that at this session of the Imperial Council a resolution be adopted authorizing the establishment of a hospital for crippled children to be supported by the nobility of the Mystic Shrine of North America on an annual per capita basis and to be known as the Shriners' Hospital for Crippled Children."

In this manner, Kendrick eliminated one of the strongest objections to his original idea. He had taken out the word *home* and substituted the word *hospital*, an institution to all intents and purposes an exact duplicate of the Scottish Rite Hospital in Atlanta. Many of the representatives had freely expressed themselves about establishing an orphan asylum. They didn't like it. But a hospital where crooked bodies could be straightened—well, that might be different. Then, too, Kendrick in his new resolution reduced the annual per capita tax on the Shriners from five to two dollars.

As the new resolution was read, the assembled nobility of the Shrine murmured noticeably and then the venerable William Bromwell Melish of Syrian Temple rose to his feet. Graying, and inclined at times to be peevish, he was nevertheless still the hard-headed businessman who had guided the Shrine out of the morass of near bankruptcy in the middle nineties. He was still the respected senior Past Imperial Potentate.

"I want to present my views on this matter," he said, "and I do so with some reluctance, but I do so with the responsibility resting on me as representing the temple to which I belong. I think that this project is one that we ought not to go into at this time. I think it has not had enough consideration . I doubt its practicability. . . . I believe it to be a project that is not within the province of the Order of Nobles of the Mystic Shrine as it is contemplated, for this reason: It is proposed that this home, if established, or number of homes, if established, shall start out to take care of every crippled child that there is in the United States, and care for them by the Order of the Nobles of the Mystic Shrine; not the crippled children of Shriners, or children of any sort that are now the wards of the several temples, but to go outside of this Order and to take every child that may be admitted under the rules that may be established, with a knowledge before us now that there would probably not be more than five per cent of them that had anything to do with the families of Shriners. I don't think that a burden of this sort ought to be put upon this Order."

There was more. Melish went on for more than fifteen minutes. It was cold, simple logic. The Shrine, or the Shriners, he said, should not undertake a project involving millions of dollars without the entire nobility having a chance to make its decision. The Imperial Council had no right to select seven men from its membership and give them carte blanche to commit the Shrine to the expenditure of untold sums.

As he sat down, there was a nodding of heads among the delegates. His argument had been sound. There was no animosity toward Kendrick. His motives had not been questioned. Then, from his seat near the front of the city auditorium, arose Forrest Adair. He was a striking man, with a heavy black mustache and thick black hair. Like Melish, he was a power in all of the Masonic circles of his home state. But unlike Melish, he was inspired. He could forsee the opportunities that would lie ahead.

"I arise, unlike my friend, Past Imperial Potentate Melish, with reluctance, but with enthusiasm," he said.

A hush fell over the auditorium as if the representatives could sense what was to come. Adair continued:

"I was lying in bed yesterday morning, about four o'clock, in the Multnomah Hotel, and some poor fellow who had strayed from the rest of the band—and he was a magnificent performer on a baritone horn—stood down there under the window for twenty-five minutes playing 'I am only blowing bubbles.'"

There was laughter, for even though it was prohibition days, there was still plenty of Zemzem water and camel's milk available, and the representatives could understand what had happened.

"Do you get it?" Adair asked, and there was more laughter. "And after a while, when I dropped back into peaceful sleep, I dreamed of a little crippled children's hospital, run by the Scottish Rite fraternity in Atlanta, Georgia, which has been visited by a number of members of this Imperial Council, and I thought of the wandering minstrel of the early morning, and I wondered if there were not a deep significance in

*Sam P. Cochran, Hella
Temple
1922–1934*

*Freeland W. Kendrick,
Lu Lu Temple
1934–1950*

*Harold Lloyd, Al
Malaikah Temple
1963–*

*Galloway Calhoun,
Karem Temple
1950–1962*

*Walter G. Seeger,
Osman Temple
1962–1963*

*Harvey A. Beffa,
Moolah Temple
1952–1953*

*Peter Val Preda, Cairo
Temple
1976–1977*

*C. Victor Thornton,
Moslah Temple*

the tune that he was playing for Shriners—'I am only blowing bubbles.

"We meet from year to year; we talk about our great Order; we read the report of the hundreds of thousands of dollars that are accumulated and loaned to banks and paid us for our mileage and per diem, and on our visitations we stop in some oasis and we are taken in an automobile by a local committee, and he first drives us by and shows us, 'This is our temple, our mosque. It is built of marble brought from Maine or Georgia. The lot cost fifty thousand dollars; we could have sold it for two hundred thousand before we built upon it. The building cost us a million, and it could not be put up now for two and a half million.'

"What is that wonderful hospital over there?"

" 'That is the hospital of the Sisters of St. Mary.'

" 'What big school is that in the distance?'

" 'That is a school erected and maintained by the Catholic church.'

"And we get here and we hear the baritone. That fellow told us what we are doing."

The hush over the auditorium deepened. Already, there could be no doubt that Adair was delivering an inspired message, a message that was to become known wherever Shriners gathered as the "bubbles" speech. One member who heard it was so shaken that in later years he purchased three copies of Sir John Millais' famous painting of a boy blowing bubbles, one of which now hangs in the Greeneville, South Carolina, unit of the Shriners' Hospitals. But once started, Adair did not let up. There are, he said, four hundred thousand cripples in the United States "and unfortunately they are in the alms houses; they are in the homes; they are mendicants; they are paupers; and the best alms you can give is that which will render alms unnecessary.

"My Brother Melish goes back to these other resolutions which have been postponed from year to year, while we blow more bubbles and sing again 'Hail, Hail,

the Gang's All Here.' This resolution has been changed.
It does not establish, Brother Melish, a home. The word
there is 'hospital; the Shriners' Hospital for Crippled
Children.' I presume that any intelligent committee
that may be appointed by the incoming Imperial Potentate will provide rules that, in the first place, no child
be admitted unless in the opinion of the surgeons, after
careful examination, its trouble can be corrected or
benefited."

At the Scottish Rite hospital, Adair said, no feeble-
minded were admitted. He said that the Atlanta institution had started with only eight thousand dollars in
capital, but that it had had no hard time getting
money—all it wanted—"as long as God Almighty con-
tinues to put an occasional drop of the milk of human
kindness in our blood."

Adair described some of the work that had been done
in Atlanta, naming the names of the children whose
crooked bodies had been improved. He said:

> This resolution merely recognizes the fact that we appre-
> ciate that the responsibility is upon us, and while we have
> spent money for songs, and spent money for bands—and
> they mean so much to us, let us keep it up—you cannot
> put your finger on a thing that I know of that has been
> done for humanity that can be credited to the Shrine as
> an organization. If this is established, these little rules and
> regulations that Brother Melish is so afraid of, will be taken
> care of by a competent committee. If they don't do it right
> and devote themselves too much to Catholic children, the
> Negro children, we can fire them and get another commit-
> tee. I apprehend we will not want to restrict it to the
> crippled children of Shriners. We don't. The first prerequi-
> site with us is that the child's trouble may be corrected
> or improved. The second prerequisite is that they shall
> be financially unable to pay. You could not get your child
> in that hospital [Atlanta] if you would pay a thousand dollars
> a week, because you would be depriving some little pauper
> of a bed.
>
> I want to see this thing started. For God's sake, let us
> lay aside the soap and water and stop blowing bubbles

and get down to brass tacks. . . . Let's get rid of the technical objections. Let's blow all the dust aside. And if there
is a Shriner in North America, after he sees your first crippled child treated, in its condition, and objects to having
paid the two dollars, I will give a check back to him for
it myself.

I hope that within two, or three, or four or five years
from now we will be impelled from the wonderful work
that has been done, to establish more of these hospitals,
in each reach of all parts of North America, and let it be
known that while our friend, the enemy, is now about
the only institution that is establishing hospitals and schools
and things of that kind for the benefit of humanity, the
Shrine is going to do them one better. And every argument
that Brother Melish makes, every argument that Brother
Melish has presented against this, is, to my mind, an argument in favor of it.

Adair sat down to thunderous applause. There was
no doubt of his feeling of the session. He was followed
by others—Noble Robert Colding of Atlanta; Noble
Opie of Ararat in Kansas City; Noble Charles E. Ovenshire of Zuhrah in Minneapolis; Noble Edward C. Day
of Algeria in Helena; Noble Henry Lansburgh of Almas
in Washington; Noble F. F. Whitcomb of Tangier in
Omaha; and Noble J. Harry Lewis of Osman in St. Paul.

Then, just as Deputy Imperial Potentate Garretson
was about to put the question to a vote, Kendrick offered a brief appeal.

"The time has come," he said," when we should do
something big. And what can you do as big as to furnish
a hospital for a poor little crippled kid? Suppose it is
black; suppose it is Catholic; God put it here on earth
and it is up to us to help it. And it means Canada as
well as the United States, for our jurisdiction is North
America."

Again there was applause and then silence as the
representatives waited for a vote. Now Melish once
more rose to his feet. "I want to say just one word,"
he said. "I think I know how this thing is going. I think

the duty of us all, the duty of myself first, is that if action is to be taken today, as it is, upon this matter, that we want to go before the world showing that the vote was unanimous, and this is the way I am going to vote."

And so he did. The vote was unanimous.

There is just one additional note of the Portland session at which the hospitals were approved. In later years, at least four temples claimed as their own the wandering minstrel who played, "I'm Forever Blowing Bubbles." The song is being played constantly at Shrine functions.

18

Temples of Baby Smiles

By action of the Imperial Council at Portland, the Shriners had put themselves in the hospital business and a highly specialized hospital business at that. The committee of seven appointed by Imperial Potentate Ellis L. Garretson of Afifi Temple in Tacoma, Washington, knew nothing about hospitals. Only one of the seven men was a doctor. Furthermore, they had only the vaguest idea of what was expected of them; and, as it developed during the year, there was wide variation among the committee members on that point.

Garretson did not announce his appointments until nearly four months after the project was approved, and when he did there was some clucking of tongues and raising of eyebrows. Named as chairman of the committee was Sam P. Cochran of Hella Temple in Dallas, an outstanding Mason and Shriner, but also a devout Christian Scientist. There were some of the leaders in the hospital movement who thought that he might not devote himself to the hospital movement because of his faith, but they were mistaken. Cochran continued as chairman of the hospital movement in its various legal entities for twenty-four years. He worked long and hard in that difficult period of establishment.

Appointed with Cochran on that first committee of seven were Philip D. Gordon of Karnak Temple, Montreal; W. Freeland Kendrick of Lu Lu Temple, Philadelphia; Bishop Frederick W. Keator of Afifi Temple, Tacoma, Washington; Oscar M. Lanstrum of Algeria

Temple, Helena, Montana; John D. McGilvray of Islam Temple, San Francisco; and John A. Morison of Kismet Temple, Brooklyn.

By direction of the Imperial Potentate, the committee met in St. Louis, October 30, 1920. The problem was where to begin. The committee had been instructed to build a hospital for crippled children. But what crippled children? Where were they coming from? Where would they be treated? By whom? The one man who might have guided them—Forrest Adair—had not even been made a member of the committee. For two days, the seven men talked about the task they had accepted, and about the only concrete result was agreement that they should seek some advice, which they proceeded to do. A subcommittee talked with leading orthopedic surgeons at Vanderbilt, Louisville, and Washington University clinics; and they talked with the great Mayo brothers at their clinic at Rochester, Minnesota. Al Chymia Temple in Memphis already was engaged in helping with the erection of a crippled children's hospital in Memphis, and the committee looked over the work being done in that city.

After six months of work and research, six of the seven members agreed that a hospital should be built somewhere in the Mississippi valley—near a medical school—and by the time the 1921 session of the Imperial Council was held in Des Moines, Iowa, these six were agreed on a plot of land adjacent to the Barnes Hospital and Washington University's Medical School in St. Louis. John Morison, who had been elected secretary of the committee, disagreed. If, as Adair had pointed out in Portland, there were 400,000 crippled children in the United States alone, one small hospital wouldn't help much. It was not the way the Shriners did things. It would be far better, he argued, to build no building at all, but simply allocate money to pay for surgical services for crippled children in local communities all over North America.

After more than four hours of debate, the members of the Imperial Council turned down the minority report and decided to erect a building. They accepted Cochran's majority report after he read a letter from Nathaniel Allison of Washington University, president of the American Orthopedic Association. "The plan you are considering," Allison wrote, "seems to me, and I am sure appeals to the great majority of our members, is one that makes it possible to take the first step toward the national solution of the problem of the cripple."

But perhaps the clinching argument came in a telegram from Dr. William Mayo, himself a Shriner. He said: "I approve of the principle of the building of Shrine hospitals for the care of crippled children. Several should be built. . . . The plan is laudable and worthy of the great body of Shriners."

Well, now! Here was something new. Not one hospital, but several hospitals. Not fifty or a hundred or a thousand crippled children, but tens of thousands of crippled children. Not one hospital to which children would travel hundreds of miles for treatment, but several hospitals located in various sections of the North American continent. Somehow, this caught the fancy of the Shriners. It was big. It was worthy of them. As long as they were going to do this thing, they would do it right.

And so, at Des Moines, Forrest Adair brought in a new resolution on the last day of the session. He would have that Imperial Session elect a committee of seven, clothed "with full authority to select and purchase sites, and to erect and maintain hospitals for the treatment of poor children afflicted with club feet, curved spines, tubercular spines and joints, infantile paralysis and such diseases and deformities that come within the scope and province of orthopedic surgery; said hospitals to admit no pay patients, but only those whose parents or guardians are financially unable to pay for such treatment. . . . These hospitals shall be located in various parts of the jurisdiction as rapidly as the funds may be available."

Of course there was discussion. Some Shriners argued that the Shrine shouldn't set up the hospitals and tax the Shriners to maintain them and still deny access to their services for the Shriners themselves, whether they could pay or not. But Adair argued that such a system wouldn't work. If some patients paid and others did not, he said, human nature would automatically give the paying patient better service and treatment. Other representatives, no doubt imbued with another great light, demanded that the word *charity* be eliminated from the resolution and that all references to the "poor" be stricken out. And thus what was delivered at Des Moines was not the "Shriners' Charity Foundation" but "The Shriners' Hospitals for Crippled Children," a gift from men with merry hearts and reverent minds.

Elected to succeed Morison as a member of the committee was Forrest Adair, and in the year that followed, the accomplishments were almost unbelievable. Imperial Potentate Ernest A. Cutts of Alee Temple of Savannah, Georgia, was able to report to the 1922 Imperial Session of San Francisco that during the year he had spoken to 250,000 Shriners and that the Shriners had taken the hospital movement to their hearts. It was an inspiration to him, and he ordered the trustees to speed up their work. And they did. The committee incorporated the Shriners' Hospitals for Crippled Children under the laws of Georgia and the Dominion of Canada. They set up rules and regulations for operation. There would be local boards to operate the various hospitals under the Imperial Board of Trustees. The hospitals would be under the direction of a staff orthopedic surgeon and a competent hospital administrator. The surgeon-in-chief at each hospital would be selected not by the Board of Trustees but by a board of nationally known orthopedic surgeons—surgeons, as

Cochran told the San Francisco session in 1922 "that you could not buy for money." All five of the advisory surgeons (including Dr. Hoke) assembled in San Francisco, at their own expense. Through the long history of the Shriners' Hospitals, not one member of the international Advisory Board of Surgeons has ever received one penny for his services.

The committee also set up rules and regulations for the admission of crippled children to the hospitals, and it was here that the committee, under the tutelage of Adair, adopted in the simplest possible language the Atlanta plan: that to be admitted a child must be from a family unable to pay for the orthopedic treatment received; must be under fourteen years of age; must not be mentally incompetent; and must be, in the opinion of the surgeons, one who could be cured or improved. The hospitals were not to become asylums for indigent incurables. They were to be hospitals in the finest sense, hospitals for the curing or helping of children who otherwise would go through life saddled with their deformities and their pain.

There has never been a change in that policy. No patient at any Shriners' Hospital has ever paid one penny for any service received. The doors have been open equally to Jews, Catholics, Blacks, Mohammedans, Orientals, foreigners and even an occasional child of a Shriner.

With the preliminary difficulties out of the way, the committee began the laborious task of selecting sites for the hospitals. St. Louis was still the first choice, but there were legal problems in connection with acquiring the property, and construction was delayed for several months. Thus, while the St. Louis unit was the original hospital, it was not the first hospital to get under way. That honor went to Shreveport, Louisiana, and El Karubah Temple. The cornerstone of the Shreveport unit was laid by Imperial Potentate Ernest A. Cutts on May 12, 1922, and it opened its doors to the first patient on September 16 of that year in a remodeled house adjacent to the Masonic Temple.

So hard did the committee work during the second year of its existence that it was able to report to the Imperial Shrine session in San Francisco on June 13, 1922, that locations had been selected for ten hospitals and that construction was underway at most of them. Eventually, the Shrine erected seventeen hospital units in the following cities: Shreveport; St. Louis; Minneapolis-St. Paul; Montreal; Portland, Oregon; San Francisco; Los Angeles; Spokane, Washington; Salt Lake City; Philadelphia; Honolulu; Springfield, Massachusettes; Mexico City; Lexington, Kentucky; Chicago; Winnipeg; Manitoba; and Greeneville, South Carolina.

Thousands of Shriners who arrived in San Francisco a few days before the opening of the 1922 Imperial Session on June 13, were present when the cornerstone was laid for the hospital unit there, and when the session itself opened, it was evident that there would be no debate. The Imperial Council had been "sold" on the movement, and for that matter so had much of the rest of the nation. National magazines and newspapers were keeping the public apprised of every Shrine hospital activity.

In his report to the Imperial Council in 1922, Cochran had a prophetic vision of the days ahead:

"I believe that time will demonstrate that you have set an example and outlined a plan of development which will lead, in the course of time, to the institution of a great plan of humanitarian care of all those classes of people whom we find in every city and among all populations who become objects of charity or affectionate care on the part of the people among whom they live. This work is going to practically elminate from the streets of your cities in the course of the next generation or so the crippled child."

And so it has. It has not been easy. There can be little doubt that the pioneering efforts of the Shriners to aid the destitute crippled child has motivated other organizations, including various units of government, to give attention to the problem. Experts in the field have learned that while the crippled child has not been eliminated and probably never will be, it can be helped and is being helped.

Meanwhile, in Greeneville, South Carolina, W. W. Burgiss, a philanthropist, was so impressed with the work the hospital movement was doing that he built and bequeathed an entire unit to the Imperial Board of Trustees. His gift amounted to more than $350,000, but nowhere does his name appear in the hospitals except in the "Book of Gold," a book composed of pure gold sheets, on which is inscribed the name of every donor to the hospital movement. A similar "Book of Gold" is enshrined in every hospital operated by the Shriners. Hundreds of donors have bequeathed millions of dollars, maintained as an endowment fund for the operation of the hospitals, which now costs almost fifty-seven million dollars a year. Many of the donors are Shriners, many of them are not. The Roman Catholic Bishop of Wichita, Kansas, wrote to the chairman of the board of the St. Louis hospital unit about a Catholic boy from Wichita, named Jerry: "Certainly the Shriners' Hospital in St. Louis as well as the members of the Shriners' organization in Wichita are deserving of orchids and congratulations for the magnificent care of this dear little boy. It is a medical wonder that a little fellow like Jerry, born without arms and legs, can be equipped to take his normal place in his home and later on in society. I have never failed to send in my check to the Shriners when they conduct the annual circus here to raise funds for the wonderful Christlike work they are doing for handicapped children." The letter was signed by the Most Rev. Mark. K. Carroll.

And in addition to the Shrine Circuses held all over the United States and Canada to raise funds for the hospitals, more than forty annual football games are played. One of the more notable ones is the Los Angeles North-South game, played between high-school stars from the north and the south of California, which draws more than 100,000 patrons. Another was the North-South College All-Star game in Miami. The "Oyster Bowl" is promoted by Khedive Temple of Norfolk, Virginia, and played in the Municipal Stadium in that city. In twelve years, it earned more than $800,000 for the endowment fund and tremendously more as of today. In Charlotte, North Carolina, Oasis Temple promotes a game between all-star high-school seniors from both North and South Carolina, and one can only surmise what the Governor of North Carolina says to the Governor of South Carolina after the game is over. The Maple Sugar Bowl Game played at Dartmouth, the Pretzel Bowl at Reading, Pennsylvania, etc. The list could go on, but the most famous and the first of the Shrine games is the East-West College All-Star game, promoted by Islam Temple in San Francisco, a game that has been called "footballs finest hour and the granddaddy of all-star college football games."

Every year since 1925 the best of the nation's collegiate football players assemble in San Francisco during the holiday season, giving up their vacations at home to play a game which has as its motto, "Strong legs run that weak legs may walk." During all that time, not one player has received one cent more than his expenses. Not one of the Shrine leaders who direct the game has ever received a penny. None of the coaches or officials have been paid. The entire profit of the venture originally went to the San Francisco unit of the hospital system, but in later years after the San Francisco hospital had become self-sustaining, the funds were turned over to the general endowment fund for distribution to all hospitals, but with emphasis on the Los Angeles unit. At the time that the San Francisco hospital became self-supporting, the chairman of the local board of trustees was John McGilvray, one of the original national trustees and in later years the vice president of that group. And like others on that first board, including Bishop Keator, Dr. Lanstrum and the others, he gave of his own treasure to make the hospitals the "world's greatest philanthropy."

The game is really the by-product of a fun festival that was called a baseball game between the Nobles of Islam Temple and the San Francisco Elks. The earnings of that game were divided among the charities of the two fraternities. But the Shrine hospital needed something more, and Captain E. Jack Spaulding suggested that possibly a football game between the two fraternities might be arranged. Still, the human wreckage that might result when older men started committing mayhem on the gridiron was hardly to be countenanced, and as a substitute the nobility of Islam Temple created the All-Star game with William Coffman as director. He retired and is now deceased.

The Shrine East-West game provides one of the greatest football classics in the nation. Some of the greatest stars the game has ever known have appeared. But the Shrine East-West game is more than just a football game. It is a classic of love and sacrifice for a goal that transcends the yards gained, the passes thrown or the runners stopped. This is a game played that Joe, with two clubfeet, may walk and even run and play like other children. It is played for little Mary, who lies in a plaster cast as the curve is removed from her spine. It is played for Ralph and Ruth, Nancy and Bill, Sue and Dick—white, black, yellow, Protestant, Jew, and Catholic—who lie in the Shriners' Hospitals, and for others who are waiting to reach that Mansion of Mercy.

And it should be stated right here that one young man, whose deformities were corrected in the San Francisco hospital, eventually played in one East-West game.

The procedure of the game is always the same. By

the middle of October, the players have been invited, and according to their own lights have accepted or rejected the invitation. Arriving in San Francisco, the players of both squads are taken to the hospital to meet the little boy or little girl who has adopted him for the time of the visit to the Golden Gate. Each child has a pipe-cleaner image of a football player, dressed in the colors of the school he represents. The little patient sings the school song as best he or she can. They have a cup of tea together and become friends. And it isn't always easy. Many a strong, stalwart football star, seeing the twisted bodies, the plaster casts and the smiling faces for the first time, suddenly excuses himself, walks through the front door of the hospital and finds a place to cry. Cry unashamedly. And vow that in the game ahead—well, it is best illustrated by a story written by Bud Spencer, sports editor of the San Francisco *News*, of Joe Sullivan, twenty-one-year-old, crew-haired halfback from Dartmouth, who shyly approached his hostess and said:

"Hello, Princess."

"Hello," she answered.

The little girl sang her song and showed Joe her miniature painted in the oak green of Dartmouth. He leaned down so that she could pin it on his lapel. And then they waited. Uncertain, bashful. But in a moment, as is a woman's ways, the girl broke the stalemate by reaching under her pillow and bringing out an added gift.

"Here," she said, and handed Joe a leather case.

Joe turned it over once or twice, not knowing quite what to think.

"I made it," she told him, a queer mixture of pride and shyness in her voice. "I made it just for you. I knew you were coming. I even know your name. Your name is Joe Sullivan and it's a key case."

The next day, the East team moved to Santa Clara University to begin training for the New Year's Day game. After each day's scrimmage, when the big fellows had showered and had their dinners. Joe went off alone and wrote to his "princess." And Joe couldn't forget what the nurses had told him. His "princess" needed something more than science and medicine. She had been a very sick girl. Sometimes, Joe kept thinking, inspiration can do more than all the other things put together. Then Joe was hit with an idea. He knew the game was to be televised, and he knew his "princess" would be watching. So he wrote to her that on Saturday, every play he made would be strictly for her. "And don't be surprised if I intercept a pass or two just for you." And he did.

All through the afternoon, his "princess" was the happiest girl in the hospital. That Joe was playing one of his greatest games just for her was a secret locked in her heart, but the nurses immediately noticed a turn for the better in her attitude. A few weeks later, they wrote to Joe that she was taking her first steps in the therapeutic pool.

Other Bowl games followed the San Francisco experiment. But San Francisco led the way. It is spectacular as the colorful Shrine parade units fill the field before a game. It is spectacular with the brilliant play of the young athletes, whose names are known by every follower of the autumn sport—names like Johnny Lujack, of Notre Dame; Herb Joesting and Bronco Nagurski of Minnesota; Bob Waterfield of U.C.L.A.; George McAfee of Duke; Brick Muller of California. In all, more than 125 schools have contributed more than 1,600 players to the contest , and as the New York *Sun* once said editorially: "There has always seemed something peculiarly fitting in the bringing together of fine young athletes in a laudable attempt to do something useful for physically handicapped boys and girls."

And so it has.

19

They Play and Sing

No one knows the thousands of hours, days, weeks and months that have been spent by the national and local boards to make the Shriner's Hospitals what they are. The men gave unstintingly of their time and talent. Without exception, they were men of vision and, like Dr. Hoke in 1914, were inspired by an almost fanatical zeal to be of service. As the years passed, and one after another the original board members passed into the unseen temple, new men were appointed and eventually elected by the Imperial Council. And with each passing year, there was more and more to be done by both the local and national boards. At the national level, the hospitals had become truly big business as the board appropriated and administered almost seven million dollars for operations alone. And the local boards, composed of leaders of their communities—bankers, industrialists, lawyers, doctors, businessmen—devoted more and more of their time to the handling of their local affairs. In many cases it was a full-time activity. And the competition for membership on the national board became almost as keen as competition for membership on the Imperial Divan.

With the retirement of Sam P. Cochran in 1934 as Chairman of the Board of Trustees of the Shriners' Hospitals for Crippled Children, W. Freeland Kendrick was elected to that post. He retained it until 1949, when he, too, retired, to be succeeded by Galloway Calhoun of Tyler, Texas, the Imperial Potentate in 1948–1949 and a member of Karem Temple in Waco, Texas. During the years, the Georgia Corporation had given way to the Colorado Corporation. The Imperial Potentate, the Deputy Imperial Potentate, the Imperial Chief Rabban, the Imperial Treasurer, and the Junior Past Imperial Potentate were made members of the governing board. But the changes in operating procedures were rare and, even then, largely to simplify the work. The children were not affected.

The first patient to be admitted back in 1922 was a little girl from the red clay country south of Shreveport, Louisiana, a tot with a club foot who had learned to walk on the top of one foot rather than the sole. The first child to be admitted in Minneapolis was a Blackfoot Indian boy, suffering from the deformities of polio. Since that time, more than 220 thousand children have been treated. Some of them remained for months in the various hospitals. Others received treatment in the out-patient clinic. There have been 2,265,078 clinic visits as of 1979. Many of them received surgery in techniques developed in the Shrine Hospitals and now accepted by orthopedic surgeons as standard. Thousands of the children have been fitted with arm and leg braces and artificial limbs, most of them made by expert technicians in special workrooms in the hospitals. The results have been astounding. It is almost impossible for the lay mind to conceive of the work that has been done, the results that have been achieved and the happiness that has been created.

No one knows how many million man-hours of work have been contributed, not only by the paid staff in the various hospitals, but by Shriners and their wives who work as volunteers in many ways to contribute to the program. And from these millions of hours of work, thousands of children have been and are permitted to lead normal lives, who otherwise would have become mendicants or public charges, destined to go through life in pain and misery, wards of poor administrators, suffering from shame and defeat. Walter M. Fleming, who was himself a doctor, would have been proud to have seen the glory that came to his Order that was organized for fun and frolic, and then paraded its way into the hearts of Americans everywhere.

From the very start, the hospitals kept accurate records of the patients, and it is to the everlasting credit of the management that not once since that September sixteenth in 1922 has there been the slightest defamatory remark made about the hospitals. There has been only praise, praise of the highest order, praise from the medical profession, praise from those who have a different religion or nationality or color from the Shriners themselves.

Since the hosptial records are couched in medical terms, they do not reveal the true story behind many of the patients. They do not reveal the story that can be learned only by visiting one of the hospitals and seeing the children and talking with them. You can see a boy of seven without either arms or legs feeding himself with a contraption manufactured in the hospital. He has learned to control it with his back muscles. There was a little girl lying on a plain plank board, and she had been strapped to it for three months, as each day the surgeons forced her twisted body back to normal. She would be there three more months but she was happy and smiling. You can see boys and girls whose entire lower extremities were encased in grotesque plaster casts, but they would leave the hospitals, walking erect instead of crawling on hands and knees, which is the way they entered.

The deformities of the children are not pleasant to think about, but it's wonderful to see the children themselves. Somehow—perhaps through some angelic power—the staff in the hospital is able to instill in these unfortunate children the hope for a normal life. Even while they are the guests of the hospitals, they begin to lead that normal life. They go to school. They engage in handicrafts. They play and sing. They watch movies and television and listen to the radio. Their food is better—and there is more of it—than in most homes in America. Many of the famous stars of the stage, the movies, radio and television have visited the hospitals and entertained the children. Roy Rogers with Trigger and Red Skeleton, both of whom are Shriners, visit the hosptials many times each year. There are Boy and Girl Scout troops. There are playrooms and playgrounds. There are pretty dresses and dress-up suits for those special occasions.

Literally thousands of children have achieved success in life as a result of the work done at the hospitals. Dozens of boys have become doctors. Scores of girls have become nurses. One girl became a medical missionary in Africa. Many are priests, ministers, dentists. Others enter into the work-a-day life for which they are equipped. They marry and have children, and there have been several cases where the daughter of a former patient has entered a hospital, troubled with the same congenital deformity that afflicted the parent.

And frequently Shriners maintain their interest in patients after they are dismissed. For example, an Americana Y.M.C.A. worker from Kansas City was sent to São Paulo, Brazil, and there he encountered a poorly paid teacher, whose daughter—a pretty little thing—was afflicted with a congenital hip deformity. After much letterwriting she was admitted to the Philadelphia hospital. Her father obtained a teaching job in Philadelphia and together they learned to speak English. After she was dismissed from the hospital, she returned to her home, became a dental technician and met a young dentist. They each received scholarships to the University of Rochester to complete their education. When they arrived in New York, they were met by the Shriners from Mecca Temple and entertained there. When they arrived in Rochester, Damascus Temple took over, arranged their wedding for them—and then gave them a reception. Their whole happiness, it might be said, could be traced to the Shrine.

As the years passed, the malcontents who had resented the two dollar and later five dollar assessment realized they had been wrong. The Shriners not only accepted the fact that they had the hospitals, but prided themselves on it. Almost every weekend, some of the temples near the various hospitals would arrange entertainments for the children. The bands played. There never was a time when a toy was not available for one of the tots, and after every case of major surgery there was an extra toy which the child prized most of all. Many of the former patients still have as many as ten or twelve toys, representing the ten or twelve operations they endured, always smilingly.

The towns where the hospitals were located also took them to their hearts. In Greenville, South Carolina, a local barber visits the hospital every week to cut hair—free of charge. In another hospital, the town's theater owner makes a film available and an operator to run the machines which had been contributed by the local Shrine temple. School boards provide teachers, and the local hospitals and even the Navy joined forces to provide blood and bone banks, all free.

This, then, was the "soul" the Shrine had been seeking all the years of its existence. This was the glory toward which they had been parading since that first procession from the Dennison House to the Scottish Rite Cathedral in Indianapolis in 1887. Wonderfully enjoyable accomplishment.

20

Presidential Participation Again

By June of 1923, the Shrine had come a long way from that first meeting of the original thirteen in New York on that June night 1871 when the decision was taken to found a new Order. The Shrine could boast of a half-million members, only one of whom had been a member of fifty years. He was the venerable James McGee, No. 28 on the rolls of Mecca Temple. The Shrine owned scores of temples scattered across a continent. It owned a chain of hospitals, some already in operation, others under construction and still more to come. And the Shrine prided itself that among its membership was the President of the United States. In tribute to Warren G. Harding, the forty-ninth annual session of the Imperial Council was held in Washington, D.C., June 5–6–7, 1923.

Still bigger and better sessions of the Imperial Council were to come in later years as both the Shrine and the cities grew, but until 1923, there had never been a session like that one. There are still some of the old-time Shriners who have been attending sessions for fifty years who declare the Washington meeting was the biggest, gaudiest and most spectacular of all that have ever been held. Certainly it was among them. The 1965 and 1967 Washington sessions surpassed in number of attendance and spectators.

Three of the most famous names in American history were to play a part in that session—the President, a member of Aladdin Temple in Columbus, Ohio; General John J. (Black Jack) Pershing, Army Chief of Staff, wartime commander of the allied forces, and a member of Sesostris Temple in Lincoln, Nebraska; and John Philip Sousa, most famous of all band conductors and a member of Almas Temple in Washington.

In January of 1921, Leonard P. Steuart, later to become Imperial Potentate and Imperial Treasurer, had just been elected Assistant Rabban of Almas Temple, and with other members of the Divan of that temple he began making plans for entertaining the Imperial Session in 1923 in Washington. The invitation actually was presented to the Imperial Council at its 1921 session in Des Moines, and included as a part of that invitation was a letter from the White House. It said:

"Your letter informing me that Almas Temple, Ancient Arabic Order Nobles of the Mystic Shrine, intends to invite the Imperial Council to meet in Washington during June of 1923 has interested me very much. Of course, being President of the entire country, it would not quite be proper for me to indicate a special preference for any particular city as a location of such a gathering, but being, during the Presidential term, a resident of Washington, I am very glad to say to you that if the Imperial Council shall determine to hold the Imperial Session in Washington, you can be assured of my great pleasure and readiness to make every possible contribution to the success of the occasion."

No action was taken on the invitation at the 1921 meeting, but it was the consensus that when the invitation was presented again in San Francisco in 1922 it would be accepted.

Scores of committees from Almas Temple went to work immediately, determined to make the affair a wing-ding that would never be forgotten. And even before the great day arrived, it was apparent they had succeeded. The Washington *Post* printed a seventy-two-page special edition, devoted entirely to the Shrine. Pennsylvania Avenue from the Capitol to the

White House was decorated with hundreds of lighted arches. An ingenious loudspeaker system was set up so that the million or more people who would watch the parades would know what was going on, and later could dance in the street to the music of the world's famous bands.

On the Sunday before the opening of the Imperial Session, special church services were held throughout the city; and it seemed that the entire city gathered around the Masonic Temple in the afternoon for a sermon and songs by the chanters of Zuhrah Temple. Temples as far away as Pittsburgh entertained the various pilgrimages on their way to Washington, and it appeared that Baltimore's Boumi was as popular as Washington itself.

On Saturday night before the opening of the session on Tuesday, June 5, prohibition agents made a series of spectacular raids on bootleggers and speakeasies in the city, but they confiscated only a few cases of beer and a small amount of corn whisky. As a matter of fact, the Shriners had learned that alcohol was not necessary for them to have fun. The Washington *Post* commented after the Shriners had been in town one day "there was only one limitation of the extent to which the throngs went in enjoying themselves and that was the limit, or rather the abjurgation placed on them by their leaders—that their pleasures be without intemperance, the jollity without coarseness and their happiness without sin." As a result, every kind of clean pleasure ever found was to be found in Washington. Pennsylvania Avenue swarmed with Shriners and townfolk alike, and the Shriners entertained in their own local fashion. There were Indian dancers from New Mexico, cavorting next to square dancers from Missouri. The people were having so much fun that uniformed patrols could not drill and bands could not march.

The aircraft carrier *Langley* arrived in the Potomac

River to participate in naval demonstrations, and the army air service—attempting to gain attention—flew two bales of cotton from Atlanta, Georgia, to New Bedford, Massachusetts, where it was manufactured into Masonic aprons and then flown back to Washington, where they were presented to Imperial Potentate "Sunny Jim" McCandless of Aloha Temple (Honolulu) for distribution as mementos of the great occasion.

On Tuesday morning, the great escort parade was held before the amazed eyes of thousands of persons. The Washington *Post* observed that there never had been a parade like it in the history of the city, and in the reviewing stand, beside the Imperial Potentate, were President Harding, Mrs. Harding and General Pershing.

The parade was so long that McCandless sent Deputy Imperial Potentate Conrad V. Dykeman to Keith's theater to get the session under way. The opening ceremonies had been scheduled for 10:30 A.M., but McCandless, Almas Potentate Steuart and the President did not take their places on the stage until almost two o'clock. Noble Harding told the nobility:

"Your exceptionally courteous patience in waiting for the Imperial Potentate and myself, you may be sure, is greatly appreciated. It was not in our hearts to keep you, but we sat in fascination watching the most wonderful parade it has ever been my privlege to see. . . .

"I like the atmosphere of fraternity. I rejoice in the knowledge that I am addressing a body where every heartbeat is loyally American, where every impulse is American, where every commitment and consecration are to the Republic and its free institutions. . . ."

The President spoke for twenty minutes, interrupted frequently by applause, about the joys of fraternity and the blessings of Masonry in particular.

The George Washington National Masonic Memorial was under construction in nearby Alexandria, Virginia, during the time of the Imperial Council session, and

Library of Congress

President and Mrs. Harding and General Pershing, Washington, 1923

the Imperial Council visited it in a body. They also went on to Mount Vernon, where McCandless laid a wreath on the tomb of Washington. McCandless and the Imperial Divan were greeted by Governor E. Lee Trinkle of Virginia who declared: "This is still the land of Washington. May I not hope that you and through you all the Shriners of the earth may be baptized with the spirit of American patriotism."

On Tuesday evening, June 5, 1923, the President attired in evening dress and a fez, attended the Imperial Potentate's banquet, and afterward at his request, he toured Pennsylvania Avenue in a White House car with McCandless and Steuart. Thousands of persons had gathered in the street all the way from the Capitol to the White House for the merrymaking and the dancing. The Presidential car left the Willard Hotel at 11:20 o'clock and proceeded slowly along "the road to Mecca" toward the peace monument, up the avenue on one side and back to the White House on the other. Whenever he was recognized—and it was unusual to find the President wearing a fez—he was given a rousing cheer. On Wednesday afternoon, the President and Mrs. Harding gave a garden party at the White House for members of all the Ohio Temples, and on Thursday he opened the White House to all the Shriners. They swarmed through the entire lower floor, making themselves at home with Noble Harding. The occasion was unprecedented in all the history of the White House. No tickets or invitations were required—only the password of a Shriner to be a personal guest of the President.

Library of Congress

The Famous Conductor John Philip Sousa, Noble of Almas Temple

There was a great night parade on Wednesday night, again reviewed by President and Mrs. Harding, and on Thursday night there was a mammoth pageant and parade, depicting the great Masons in American history, including, of course, Washington, Paul Revere, Putnam, the Adamses and scores of others. The evening was climaxed by a ten-thousand-dollar fireworks display at the foot of the Washington Monument, which Noble Harding and his guests watched from the south portico of the White House.

With the last burst of shells, thousands of people swarmed out of the stands. The crowd formed a milling mob from Eleventh to Fifteenth Streets and the police were helpless to control them. At the time, a false fire alarm brought screaming engines into the street and a panic was narrowly averted. But none was hurt, and the bands struck up and dancing went on until daylight in Pennsylvania Avenue.

One of the outstanding features of the session was a massed band, performing in the American League baseball park. It was a band of chosen musicians from every Shrine band present, and it was conducted by Sousa in the first performance of his new march, "The Shriners."

The Shriners were all having so much fun that it was difficult for the Imperial representatives to get down to work, and actually not much was accomplished in the official meetings. But there was one debate, which went on for almost four hours, on the old question of whether or not the Shrine should be incorporated. The proponents felt that only by incorporation could the rights and privileges of the Shrine, its emblems, badges, Ritual and even the fez itself, be protected from the Ancient Egyptian Order of Nobles of the Mystic Shrine, which was incorporated. But in the end, the opponents, who argued that the Shrine was a fraternity and not a business, won out, although the subject was to come up again and again over the years.

And so the 1923 session of the Imperial Council reached its end. There would never be another one exactly like it. But the President, Vice President and First Lady participated in the 1967 session, all at the same time, with Orville F. Rush as Imperial Potentate. Noble Harding had a whale of a time for four days, and he enjoyed every minute of it. It was his first and last Imperial Council session. He died in San Francisco August 3, 1923, just two months later. A great and active Mason and Shriner.

21

Dreams of Grandeur

The twenty years that followed the Washington session of the Imperial Council were years of plenty—and then depression and war. The Shrine troubles of the thirties were brought on, to a large extent, by the plenty of the twenties.

The membership when the Shrine met in Washington was almost 550,000. By 1927, it had grown to 580,000, the high-water mark of the period. Temples were prosperous, the nation was on a binge, and the Shrine was a part of it. When the Shrine met in 1924 in Kansas City, the Kansas City *Star* reported that the decorations were the most lavish in the history of the Order. Entire areas of the city were roped off to take care of the throngs. The *Star*, which had reported Shrine activities in two columns in 1901, now devoted almost the entire paper to the session and its activities. Sousa was on hand again to conduct the massed bands. The nobility arrived en masse. If there was Zemzem water about, it was not in physical evidence; but the gaiety was spontaneous and the *Star* said: "This is no time for the killjoy and the solemn face. It simply cannot be done. Such enthusiasm! Such rollicking spirits! Who could hold out against it?"

In 1925 and 1929, Al Malaikah Temple of Los Angeles entertained the Shriners in two of that city's gaudiest affairs. In 1925, the great Los Angeles Coliseum was converted into an immense Moorish palace, with thousands upon thousands of lights in myriad colors—the greatest lighting event in the history of the world. But, in 1925, it also rained. And it rained again. The parade had to be postponed. The Shriners swamped the sporting-goods stores. The most popular costume was a bathing suit. Some of the Shriners put on water wings which, according to the *Times,* made them look like dear little Cupids with red panties. The city of Los Angeles had erected a major railroad city, and scores of special trains arrived from all over the continent, many of them decorated in gaudy colors. Some were complete with radio and loudspeaker systems.

In 1926, the Shriners were the guests of Past Imperial Potentate Freeland Kendrick, who had become Mayor of Philadelphia and was presiding over the sesquicentennial celebration of the signing of the Declaration of Independence. The Shriners took over the staid city, and Kendrick helped them do it. The 1927 and 1928 conventions were held in Atlantic City and Miami, where there was ample playground for the Shriners and their families and also plenty of hotel space; but in 1929, as we have noted, the Shriners were back in Los Angeles again for an even bigger and gaudier affair than that of 1925.

The great efforts at lighting in 1925 were surpassed as great searchlights moved like giant fans over the 100,000 persons gathered in the Coliseum. Four hundred thousand more tried to get in and couldn't. The floats were as beautiful as those in the rose parade in Pasadena and there were more of them. The movie industry participated for the first time, and among the stars prominent in the affair were Wallace Beery, himself a Shriner, who was the vice-chairman of the affair. Other were Monte Blue, Ann Pennington, Leo Carrillo, Bessie Love, Laura LaPlante, Conrad Nagel, Louise Fazenda, Joe E. Brown, and Jean Hersholt. Almost every temple had a bathing suit brigade, reminiscent of 1925, but the weather in 1929 was perfect. One group wearing bathing suits was sprinkled by a fire company when it approached the station house.

It was a great fling and the boys enjoyed it, not knowing there was trouble ahead for the nation, for the temples at home, for the hospitals and for the Imperial Council.

The first real evidence that the temples were facing financial difficulties came in the 1925 report of Imperial Potentate James E. Chandler of Ararat Temple (Kansas City). "The conditions of the present day are very different," he said, "from those prevailing several years ago. I find that temples about the jurisdiction are having difficulty in maintaining themselves properly because of insufficient income. In order to bridge over these gaps the membership is being constantly asked to subscribe money, or buy tickets to various entertainments instituted for the purpose of raising funds."

Chandler then recommended that legislation be enacted forbidding any promotional scheme which had connected with it a gambling device, a lottery, raffle, prize contest, or gift enterprise. Actually, most of the fund-raising enterprises were for the purpose of sending the uniformed units to the Imperial Council sessions, and that was getting to be an expensive proposition. The Imperial Council agreed with Chandler after a long debate and forbade the money-raising operations. To compensate the temples for these losses, also as recommended by Chandler, the Imperial Council ordered that minimum dues in the Shrine be set at ten dollars, with an additional two dollars for the hospitals. This precipitated bitter debate. Some temples argued they didn't need the money and should not be forced to assess it under those conditions. Others argued that it was unfair to assess the entire membership to send a few of the boys in the uniformed units on a four- or five-day vacation. In the end, Chandler won his point, but he had to agree that one dollar of the five-dollar increase should be forwarded to the Im-

perial Council as the annual subscription price of a
new national Shrine magazine, which he also recommended and which after more long debate the Imperial
Council established.

There were problems in connection with the founding of the Shrine Magazine. First, there was the problem of *The Crescent,* a magazine devoted to the shrine
and published by J. Harry Lewis, Past Potentate of Osman Temple in St. Paul. At one time Lewis had had
a circulation of about 60,000 copies, but when the idea
of a Shrine magazine was first broached, his circulation
began to fall off. In 1952 it was down to about half
its top figure. Lewis felt, and the Imperial Council
agreed with him, that if the Shrine was to establish
its own magazine, he should be paid for his assets. The
major hurdle, however, was the fact that some of the
Shriners didn't see the need for such a magazine, even
if the Elks, the Moose, and other fraternal organizations
had found them not only eminently satisfactory but
profitable. One of the opponents of the magazine argued that, if the Shrine was to assess each member a
dollar a year for the magazine, it would be much better
if that dollar went to the crippled children. But under-
lying most of the argument was the fact that the individual temples were somewhat jealous of their position and wanted no encroachment of the national
organization beyond its present position. One of the
debaters argued that the position was similar to the
division of authority between federal and state gov-
ernments.

The debate went on for more than two hours, and
after considerable parliamentary maneuvering the proposal was defeated by the representatives. But an hour
later there was a motion to reconsider, and after another hour of debate the magazine was approved.
Chandler was appointed chairman of the publication
committee by Imperial Potentate James C. Burger of
El Jebel Temple (Denver), who along with Deputy Im-

perial Potentate David Crosland of Alcazar Temple (Montgomery, Alabama) became a member of the committee. They hired Fred O. Wood of Kansas City as general manager. By the time the 1926 session of the Imperial Council was held in Philadelphia, the committee had two issues of the magazine off the presses. And it was a pretty good magazine. There was a short story directed toward men. There was a page of Shrine history by the venerable William B. Melish. There were news from temples, a message from the Imperial Potentate, and other features designed to meet the needs of the Shrine in the dissemination of information.

There was more grumbling and bickering, however, much of it inspired by the Recorders of some ninety-eight temples, who felt the method of collection of the dollar-a-year subscription price was involved and dangerous. But in the end, the Imperial Council went along for another year. By the time twelve more issues had been printed and distributed, the Imperial Council had little to distract it with respect to the magazine, but in 1928, at Miami, a bombshell exploded and Chandler and his committee were unprepared for it.

The printed report circulated among the representatives showed that the magazine had a profit of $113,015 for the second year of its operation, but no sooner had Chandler moved the adoption of the report than Noble Arthur H. Diamant of Mecca Temple demanded to know where the profit might be. The Shrine, he said, had contributed $1,100,000, and if the magazine actually was showing a real profit, some of the money should be in the coffers, whereupon Imperial Potentate Clarence M. Dunbar admitted that the magazine had not shown a real profit. Yet, what Dunbar and everyone else in the convention missed was that the money paid by Shriners to the magazine committee was not a contribution at all. It was a subscription price for the magazine. The point was that for two years a group of the nobility had objected to having the magazine forced upon them. If it was worth the money and they wanted to subscribe, that was one thing, but to be forced to subscribe was another.

This hard core of opposition had three resolutions ready when the magazine report was filed. The three resolutions came from Alcazar (Past Imperial Potentate Crosland's temple), Syrian (Past Imperial Potentate Melish's temple) and from Noble Lee Thomas of El Karubah Temple (Shreveport). All of them were designed to accomplish the same thing—the liquidation of the magazine. This was the bombshell. Chandler and his committee did not know it was coming and they had not assembled facts and figures to combat the issue. And they couldn't get them ready in time for the debate that followed the presentation of the resolutions through the Jurisprudence and Laws Committee.

The 1928 session ordered the liquidation of the magazine. In the end, the Shrine paid several hundred thousand dollars to buy out the contracts of the personnel, the paper manufacturer and the printing firm. But the Shrine was not out of the magazine business. In later years, there were many Shrine leaders who felt the 1928 session had made a grave error in eliminating the publication, but it was done, never to be revived.

The curtailment of the magazine had not been the only controversial issue before the 1928 session of the Imperial Council. Imperial Potentate Dunbar during his year of service had managed to travel widely and visit almost all of the temples. He had witnessed great enthusiasm among the nobility. He had observed scores of ceremonials at which thousands of new Nobles were created, but he had also noted a net decrease in total Shrine membership of more than five thousand as temples suspended members of the nobility for non-payment of dues and thousands more took demits. He had presided at the dedication of one new mosque and he had noted others in process of construction, but he also had noted severe financial difficulties for some of those temples that had overextended their financial position. He made note of the fact that the enthusiasm of many Nobles, particularly officers of temples, to create beautiful buildings was leaving those temples in dire financial distress. It was his position that, if and when those temples defaulted on their building bonds, the Shrine as a whole would be injured. He also noted that the act of the temples in assessing their membership in order to meet their contracted financial obligations was creating almost insurmountable problems, including loss of membership.

Like some other Imperial Potentates, it would appear that Dunbar was close to a prophetic vision. Even though the country was just entering its greatest era of prosperity, Dunbar could see difficulties ahead, and to prevent those difficulties he recommended the passage of a resolution, presented by Past Imperial Potentate Burger, designed to limit the authority of a temple to contract financial obligations beyond its ability to pay. Technically the resolution provided that a temple could not enter into a building or other program in which the financial obligation exceeded ten dollars per member without first obtaining the approval of a special committee of the Imperial Council.

There was great debate on the issue. The opponents contended that this was an invasion of local rights by the Imperial Council, but in the end, the resolution passed.

The high point of Shrine membership of the period came on January 1, 1927, when there were 587,133 Nobles. From that point, there followed a gradual decline to 517,827 on January 1, 1932, and a precipitate decline to 306,470 on January 1, 1942. But when the Shriners met in Los Angeles in 1929, there had been no evidence of the troubles ahead. Leo Youngworth of Al Malaikah Temple became the Imperial Potentate and devoted himself to his task. At the 1930 session in Toronto, Ontario, he obtained more publicity for the Shrine than it had ever had before.

22

Symbol of Good Will

There was one major defect in the fabulous 1929 convention in Los Angeles. It was so stupendous, so glamorous, so beautiful, so big that there were no invitations for the 1930 meeting. No other city felt that it could prepare such an Imperial Session and that the city and the temple might suffer by comparison. But Shrinedom and other temples failed to realize the capabilities of the new Imperial Potentate, Leo V. Youngworth.

Youngworth was a fraternity man. He had worked long and diligently in most of the various degrees of Masonry. He had lived with the Hollywood show, which was in its heyday. He was a lawyer by profession and like Kendrick had more than the average share of showmanship in his makeup. The Imperial Council left to him the selection of the time and place for the 1930 session.

It was not until August 21, 1929, a little more than two months after the Los Angeles session, that he made an official visitation to Toronto. After several conferences with the officers of Rameses Temple while he was there, an official invitation was issued and accepted for the 1930 session, to be held June 10, 11 and 12. To Youngworth, the Toronto session was a challenge. Perhaps it could not emulate the glamour of Hollywood, but there were other attractions. It would add an international flavor absent since the session of 1888, and of course there was no prohibition in Canada.

With Toronto selected as the convention city, the

director general was appointed along with his various committees and Youngworth began to dream.

"I was impressed with the wonderful possibilities," he reported to the Imperial Council, "of making this session of the Imperial Council an outstanding Masonic demonstration. The fine feeling of our Canadian neighbors and their kindly attitude toward our own country prompted a desire to do something that would further develop the fine friendship which has existed between our English-speaking peoples for so many years. The thought occurred to me that it would be a great object lesson to the world to have the Governors of the various states of the United States and the Premiers of Canada, the Grand Masters of the various states and provinces, as well as the representatives from Cuba and Mexico, assemble in Toronto and join with us in a meeting that would be outstanding in its accomplishments."

With this thought in mind, he called his Divan together in Philadelphia on October 2 to discuss these various possibilities, and the Divan was just as enthusiastic as Youngworth himself. The stock-market crash of October 29 was still almost a month away. While there were some indications that the future would not be as bright and rosy as some people seemed to think, there certainly was no indication of panic. True, the farmers were suffering, but this was a periodic phenomenon and no cause for particular concern. True, the Shrine membership was shown to be declining somewhat, but again it was certainly not serious enough to worry about.

Among other ideas that Youngworth offered to his Divan at the Philadelphia meeting was one that the Shrine should create a magnificent "peace monument" to be erected along the shores of Lake Erie, eternally facing across the border to the south. The Great War was only twelve years behind the world and everyone was looking for something that would prevent another such holocaust. The peace monument would serve not

only to commemorate the 150 years of friendship between Canada and the United States, but would serve
also as a memorial to the entrance of ancient Free and
Accepted Masonry into the continent of North America. And what better organization could offer such a
monument than the Shrine, which was the only Masonic organization with international jurisdiction?

Questionnaires were sent to the several temples, and
95 per cent of them endorsed the entire program as
enthusiastically as had the Divan. With this support
behind him, Youngworth contracted with Noble
Charles Keck, a noted sculptor and a Noble of Kismet
Temple (Brooklyn) to erect a monument to cost no
more than $55,000 and to be unveiled on the last day
of the Toronto session.

Youngworth worked incessantly toward the project.
He conferred with President Herbert Hoover and
Prime Minister Mackenzie King and won their cooperation. Finally the great session arrived. Two hundred
weary Sons of the Desert were admitted into the Oasis
of Rameses on Saturday, June 7. The Shriners from
all over North America—depression or no depression—
began to arrive on both Saturday and Sunday. On the
Sabbath, the giant stadium at the Canadian National
Exhibition grounds was filled to overflowing as the
chanters of several temples participated in a giant
open-air religious service.

It was an auspicious beginning of the 1930 session
of the Imperial Council. It was friendly, international,
religious and fraternal. And the glamour was added
on Monday, June 9, when Youngworth arrived with
two special trains from Al Malaikah Temple. The *Globe*
described it: "The sight of the first rank of marching
Shriners, swinging up from the Bay Street subway and
turning onto the broad thoroughfare of Front Street
displayed a richness of color and light. The sun came
out from behind the clouds and struck the marching
ranks. They reflected the beams of gold and red, glint-

ing and shimmering like even waves of light, with Union Jacks fluttering in the breezes from ranks of spears."

And the Shriners really were having a whale of a time. They had so much fun that there wasn't a single Shriner present when the Toronto police raided a gambling hall that had been set up especially for the convention by some thugs from the United States who had expected to make a killing. When the police arrived the gamblers were sitting around trying to think of some way of drumming up some business.

Toronto contributed immensely to the session. Seven thousand schoolchildren paraded for Imperial Potentate Youngworth, and a children's choir gave a concert in the Coliseum that the *Globe* called splendid. And, of course, the Shriners entertained their Canadian friends. One fat Shriner had a toy balloon that he used to play a flute. There was the proverbial six-foot-seven Shriner pulling a toy cannon, and occasionally shooting it off. Two Shriners with a combination hurdy-gurdy and calliope blocked Young Street traffic for a half-hour.

On Wednesday a cold downpour of rain delayed the parade, but the Shriners continued to have fun in the hotel lobbies. Street cleaners tried in vain to sweep the wet streets and clear them of paper ribbons that floated down from the hotel rooms.

And then the rain ceased, and the great night parade of Wednesday moved on time. The *Globe* wrote: "The greatest spectacle that this city or perhaps any other city ever witnessed kept what seemed to be half the population of Toronto awake and out of bed for hours after midnight. The procession was a river of light, flowing between great human banks with the golden moon overhead scarcely visible against the display of skyrockets that fountained up streams of multicolored sparks to the sky."

But it was all just a prelude to the big event on Thursday afternoon, the dedication of the peace monument. At the opening Governor Albert Ritchie of Maryland declared that "here if anywhere will dawn the peace for which the world is waiting." Youngworth in his address of presentation declared that "our hope must be that somewhere and somehow these mutual understandings shall be arrived at, that war will be impossible and that universal peace will be enthroned." He called on 600,000 Shriners to continue in thought, word and deed their support of world peace. This moment, he said, "symbolizes our longings for international harmony to the end that universal peace and good will may rule the thoughts of the world's peoples. Our only fight is for one God, for home and for humanity against all forms of radicalism, realism and anarchy."

Prime Minister King spoke by radio from Ottawa and said: "I should like to add the thanks of the Canadian people as a whole for the inspiring monument which your Order is erecting on the shores of Lake Erie and which you are now about to dedicate in the cause of peace. It is indeed a worthy addition to the art treasures of the province of which Toronto is the capital city. It will be cherished by Canada as a national possession and by our continent as an abiding symbol of international good will."

Secretary of State Stimson, speaking for President Hoover from Washington, said that "during the past year earnest efforts toward the creation of a lasting peace have been made by some of the great nations of the earth and your influence has been powerfully asserted behind these efforts. The impressive monument you are unveiling today signifies your consecration to this cause. I am therefore happy to greet you and bear witness to the sentiments with which the government and the people of the United States accept the encouragement and the assistance of your great Order. That this meeting, composed so largely of United States citizens, should take place on Canadian soil is in itself significant. Our two nations have been offering to the world an example and practical demonstration of the benefits in the direction of lasting peace which can grow from a treaty of naval limitations."

Mrs. Youngworth unveiled the statue, and in accepting it, Mayor Wemp of Toronto said: "The motto of your great order is 'peace be on you,' and 'on you be the peace.' This with you on this great occasion is no mere gesture, no empty phrase. You have put your creed into your deed and have erected, dedicated and consecrated this lasting memorial as an altar of sacrifice and a stone of remembrance to those of our sons and daughters who passed by the path of duty of immortality in the cause of peace. Your generous gift, so nobly conceived, so worthy of the great cause, so expressive of the ideal of harmony and concord is gratefully accepted by this city as a sacred trust, as a great object lesson, unifying and vivifying, that animates all. May the life of our two nations flow in one gracious river, the confluence of many streams to the ocean and haven of peace and prosperity. And may there be no ebb to that tide of international amity which is now flowing so full and clear and strong between our two nations."

Symbol of Good Will.

23

Great Depression Impact

The years of the great depression were the most difficult for the Shrine since the first ten years, when Dr. Walter M. Fleming held the struggling organization together by hard work, the strength of his own character, funds from his own purse and his indomitable will for success of his brainchild. The Imperial Potentates who carried the burdens of the Shrine during the depression were without exception equipped with the same character and will as Fleming, and that they did not contribute to the finances of the Shrine in those trying years was due only to the fact that the fraternity had grown so large that any contribution they might have made would have been insufficient.

Beginning with Clarence Dunbar (Palestine) in June of 1927, and including Thomas C. Law (Yaarab) in July of 1942, all of the Imperial Potentates devoted most of their time to assuaging the wounds of the temples, incurred in the lush days of the Roaring Twenties, and to devising ways and means of holding the Order together. Dozens of ideas were submitted, argued and debated at the Imperial Council sessions and some positive changes were made, most of them helpful. The Imperial Potentates who served following Dunbar were Frank C. Jones (Arabia), Leo V. Youngworth (Al Malaikah), Esten A. Fletcher (Damascus), Thomas C. Houston (Medinah), Earl C. Mills (Za-Ga-Zig), John N. Sebrell (Khedive), Dana S. Williams (Kora), Leonard P. Steuart (Almas), Clyde I. Webster (Moslem), Walter

S. Sugden (Osiris), A. A. D. Rahn (Zuhrah), Walter D. Cline (Maskat), George F. Olendorf (Abou Ben Adhem), and Law.

The problems they faced were manifold, among which was the fact that the Shrine had no Masonic standing as such. True, the law of the Shrine required that all members must be members in good standing of a Blue Lodge of Masons and/or the York or Scottish Rites. But after the stock-market crash of 1929, many members of the Shrine found they could not continue the expense of paying dues in all of the bodies requisite to the Shrine. Some of them, the Shrine liked to feel, would gladly have continued the payment of the Shrine dues if they could have dropped the others. But the Shrine would have no part of that. The result was that demits and suspensions mounted sharply. And what puzzled the Shrine officials the most was the fact that there were far more suspensions than demits. The largest number of demits in any one year was 11,200 in 1932. But suspensions reached the fantastic total of 27,000 in 1931; 33,000 in 1932; and 45,000 in 1933. That was the high water mark, but still there were 33,000 suspended in 1934.

The Shrine was certainly no different from other fraternal bodies. The Masons themselves lost heavily. So did the Scottish and York Rites, the Knights of Columbus and the Knights of Pythias. But the fact was that the various Masonic orders were the largest and wealthiest. The Blue Lodges, the Rites and the Shrine—sometimes individually and sometimes collectively—had entered into stupendous building programs for temples, cathedrals and mosques. After all, in the lush days of the twenties, they could foresee sufficient income to pay off bonds and mortgages. They did not foresee the huge loss of membership incident to the depression. No organization was more affected by this loss than the Shrine; for in addition to the mosques that had been erected, the Shrine also was committed to the support of its hospitals and, with the loss in membership, the income for the operation of the hospitals was curtailed by just about one-third. Yet the hospitals had to be kept in operation at all costs. It is even possible that the existence of these hospitals is what held the Shrine together at all during part of the time of the depression.

And yet, despite the losses, the extravaganzas of the Imperial Sessions continued. They may not have been as large as some before and some that were to follow, but they took place just the same. The 1931 session was held in Cleveland and the escort parade lasted more than four hours. The city was decorated in fantastic colors and lights, and the night parade brought a sense of awe to the more than many thousand persons who watched it. In 1932, the Shriners moved on to San Francisco, where Islam Temple had imported movie stars from Hollywood to add glamour to what might otherwise have been a dull affair. President Herbert Hoover sent a message to the Shriners in 1932 that he expected them to help get the nation back on its feet. The Californians proclaimed there was no depression and that the 1932 session would be the means of starting the nation back toward recovery. But it was not to be. Things were getting worse.

Time after time during the depression years efforts were made to change the Shrine law on jurisdictional lines, and each of them failed. The matter of state lines was particularly annoying. Every temple was fighting for every member it could possibly obtain. To do otherwise, they argued, might lead to temple bankruptcy. Syrian Temple in Cincinnati pleaded for the right to create Nobles in the Kentucky towns across the Ohio River. Wheeling wanted some jurisdiction in Ohio. Davenport, Iowa, wanted to create Nobles residing in Illinois. And so it went. But the Imperial Council turned a deaf ear to all such proposals that did not bring with them agreements between temples in adjoining states.

The Jurisdictional Lines Committee, however, was kept busy enough rearranging territory within the respective states. It was argued that, where jurisdictional lines were held absolute, it frequently developed that a prospective member of the fraternity would not join because he would be required to travel too far to reach his temple when actually there was one closer at hand, but forbidden to him because of the exclusive jurisdiction maintained. It appeared that the officials of some temples would rather lose the prospect entirely than to sacrifice him to a sister temple.

During all of this time, one temple after another lost its holdings. Several mosques in cities all across the nation were sacrificed to the bond or mortgage holders, and occasionally they were taken over for unpaid taxes. One temple became so involved with mosque and country club property that it surrendered its charter and immediately was granted a new one under a different name. No one suffered and the Shrine was never criticized. It was an action that had to be taken.

Debates continued year after year over whether to reduce the minimum dues required by the Imperial Council, but no action ever was taken.

If the temples were having their difficulties, so was the Imperial Council, which was supported by membership contributions collected by the local temples. Every year during the depression the reserves of the Imperial Council treasury were being depleted. The law provided that each temple must contribute fifty cents a year from each member for the support of the national organization, particularly the Imperial Sessions. And each year, as the membership decreased, there was a further reduction in the income of the Imperial Council. But the Imperial Council did not change its ways.

It was argued—and correctly so—that the plan of representation for the various temples was set up for times of plenty. That is, each temple had representatives according to its membership, most of them with four or more. Each representative received fifteen cents a mile, one way, to pay his railroad and Pullman fare to the session, plus an additional fifteen dollars a day for three or more days at the session. Whenever the sessions were held in the Middle West or the East, it was comparatively inexpensive, for most of the temples were in that part of the country; but when the Imperial Session was held on the West Coast, the cost doubled, because of the additional travel expense. For example, the Imperial Session in San Francisco in 1932 cost more than double the expense incurred in the 1930 session in Toronto and the 1931 session in Cleveland. Despite statements to this effect in debate on the issue, the Imperial Council held three sessions on the West Coast during the decade of the depression—1932 in San Francisco, 1936 in Seattle, and 1938 in Los Angeles. But the only concession the Imperial Representatives ever made was to reduce the mileage pay from fifteen cents to ten cents a mile.

In 1936, the Imperial Council treasury was further depleted when Freeland Kendrick, who had succeeded Sam P. Cochran as chairman of the hospital board of trustees, declared that the hospitals needed financial help. The contributions had been so reduced by the reduction in temple membership that they simply could not continue to operate unless something was done. Many suggestions were made. One was to increase the hospital contribution of the remaining membership, but to this the temples cried out in horror. They would lose even more members, they said, and instead of providing more money for the hospitals, it would provide less. Another suggestion was that the representatives contribute half of their per diem pay for the Imperial Sessions. That also was turned down. In the end, the Imperial Council simply appropriated $100,000 to the hospital board from the Imperial treasury and provided no method to replenish the coffers.

Still, somehow, the Shrine managed to struggle through. Imperial headquarters cut its expenses. The Imperial Potentates didn't travel as much as some of their predecessors. When mosques, temples or cathedrals were lost, the Shriners held up their heads, stuck out their chins and fought ahead in smaller quarters. Those who maintained their membership seemed to have about as much fun as ever. Of course, the ceremonials were smaller. There were fewer candidates. The audiences were smaller because of the costs of travel. Some temples reduced their ceremonial sessions to two and even one a year—a few had none at all.

Prohibition was ended and Hitler had moved into power in Germany and was creating something of a disturbance. Another man by the name of Stalin had been making his influence felt from the Kremlin in Moscow and another Shriner had become President of the United States, the first since Harding who had even been a Mason. Franklin D. Roosevelt had been made a Shriner in Cyprus Temple in Albany while he was Governor of New York, and though he did not work at the business of fraternity as Harding had done, he nevertheless was a Shriner and he let it be known. He sent Attorney General Homer S. Cummings to deliver his personal welcome to the Nobles at the Imperial Session in Washington in 1935. The President's letter said:

Fellow Nobles of the Imperial Council of the Mystic Shrine:

I take the very greatest of pleasure in extending to you a most hearty welcome on the occasion of this decennial pilgrimage to the capital of your country—the Mecca, not only of the more than one hundred temples of your organization, but of the more than one hundred millions of our citizens, whose interest, cooperation and loyalty are vital to the successful functioning of our American Democracy.

Every genuine organization has its own merits—its own distinct contribution to make. You Nobles of the Mystic Shrine, in your devotion to the maintenance of hospitals

for crippled children and to other enterprises of philanthropic endeavor are daily attaining to the lofty standards
implied in the titular designation of your members. But
you do not thus carry, as mere duty, your share of the
social load: you appreciate that the problems of life are
too serious always to be taken seriously; and you practice
the belief that gaiety of spirit is a healthful reinforcement
of the things that make life sane and sound.

In this spirit Washington receives you; the preparations
made throughout the length and breadth of the city are
the visible evidences of the warmth of its feeling for you.
The capital of your country invites you to relax in the cor-
diality of its welcome: that you may be fortified to renew
that journey, which, as we all know, will lie through both
oasis and desert, but which can never be entirely the one
or the other.

Fellow Nobles, I bid you welcome to Washington.
Franklin D. Roosevelt.

There was no doubt that Washington had gone "all-
out" to entertain the Nobles. The Washington *Herald*
reported that "all the colorful Oriental pageantry,
thundering drums and music and intricate marching
and counter-marching have come to town to make
Washington forget the New Deal, at least until Friday."
There were boat races, prize fights, golf tournaments,
pageants and the Navy brought its ships up the Potomac for the nobility to see. The city was brilliantly
lighted as it had been in 1923. Robert Smith, who later
was to become general counsel of the Shrine, was the
Potentate of Almas Temple and the director general
of the convention, and Leonard P. Steuart, a former
Potentate of Almas, was to be installed as Imperial Potentate. To protect the nobility, detectives were imported from cities all along the Eastern seaboard,
including two hundred that Mayor La Guardia (himself
a Shriner) brought from New York.

Just as the Shriners began to arrive in Washington,
the city's taxi drivers went on strike, and although the
strike was settled some thirteen hours later, it did cause

considerable jamming for a time. Altogether, thousands of Shriners invaded the city, determined to have a good time. And they did. One be-fezzed Noble, carrying a large Shriner doll, stopped traffic as he gathered a bunch of pretty girls around him and offered to sell a Shriner for a dime. After collecting a handful of dimes, he would grab another Noble from the crowd and shout, "Here he is, girls. Have a good time." Eventually all the dimes he collected were turned over to the hospitals.

When the escort parade began to move on Tuesday morning, the crowd was somewhat smaller than had been expected, for government offices had refused to permit employees to drop their work for the event. Charles Fullaway, administrative assistant in the Bureau of the Budget, said: "President Roosevelt has not issued an order for departments to close and in the absence of such order, the offices should not close." And they didn't. The President, himself, did not see that parade, which was one of the largest in Washington history at that time, but he did review, with Mrs. Roosevelt, the night parade on Wednesday. Unfortunately, it poured rain, but President and Mrs. Roosevelt were protected by a canvas canopy, and they and others on the reviewing stand were about the only ones to see the parade, which was abbreviated by the storm. There was so much scheduled for the three days of the Imperial Session that it could not be postponed, and since this was the only event in which the President could participate, the director general could not call it off. Only nineteen temples sent their bands and patrols into the rain. Fifty-four others failed to show up. By the time the marchers reached the reviewing stand, their brilliant uniforms were soaked, many of them ruined.

The weather turned bright and brilliant on Thursday and a third parade was held that night to escort Imperial Potentate Steuart to the pageant, but the President had left earlier in the day to attend graduation exercises for the cadets at West Point and only Mrs. Roosevelt was in the reviewing stand to represent the White House.

Despite the rain, it was a successful convention, and the Washington *Post* was inspired to say editorially:

> Pageants, parades and purple pants. That is an alliterative phrase that goes a long ways in describing Washington in this week of grace. Staid Washington, scarcely out of mourning for the death of the blue eagle, is throwing back its dull and heavy veil of legislative cares and learning to laugh and play, for about 60,000 men are here with an equal number of smiles on their faces, and there is nothing more infectious than a grin of good fellowship. . . . The colorful fanfare incumbent on bringing the mysterious East to the heart of a planned economy seems somehow to emphasize the essential Americanism of our vivacious visitors. The backbone of America is nonetheless apparent because of the rakish trappings with which it is concealed, and though carefree jollity is the password of the Shriner during this one week, constructive charity is the watchword that binds him to his brother throughout the year when they are scattered from the Atlantic to the Pacific.

Two months after the meeting of the Imperial Council, Congress passed and the President signed new legislation creating the social security program, which was to have a profound effect on the management of the Shrine and its hospitals. When the income tax laws had been formulated, fraternal organizations (after a considerable battle) had been exempted from paying the levies; but when Congress passed the social security law, only charitable organizations were exempted. When the Imperial Council met in Seattle in 1936, Noble Thad Landon of Ararat Temple (Kansas City), the general counsel of the Shrine, placed before the representatives a proposition that the Colorado Corporation be made into a purely charitable organization for the operation of the hospitals and that a new corporation be formed in the state of Iowa that would be purely fraternal. This was approved by the representatives and the two-corporation system was set up in December of that year.

The dual-corporation plan also served another useful purpose. As the work of the hospitals became better known to the people of the United States and Canada, hundreds of men and women (many of them neither Shriners nor Masons) began to remember the Shriners' Hospitals for Crippled Children with outright gifts and bequests in their wills. Since these funds were to be used exclusively for the hospitals and not for the Shrine itself, the dual corporation was a much more satisfactory operation. By 1955 the gifts, bequests, contributions from special fund-raising programs such as the football games and the annual assessment to all Shriners had built up the endowment of the hospitals to the point where their operation would be assured, even if another major depression reduced the membership of the Shrine as it had in the thirties.

The establishment of the Colorado and Iowa Corporations was accepted and approved by the Imperial Council at its session in Detroit in 1937, when the Shriners staged their usual glittering parades despite the depression. The low point in Shrine membership because of the depression was still to be reached, but the bands and patrols turned out in full force, many of them in new uniforms, which prompted Imperial Potentate Clyde Webster to remark that this was a good sign.

Instead of presiding over the Imperial Session in Detroit, Imperial Potentate Webster had looked forward to being elected there. But it was not to be. In 1936 in Seattle, the Imperial Council had elected Hugh M. Caldwell of Nile Temple (Seattle) as the Imperial Potentate, but after having served through the Imperial "line" Caldwell had declined the office because of business and health. His action moved Webster into the office of Imperial Potentate a year ahead of his scheduled election to that office. Caldwell, incidentally, never was permitted to call himself a Past Imperial Potentate. Instead he was elected a member of the Imperial Council for life, even though he had not earned that right by virtue of having served as Imperial Potentate.

As Webster presided, Detroit was in a turmoil. The sit-down strikes were at their height, and there was some dissension among the visitors and the homefolks. One newspaper commented, "The police who are ordinarily so active in suppressing any unusual merriment, and are always greatly disturbed when the townspeople are seen going home late and happy, seem to have been paralyzed by some sudden and mysterious power. They simply looked on and smiled, like the bartender in the play, who remarked reflectively when he sized up an awful jag, 'How I wish I could afford to enjoy myself like that.'"

In 1938, the Shrine was back in Los Angeles; and as much as anything else, the convention was a prelude to the determination of Al Malaikah Temple to present her most illustrious son as a candidate for Imperial Outer Guard. Harold Lloyd, the great comedian of the silent-screen era, had worked long and diligently as a Mason and as a Shriner to dispense cheer in a cheerless world, particularly among children. He had laid the groundwork for cooperation between Al Malaikah Temple and the moving-picture industry for the use of props and equipment in ceremonials at unusual places, including the desert itself, Boulder Dam and the Carlsbad Caverns. He had participated in the Shrine conventions of 1925 and 1929, and now in 1938 as Chief Rabban of his temple, he was made Grand Marshal of the affair. Here was a celebrity of the first rank, the first showman ever to participate actively in Shrine affairs since Billy Florence was a member of the original thirteen. And Lloyd believed devoutly in the brotherhood of Masonry and the Shrine.

The Shrine was there with all the panoply for which it had become famous, but in addition there was the pageantry that only Hollywood could provide. Mary Pickford was named the grand marshal of the parade of floats, and her assistants, who rode in the parade, were the stars of the day—Sonja Henie, Jane Withers, Alice Faye, Michael Whalen, Warner Baxter, the Ritz brothers, Tyrone Power, Tony Martin, Don Ameche, Irene Hervey, Myrna Loy, Eleanor Powell, May Robson, Allan Jones, George O'Brien, Martha Raye, Dorothy Lamour, George Raft, John Barrymore, Anita Louise and many others. In floats as spectacular as any that ever appeared in the Rose Parade, Hollywood and Los Angeles put on a parade and a pageant that would last in memory until 1950, when the most spectacular of all of them was held. The pageant in the giant Coliseum had as its master of ceremonies the ebullient and popular Jack Benny.

In 1939, at the convention in Baltimore, Lloyd's name was presented as a candidate for Outer Guard. He didn't win. He had not expected to win, but in 1940 in Memphis, Tennessee, the actor was elected to the lowest rung of the Imperial Line without a vote being taken. The other two candidates, who were to be elected in later years, withdrew when they felt that Lloyd was the overwhelming choice of the convention. Here, with the membership of the Shrine still dropping, was just the man who would add another touch of glamour so vitally needed at that particular time. He seemed to have that indefinable something that would help to return to the Shrine the attractiveness that had built it to such stupendous proportions in the twenties. In Baltimore and in Memphis, Lloyd clowned in an old Model-T Ford that had been rebuilt to do tricks, and the crowds loved it. In both Baltimore and Memphis, rain dampened the enthusiasm of some of the visitors and townspeople alike, but the parades and pageants went on just the same.

Harold Lloyd

Elected as Imperial Potentate at the Los Angeles session in 1938 was A. A. D. Rahn of Zuhrah Temple (Minneapolis), a swashbuckling, self-made lumberman from the north country, and perhaps he was exactly the man the Shrine needed in the hectic days that marked the end of the depression and the crisis in world affairs. As he took over the administration of the Shrine, he could recall that only a few months before the Japanese had bombed the American gunboat *Panay*, that the Japanese were keeping up a relentless attack on the Chinese, that the Spanish Civil War was at its height and that many Americans had gone over to fight for the Loyalists, who were being supported by Moscow. Only two months before the Los Angeles meeting, Hitler had taken over Austria as a prelude to the Second World War, and in the United States, German-American Bunds were being created. Spies were everywhere and almost everyone felt that war was just around the corner. The only question was whether or not the United States would get into the conflict. It seemed almost certain that Canada would be embroiled, which had nine Shrine temples.

On August 25, 1938, after his election as Imperial Potentate in June, Rahn issued his third general order to the nobility. It was strictly patriotic in character. "The Imperial Council of the Ancient Arabic Order Nobles of the Mystic Shrine," he wrote, "in reality lives under three flags, and the membership in consequence is divided in its allegiance. It happens that 149 of our temples owe allegiance to the Constitution and the flag of the United States. The membership of one temple owes allegiance to the Mexican Republic, and the membership of nine other temples are citizens of the great British Empire. The Imperial Potentate feels some concern, particularly about certain agencies in the United States which apparently are active in destroying respect for constitutional government, and are planning in its stead foreign conceptions of government which are diametrically opposed to the guarantees of freedom of thought and action which are the very foundation on which the government of this country rests. He is, therefore, suggesting the following resolution which he feels the temples of this country might be interested in adopting in full or in part and passing on to the nobility through their magazines and other channels of information."

In effect, the resolution pledged every Shriner to reaffirm his loyalty to his flag and to be "alert in preventing the growth of any influence on the jurisdiction which will be derogatory to constitutional government, and report any information obtained of activities of adverse persons or organizations to the Imperial Potentate, who, acting alone or in conjunction with other organizations of patriotic citizens, will, to the extent of his authority, use every means in his power, and take such action as he may deem necessary, to contribute to the defense of the liberties guaranteed to our people under the Constitution and to counteract the efforts of those who would work to destroy our present form of government."

To make the Americanism program of the Shrine official, Islam Temple presented a resolution which would memorialize Congress and the President to establish a "citizens" day in the United States, when certificates would be presented to all young people as they reached their twenty-first birthday in order to impress upon them the privileges and prerogatives of citizenship. The resolution was passed, of course. And throughout Shrinedom, patriotic affairs were being staged. The largest was that of Moslah Temple of Fort Worth, Texas, which held a giant Americanism pageant in the Texas Christian University stadium as part of the Texas State Shrine Association meeting.

This was the beginning then of the part the Shrine was to play during the following decade, a decade to be climaxed by the Shrine's Diamond Jubilee celebration in Chicago at which President Harry Truman, a Shriner, would make the principal speech, a speech in which he would condemn the ideological forces of the world that would beat a path to still another war, with a Plethora of distinguished Shriner participants.

24

Second World War Activities

By the time Walter D. Cline (Maskat) became the Imperial Potentate of the Shrine on June 29, 1939, it was apparent that the depression was almost over. It was just as apparent that the United States was moving inexorably into a wartime economy as it began production of matériel for Britain, France and the other allied nations. Prime Minister Chamberlain and his umbrella had been to Munich and Czecho-Slovakia had been dissolved. Farther south, Mussolini had invaded the Moslem country of Albania and King Zog had been forced to flee. Britain and France went on a war footing and began conscription. Every thinking American knew or at least felt that war was inevitable and the only question was "when?"

These problems made Cline's year as Imperial Potentate difficult, indeed. The list of new members was increasing, but they did not overcome the higher rate of demits and suspensions, and thus the overall membership continued to decline. There were several reasons why. One of them was the fact that most of the some 200,000 men who had left the Shrine by one means or another during the depression years were young men. This meant that most of the men remaining on the membership rolls were middle-aged or older, men at least past their physical prime. And while many of these could and did participate actively with the marching organizations of their temples, and could and did make a creditable showing in the parades, they nevertheless displayed the fact that they were older. Brutal as it might sound, the fact was that young men simply did not want to join an organization of older men for fun. They thought there were other and better ways.

Still, some seven thousand new Nobles were created during the year Cline served; and when the convention met in Memphis in June of 1940, the Shriners appeared to be just as gay, just as fun-loving, just as noisy as ever. There were the same stunts with an occasional new one; and if the parade was not quite as large as had been held in other years, it was just as brilliant and glittering. But it cannot be denied that there was something in the air, a tension that was felt by almost everyone. Cline chose deliberately to ignore the growing war fever. In his annual address, he said:

"I think as your Imperial Potentate, some word should be said about the attitude of our organization with reference to 'isms,' 'ists,' 'shirts,' and 'fifth columns.' I shall only say what I have said to some of you in numerous places. I have not appointed a committee on Americanism because I felt, have felt all year, and feel today that if the time has come when your leader, your Imperial Potentate, conscientiously feels that it is necessary or important that he select a committee to tell you to be loyal to your government, then Masonry has failed, and I am not ready to admit that all the teachings and philosophies and obligations that you men must have assumed from the time you took your Entered Apprentice degree until you passed through the Masonic Rites, either York or Scottish, in order to entitle you to wear a fez and sit in this convention, have failed to accomplish their mission."

Cline was a storyteller of some note. An oil prospector, he had made a fortune, lost it and made another. He had served during the depression years on various government boards, particularly the housing administration. He was "earthy" in his manner and in his speech. He liked in later years to tell how he was received in Memphis with all the pomp and ceremony to which an Imperial Potentate was entitled, but that as a Past Imperial Potentate, he carried his own bags to the train. Perhaps that is the reason he concluded his annual address by telling the representatives, "I would not sell the experience of being your Imperial Potentate for nine million dollars, and I would not give you a plugged nickel for the job again." He attended but one more Imperial Session. That was to cast a ballot for Hubert M. Poteat for the post of Imperial Outer Guard.

Even though Cline wanted to steer a course for the Shrine that would not involve it in the "isms" of the day, it nevertheless was clear to most of the Shriners that a patriotic fervor was spreading across the entire jurisdiction. The Shrine bands on frequent occasions were called into parades that were purely patriotic in character. In his annual report to the Imperial Council in Indianapolis in 1941, Imperial Potentate George F. Olendorf (Abou Ben Adhem) remarked that during his year he had urged the nobility to rededicate itself, individually and collectively, to the highest ideals of Americanism. "I am proud," he said, "of the patriotic position the Shrine has taken throughout its long and eventful history. Whatever the future may hold for us, I have every assurance that the Order of the Mystic Shrine will be uncompromising in its support of the democratic ideal and in those worthwhile things which brighten, sweeten and enrich the way of life."

Actually Olendorf never appeared at the 1941 convention in Indianapolis. He was taken ill just before his arrival and was sent immediately to a hospital. Deputy Imperial Potentate Thomas C. Law (Yaarab) took over. Olendorf eventually recovered sufficiently to be removed to his home in Missouri, but he died shortly thereafter.

The Indianapolis convention was a bright and splendid affair. Money once more was becoming available after the long depression and the Shriners made the most of their opportunities for fun and parading, and it was well they did. It was the last of the wondrous affairs of the Imperial Council session until after the Great War ended. Somehow, the Time and Place Committee seemed to feel that this would be true. Invitations for the 1942 session had been received from Portland, Oregon, and Atlantic City, New Jersey, and another was expected from Boston, but the committee, "giving due consideration to the uncertainties facing the country," recommended that the decision for the next session be left to the Imperial Divan.

Thomas C. Law of Yaarab Temple (Atlanta) was elected Imperial Potentate in Indianapolis, and he let it be known from the very start that the theme of his year of administration was to be Masonic Unity. Throughout his term of office, he attended every Masonic meeting for which he had credentials in his own right and others where the privilege was extended because of his official position in the Shrine. Everywhere he went, Noble Law felt that his theme was welcomed with open arms. In his annual address at the Imperial Council session (strictly business—no parades) in Chicago on June 29, 1942, Law declared that as a result of his efforts "it can be said without hesitation or apology that the spirit of the Shrine has assumed a trend which leads to a happy middle ground of mutual understanding (with other Masonic bodies) on which the seriousness of the craft and the relaxation of our Order can meet in a true brotherhood. Both are reaching the proper conclusion that the contentment which the principles and precepts of Masonry bring, added to the pursuit of happiness which the Shrine seeks, is true American democracy."

Imperial Potentate Law never abandoned this theme even after the day of infamy that came on Sunday,

The nation's only living five star general, Omar Bradley, is a Noble of El Maida Temple, El Paso, Texas.

December 7, 1941. All America, including the Shrine and its leadership, realized what the Japanese attack on Pearl Harbor would mean to the nation and its people. Law and other members of the Imperial Divan were well aware that America was unprepared, either physically or mentally, for the road ahead. When the attack came, Law was halfway through his term in office as Imperial Potentate and the nation had hardly begun to recover from the blow before it was time for the annual session. Obviously, it would be unwise, improper and almost impossible to hold a full-blown Imperial Session with all of its pomp, ceremony, parades and pageantry. In his annual call for the Imperial Session, Law said, "Due to the fact that our country is at war and due to the cost and difficulty in obtaining transportation for uniformed units, a business session only will be held." And that was confined to two days, rather than three, because of the shortage of hotel space.

Acting in the spirit of the times, the Imperial Council took steps to turn over the management of its affairs to the Imperial Divan if it should develop that, at some time during the war, even the representatives proved unable to get together for their annual session. Actually, the Imperial Session was abandoned only in 1945, but the Shriners felt they must be prepared. The only power not passed on to the Imperial Divan was the authority to elect new officers at the bottom of the Imperial line. All others were to be advanced in regular rotation with the Outer Guard and any other offices to be left vacant until a meeting of the full Imperial Council could be held.

The Shrine also put itself on a war footing. George H. Rowe of Ismailia Temple (Buffalo) presented a resolution from the New York Shrine Council which would create a War Activities Committee, designed to assist the government and the membership in every possible way during the war emergency. Rowe was serving at the time as the Imperial Oriental Guide, and he promptly was named chairman of that committee. More than anything else, Rowe and his committee over the next four years coordinated activities in the temples and promoted new ideas which in any way might help the war effort.

Elected as Imperial Potentate was a distinguished Cleveland attorney, Albert H. Fiebach, who for many years had served on the Jurisprudence and Laws Committee of the Shrine. At the very start he let it be known that the Shrine must do everything in its power to help win the war. How much the Shrine did is revealed in the reports of the Imperial Potentates and the War Activities Committee over the next three years.

Again meeting in Chicago in 1943 with only the representatives to the Imperial Council present, Fiebach reported: "With civilization standing at the very cross-roads of destiny, at a time of national crisis and peril, men are impelled to turn to the serious philosophy of life. Moved by these impulses, they naturally seek light and refuge in Masonry and the Shrine. Here they find the most congenial forum for the profession of their belief in God and of their devotion to country and flag. Symbolic Masonry has prospered as has the York Rite, the Scottish Rite and the Shrine. Last year for the first time since 1926, our Order showed a gain."

Indeed it was true. The tide had turned from the depression years. The spiritual feeling of men, particularly in scores of training camps all over the United States, had increased and with that increase had developed an apparent need for fraternalism. It was also a fact that the nation had entered into a war economy. More money was available and with more money in millions of pockets, there was a better atmosphere for the development of the Shrine and its prerequisite bodies of Masonry. Furthermore, individual temples, spared the expense of sending their marching units long distances to participate in parades, found greater activity at home. The War Activities Committee urged the local temples to participate in every patriotic parade, and they did, adding their colorful uniforms, precision marching and military music to rallies for the Red Cross, the sale of war bonds, the return of wounded troops and every other event that seemed appropriate.

In some cities, the local temple took over the management of the sale of war bonds, and in the course of four years of war, more than a billion dollars was invested by and through the Shrine in government bonds for the conduct of the war. The Colorado Corporation (the hospitals) also invested all of their available funds in government securities as a means of furthering the war effort.

In some cities, the Shrine mosques became the center of wartime activities, both as a place for work for Red

Buckingham Studio

George Washington National Masonic Memorial, Alexandria Va.

George J. Kossuth

Mechanical Parade in the Shrine Rooms of the Memorial

Cross volunteers and as a center for entertainment of all troops, but particularly Shriners and Masons. In those areas where training camps were near at hand, the mosques were the scenes of dances and other entertainments. Special committees were formed to make certain that every Mason was personally invited to these affairs. Contacts were maintained with other temples. Frequently a temple in one section of the nation would write to a temple far distant, advising them that a Shriner or a Mason had been assigned to a nearby camp. Wherever possible the visiting Shriner or Mason was made to feel at home among his brethren.

It was perhaps singularly important that the Imperial Potentate elected in 1943 was Morley MacKenzie, a Canadian and a member of Rameses Temple in Toronto. Canada had been at war two years longer than the United States and had felt more of the heartaches that go with it. But it was during his year as Imperial Potentate that the tide of battle began to turn. Mussolini had been forced to resign as premier of Italy and that nation had surrendered. George Patton and his Seventh Army had invaded Europe from the south and just one month before the Imperial Council session on July 5, 6, and 7, 1944, General Dwight Eisenhower had directed the invasion of France. Already Patton was on the march. Just as the Imperial Session was about to get under way, MacKenzie wrote to all of the Potentates of all of the temples that "these are hours of dedication. The crusading armies of free peoples have begun the greatest mission of rescue in world history . . . the encirclement of Germany—the noose that must hang their tyrannical military despots and hasten Hitler's final day of reckoning—is being drawn about the Nazis. . . . Within us all a spirit of solemn dedication, of earnest devotion, prays for Divine blessing, for protection, for courage, for fortitude."

But the war was not over, even though the end was in sight. There were still sick and wounded troops to visit. There were still entertainments to give. Almost every day, at some hospital or in some training camp, the Shriners gave band concerts. They equipped recreation halls with radios and jukeboxes. They conducted blood banks. And they bought bonds. In some temples, there was a sort of secret committee which helped the FBI and other government intelligence units as a clearing house for cloak-and-dagger activities.

Alfred G. Arvold of El Zagal Temple (Fargo) was elected Imperial Potentate in 1944, and it fell to his lot to be the only head of the Shrine in history not to have a meeting of the Imperial Council to preside over. The session of 1945 was abandoned at the behest of the government, faced with the almost impossible task of keeping the nation's transportation system moving. Even the six hundred representatives could not be accommodated, and the 1945 session was composed of the Imperial Divan and the necessary members of the various committees of both the Iowa and Colorado Corporations.

By the time the 1945 session got under way in Chicago, the war in Europe was over. The Germans had surrendered. Hilter and Mussolini were dead. In the Pacific, Iwo Jima and Okinawa had been captured. The fleets were bombarding the Japanese coastline, and the first atomic bomb was only a month away. And thus it was that the big debate among the members of the Divan concerned the amount of money that was to be expended by the Shrine in the development of special display rooms in the George Washington National Masonic Memorial in Alexandria, Virginia.

These rooms were the dearest wish of Arvold, who had spent his life in show business of one kind and another. He fought for the rooms. He organized them. Mecca Temple gave her Shrine treasures for display. But some of the members of the Divan were hesitant. They wanted to know how much money the Shrine was going to spend, and for what. Arvold knew only part of the answer, but he had faith in the future, and as a result the motion to spend $25,000 went through. Since the original investment, thousands more have been spent, largely under the guiding hand of a committee from Almas Temple and in later years from Kena Temple in Alexandria as well. The original committee obtained a mechanical parade (designed by Arvold), and when it had been decorated, the tiny marching figures appeared in Arabic garb; prancing horses and plodding camels looked exactly like the fine parades for which the Shrine had become famous. The parade was hooked up to a loud-speaker system that blared forth band music, and at a propitious moment, a crowd of visitors watching the parade in its setting before a replica of the Taj Mahal, hears a narration explaining what the fun-loving Shriners have done about helping scores of thousands of crippled children, and how others will be helped with the creation of the Shrine Burn Institutes.

From time to time, additions were made to the Shrine rooms in the memorial wing devoted to the hospitals, including a "Book of Gold," the only public recognition of givers to the hospital program; the Imperial Potentate's Room, wherein are displayed the museum pieces of Shrine history. In this room, before a huge mural depicting a caravan of Shriners before the Kaaba after their long trip across the hot sands to Mecca, are the color photographs of all past Imperial Potentates, and the current Divan.

In the parade room, hang the portraits of those world leaders who were members of the Shrine. Aladdin Temple in Columbus, Ohio, gave the first portrait of President Warren G. Harding, the first Shriner to become President of the United States. (But not the first Mason, of course.) Cyprus Temple in Albany, N.Y., contributed the portrait of Franklin D. Roosevelt, and Ararat Temple in Kansas City gave the portrait of Harry S. Truman. The Canadian Temples joined to present the portrait of former Canadian Prime Minister John W. Dieffenbaker; and in 1963, under the Shrine Room Chairmanship of Imperial Sir Orville F. Rush, four portraits of the four Presidents of Mexico who were Shriners—Diaz, Rubio, Rodriguez and Aleman—were hung.

By 1963, the tramp of more than two million visitors to the Memorial Shrine Rooms had left their imprint, and the Imperial Council authorized refurbishing under the leadership of Imperial Sir Orville F. Rush. The parade was rewired for a better electronic system, the mural repainted, better displays for the museum pieces created, a new floor installed, and the portraits of the five men who had served as Chairmen of the Board of Trustees of Shriners Hospitals for Crippled Children were hung in the hospital room.

During the refurbishing operations, the Shrine rooms committee also created a huge lighted map, delineating the location of all Shrine temples, the hospitals, and of course the new burn centers, that were created in 1962.

In the twenty years that followed the establishment of the Memorial Shrine Rooms at the curtailed meeting of Shrine leaders in Chicago in 1945, Shriners generally and the leaders in particular, realized that the end of that session was the end of another era. They had come through the war years in which the Shrine once more had distinguished itself by its service to the country as a whole and to Shriners and Masons in the camps and in faraway places. And the membership was growing once again. From the low point of 306,000 in 1942, it had grown by the end of the war to 400,000. And in the next decade alone, it would double in size, and is now nearing the million mark.

25

Shrine Law and Membership

Someone with great sagacity once said that the Second
World War was fought for the right to go to Lodge
on Tuesday night; and when the Shriners were freed,
along with the rest of the world, of their war fears
and their hopes and dreams of a better world once
more gripped their hearts, there was nothing they
wanted so much as to bust loose in a festival of fun
in the true spirit of their fraternity.

William H. Woodfield of Islam Temple in San Francisco had succeeded Arvold as Imperial Potentate at
the abbreviated Chicago session in 1945, and on July
23, 1946, the exotic city of San Francisco opened wide
its portals for the after war fun festival.

The San Francisco *Examiner* could think of no better
way to report the opening parade than to repeat the
story written in 1932, when the Shriners were last in
town:

> By Allah, 'tis a noble sight. Behold, ye unbelievers, an
> enchanted city. Sheiks of the desert smoking two-bit cigars.
> Minarets and temples alight with magic fire. Baghdad and
> Cairo. What were they compared to San Francisco in the
> grip of the Shriners. Revelry, pomp, music and marching
> patrols. It is all here again. Brighter, louder, filled with
> more excitement than in those pre-war years.

San Franciscans were more excited by the hi-jinks,
the clowning and parading of the befezzed Nobles than
they had been a year before when most of the great
diplomats of the world had congregated in the same

city to create the charter of the United Nations. It was indeed a gay and festive occasion that not only celebrated the victorious end of the war on two sides of the world, but reopened exciting vistas for the caravan of The Shrine toward some rendezvous with some destinies as yet untold.

It was even possible that Aahmes Past Potentate Governor Earl Warren (later to become Chief Justice of the United States) served as prophet when he welcomed the Imperial Council representatives to California, by declaring that America is a fraternal nation. "It is," he said, "a land of fraternities, and one of the greatest is the Shrine of North America. Nations across the waters do not understand this phase of our national life. . . . I wish all the world could absorb this fraternal spirit and put it to work. It is all that is necessary to solve the most troublesome problems of our turbulent times. . . . If the world would adopt the same attitude toward the poor, the weak and the underprivileged that the Shrine has maintained toward the crippled children of North America, without regard to race, creed or color, it would dispel most of the darkness around us. There is no gloom that cannot be driven out by the sunshine of the Shrine."

It was all so very true, but neither Governor Warren nor anyone else at the star spangled San Francisco convention could either foresee or imagine what the future held for the fraternity, including its astounding growth and the developments that went with that growth.

Because of the depression years, the Shrine along with other fraternities had seen its membership rolls dwindle to a low point in 1942; but as in all wars, the spirit of fraternalism grew with the advent of hostilities. Masons were Masons and Shriners were Shriners, no matter where you met them and no matter what their lodge or temple. When they met at a training camp, aboard ship or on the battlefield, it was almost like a message from home. By the time of the San Francisco convention in 1946, the membership was up 150,000 from the depths of the depression, all of which pleased the leadership, but which nevertheless produced problems for Everett W. Jacocks, the Imperial Recorder who maintained his office in Richmond, Virginia, and operated it with a minimal of staff.

Actually, the Shriners themselves didn't care much about record keeping and finances so long as they received a dues card, had a temple to attend once in a while for ceremonial occasions, and a set-time to join with other Shriners for band, chanter or patrol rehearsals. And for those Shriners who did not participate with the marching units, there were increasing demands for more activities. They wanted some use out of the red fez, for which they had crossed the hot sands; and having once tasted with their brethren the sparkling waters from the wells of Zem Zem and having feasted at some oasis, they wanted more of the same.

The trouble was that few mosques could accommodate their membership at ceremonials. Most of the temples were growing by leaps and bounds. Syria Temple in Pittsburgh grew during the post war years to a membership of more than 26,000. Al Malaikah in Los Angeles shot up to 22,000 and would grow still larger to become No. 1 in membership. Medinah in Chicago reached 21,000.

The result of the growth and the advent of more youth into the temples was inevitable, and Woodfield and the Imperial Potentates who succeeded him urged the creation and development of more and more Shrine Clubs, which met oftener than the temples and thus offered more fraternity and frivolity. Some erected their own club houses and a few became well-to-do. Some created units of their own, participating in temple functions and parades, and as might have been expected, produced many if not most of the new candidates who wanted to wear the crescent and scimitar, and participate in all of the activities that made the Shrine glamorous. And once a wearer of the red fez, the nobility soon discovered that glory by which Shriners had attracted the attention of the world—the hospitals for crippled children.

During this period of phenomenal growth in membership, there were many important developments, each in its own way contributing to the future of the fraternity and which taken as a whole were to contribute to another of the Shrine's rendezvous with destiny.

It is important to recall that in 1894, Benjamin Rowell of Aleppo Temple in Boston had taken over from Frank Luce the job as Imperial Recorder, and held it until 1928. It is notable that during this period, the records were adequate, but rather loosely kept at best, for the Imperial Council was not so much a national organization as it was an association of individual temples. But the advent of the Hospitals for Crippled Children changed all that. It cost a lot of money to build and operate the "temples of mercy," and strict accounting had to be made. It was at this time that Rowell employed a young Bostonian named Everett W. Jacocks to help with the details of what was rapidly becoming big business. In 1928, with the hospital program well underway, Rowell was succeeded as Imperial Recorder by James W. Price, the governor of Virginia, who promptly moved the office, records and Jacocks to Richmond. Price held the office until his death in 1943 when the Imperial Council elected Jacocks to the post, and he continued to operate from the Richmond headquarters until his death in 1947. The office had grown, and now boasted of two men and two girls as employees, but it seemed fairly obvious that it was to grow still larger because of endowment funds accumulating in the treasury of the Colorado Corporation.

At the time of Jacocks' death, Karl Rex Hammers of Syria Temple in Pittsburgh was the Imperial Potentate, and he had ambitions to be elected Imperial Recorder at the Imperial Council session in Atlantic City in June, 1948 over which he would preside; and with that in mind, he appointed Frederick Wilken, the Recorder of Almas Temple in Washington, as the interim Imperial Recorder. But Hammers never achieved his ambition.

With the growth of the fraternity, there were increasing pressures to locate Shrine headquarters in some city that would be more convenient for western, southern and Canadian as well as eastern temples. And with the coming of air transportation, members of the Imperial Divan and the hospital trustees sought a location that would be convenient for their more frequent meetings. At the same time, the burgeoning Recorders' Association had ambitions to put one of their own in the national office. To that end, the various temple recorders who also were Imperial Representatives promoted the candidacy of George M. Saunders, the Recorder of Ararat Temple in Kansas City, who had been closely associated with Thad Landon who had served with distinction as General Counsel; and with

Chicago, Ill., Offices of the International Shrine Headquarters

Frank M. Land, the founder of De Molay and already a rising member of the Imperial Divan.

In the election at Atlantic City, Saunders won over Hammers, and under instructions from the Imperial Council, moved the Imperial Headquarters to Chicago.

The Saunders election inaugurated a new era in Shrine operations. It came at a period when the fraternity was just beginning its astonishing growth that was to pass 800,000 members in the next ten years and that was to see endowment funds for the hospitals grow beyond $100,000,000 in the same period; and continue to climb in succeeding years to near $887 million.

By the decade of the sixties, the work of keeping records for the 800,000 Shriners as well as maintaining control of hundreds of estates that had been willed to the hospitals, had forced repeated expansions of the office staff and office space and it became apparent that the time was ripe for the Shriners to have an international home of their own. Past Imperial Potentate Thomas Law was appointed chairman of a committee to find such a home, which it did at 323 North Michigan Avenue, in Chicago, and it was purchased during the regime of Imperial Potentate George E. Stringfellow. Suitably remodelled, it housed staff and records, all of which, incidentally, have been micro-filmed.

A second important development that was to have far-reaching effects on the future of the Shrine came in 1942 with the retirement of Thad Landon as the Shrine's chief legal counsel. It was Landon, more than any other single individual, who had created the Shrine's corporate structure and was responsible in no small measure for Shrine law itself. Imperial Potentate Law of Yaarab Temple in Atlanta, gave long and serious thought to the appointment of his successor and finally settled on Robert P. Smith of Washington. Smith had been Potentate of Almas Temple and had served as director general of the eye-startling convention in Washington at which L. P. Steuart had been elected

Imperial Potentate. He had been elected a representative from Almas Temple to the Imperial Council and had served on the Jurisprudence and Laws Committee.

In the twenty succeeding years that Smith was to serve as General Counsel, he gave unstintingly of his time and talent, insisting that every Shrine Temple should be on firm legal ground. It was he who handled until his death in 1962 the mass of legal detail involved with the probate of estates willed by the hundreds of donors to the Shriners Hospitals for Crippled Children. And it was he who initiated in both the Iowa and Colorado Corporations the idea for the creation for institutes for treatment, research and education in the little known medical field of burns to the human body, of which more later.

But despite the manifest importance of these developments in the management of the Shrine, the fact still remained that the great mass of Shriners were primarily interested in fraternity, fun, frolic and the maintenance of their pride and joy—the hospitals.

At the same session of the Imperial Council in Atlantic City where Saunders had been elected, the Shriners promoted to Imperial Potentate a handsome, suave and dynamic lawyer from Tyler, Texas, who like Saunders and Smith was to have a profound effect on the future of the fraternity. Galloway Calhoun was a member of Karem Temple at Waco, had served as an assistant attorney general of his state, taught one of the biggest Sunday School classes in the world, was an accomplished orator and had served as Grand Master of Masons in Texas. Furthermore, it was his privilege to preside over the diamond jubilee convention of the Shriners. He chose Chicago for the setting and set about making preparations for the biggest affair the Shriners had ever seen.

Wherever he went that year from June 1948 to July 1949, he appeared before huge audiences that filled auditoriums and stadiums. Escorted by the units of the temples he visited, he literally preached before Shriners and non-Shriners alike against what he called the "cancerous sore of communism."

Sitting in the White House was another Shriner and, moreover, a past Grand Master of Masons in Missouri; and Calhoun determined, if possible, to have the president at the diamond jubilee convention. Harry S. Truman consented, and he did appear for a major foreign policy speech at an overflowing Soldier Field ceremony, but without his fez, for he was the President of all of the people of the United States.

Mr. Truman went almost sleepless during much of his stay in Chicago. He occupied, of course, the presidential suite at the Stevens Hotel, which also was Shrine headquarters, and became the victim of an old Shrine

President Harry S. Truman, a Past Grand Master of Masons in Missouri, was an enthusiastic Noble of Ararat Temple, Kansas City.

Diamond Jubilee Parade, Chicago, 1949

trick of calling "Chloe" with a loudspeaker throughout the night. Always an early riser, the President arose even earlier on the morning after his speech and banquet appearance, and departed for Washington.

The President of the United States was not the only celebrity to join with Calhoun and thousands of other Shriners for the Diamond Jubilee Shrine ceremonies. There were generals and admirals, and Ty Cobb led a contingent of prominent baseball stars. Edgar A. Guest was there with a new poem about the Shriners. Captain Eddie Rickenbacker was there with his fez. There were many actors, and Sigmund Romberg was there from the field of music.

Various Shrine bands played almost incessantly in the lobbies of all the hotels. There were impromptu dances, and all in all the pilgrims who had crossed the hot sands had a wonderful time at their Mecca in Chicago.

But it was not all hoopla and parading. There was also business for the Shriners and at this convention there were two important changes in Shrine management. To succeed Calhoun as Imperial Potentate, the Shriners elevated to that office the glamorous Hollywood comedian, Harold Lloyd. At the same time, Freeland Kendrick announced his retirement as chairman of the Board of Trustees, Shriners Hospitals for Crippled Children, and the representatives promptly chose for this most important post the retiring Imperial Potentate, Galloway Calhoun.

There was no doubt that the election of Harold Lloyd as Imperial Potentate attracted international attention to the fraternity, for he was one of the great comedians

Los Angeles Evening Herald-Express

Red Skelton, "Used Camel Dealer," at Los Angeles, 1950

of all time. In the days of the silent movies, he had made millions upon millions of people laugh. His black-rimmed spectacles had given him a trade-mark that was to last for the decades ahead, but even more important in the scheme of things, he was a devout Mason and Shriner. He had served as Illustrious Potentate of Al Malaikah Temple in Los Angeles. Always self-effacing, he lived a true family life, albeit in simple grandeur, in one of the Hollywood showplaces.

Lloyd devoted to his new job a seriousness of purpose as he visited scores of temples, but it was in Los Angeles in June of 1950 that he achieved a pinnacle not only for himself but for the Shrine. There had never been anything like it before at a Shrine convention, for not only were there the great morning and night parades by the Shriners themselves, and prime hi-jinx good enough to entertain the entertainment capital of the world, but the movie colony itself staged massive spectacles from its storehouse of talent and facilities as a

The late famed movie actor John Wayne was Ambassador at Large for Al Malaikah Temple and was a frequent participant in Shrine events.

tribute to one of their own, who had become the Imperial Potentate. They staged a float parade of their own and helped with the staging of a great pageant on the final night of the convention. Movie colony Shriners participated with their temples in the Shrine parades, among them "Red" Skelton who appeared as "Honest Red, the 'used camel' dealer."

Movie star Glenn Ford is Ambassador at Large for Al Malaikah Temple, Los Angeles.

In reporting on the great electrical pageant, the Los Angeles *Examiner* said:

Down through the years, there rarely comes to humanity a spectacle of more beauty and magnificence than the shimmering jewel with which the Shriners of North America crowned their Los Angeles convention last night—the million-dollar electrical pageant in Los Angeles Coliseum. Like a great glowing heart, the huge oval throbbed with light against the darkness of the skies above, as 100,000 spectators within the great bowl cheered and thrilled to the sight.

But it was not only the pomp and panoply of the occasion that merited headlines. Lloyd himself stood on the platform of the Biltmore Theatre at the public opening session of the Imperial Council and in simple words and sentences declared his belief:

"I am a Shriner," he said, "because I believe in the ideals on which the Shrine was founded. . . . We believe in the brotherhood of man, and in the dignity of the individual. We believe it is the function of government to preserve the rights and freedoms of the individual. We oppose an ideology that seeks to degrade human beings. We oppose any philosophy that declares the police state to be the highest human social achievement, and which would invade the sacred sanctuary of a man's conscience where only God may enter as judge.

Masonry and Shrinedom have flourished in this soil of freedom. Shrinedom has given me a greater appreciation of what it means to be an American. In the Shrine, I have found myself surrounded by men full of the joy of living, men of hope and optimism and understanding. They are loyal to the principles of Masonry and of the Shrine, for they are identical with the principles of brotherhood and liberty embodied in the ideals of Americanism. This, friends, is the Shrine, and these are a few of the reasons why I wear this fez.

In effect what Harold Lloyd had said was that, while so-called intellectuals might scoff at men who played Moslems and infidels, there was indeed fertility and stamina within its tents and mosques, erected on the sands of time, that would prompt Imperial Potentate O. Carlyle Brock to declare in 1964 that it was the "Fraternity of Destiny."

As much as anything else, Lloyd's year as Imperial Potentate, together with the fantastic convention in

Los Angeles, served as mediums to establish the Shrine in the eyes of the public as an institution of importance, recognized by all of the mediums of communication. In every location where Imperial Council sessions were held the newspapers, the radio and television devoted segments of their space and air-time to those gay be-fezzed men who wanted a good time and had it.

The trouble was that few cities could house all of the Shriners, for by 1958, there were 800,000 of them. Furthermore, the smaller temples and their individual members could not finance annual visits to the Imperial extravaganzas, and thus it was that during the decade of the fifties, regional associations of Shrine temples grew in popularity until their parades were as exciting, beautiful and glamorous in the smaller cities, as the Imperial parades in the larger ones. True, potentates and other members of the divans in the various temples, held short business sessions, but it was the fun and the parades that attracted the Shriners and the units to Norfolk, Virginia, Louisville, Kentucky, Peoria, Illinois, Jacksonville, Florida, Pueblo, Colorado, and Fresno, California, etc.

But the regional association parades did not curtail the big parades. Rather they seemed to enhance them, for each Imperial Council session became larger, the parades longer and the excitement greater.

Nevertheless, the Shrine had its problems. After the big surge of membership immediately after World War II, the rate of growth began to decline, until by the end of the "Fifty" decade it was causing serious concern to each succeeding Imperial Potentate, and it was not difficult to find the source of the problem—Masonic growth itself was declining.

As early as 1942, Imperial Potentate Thomas C. Law (Yaarab) had made Masonic Unity the principal objective of his administration but he and other Imperial Potentates who followed him were not quite sure how this was to be obtained. Law said at his Imperial session in 1942 that "generally it can be said without hesitation or apology that the spirit of the Shrine has assumed a trend which leads to a happy middle ground of mutual understanding on which the seriousness of the Craft and the relaxation of our Order can meet in a true brotherhood."

Other Imperial Potentates who followed also made a point of attaining Masonic Unity and believed the Shrine, growing large and powerful, was the medium through which unity might be attained. The Shrine was international in scope, particularly in the United States and Canada, but it still had no Masonic standing and the Imperial Council was not sure that it should have. More and more Shriners were being referred to as "high-up Masons," which in a sense was true because every Shriner must have either York or Scottish Rite prerequisite degrees; but the fact still remained that within his geographic area, the Grand Master was and is THE top Mason.

From the very beginning of the Shrine, Imperial Potentates had attempted to smooth the ruffled feathers of various Grand Masters, but because there were so many Masonic jurisdictions, some of them quite different in their practices, it was impossible to anticipate each difficulty.

Savants saw that unless there was Masonry, there would be no Shrine; and that unless the growth of Masonry was maintained, at least in proportion to the growth in population, the Shrine itself could not grow.

During his year as Imperial Potentate, Frank Land, the founder of DeMolay, gathered statistics to show that too many Shriners had gone through the Blue Lodge and one of the Rites just to become a Shriner; and he told the Imperial Council that 92 percent of Blue Lodge Masons failed to return to their own or another lodge after receiving the degrees and that 95 percent seldom attended the meetings of the Rites.

Imperial Potentate George M. Klepper reported to

the Imperial Council in Chicago in 1963 that in 1961, 27 state Masonic jurisdictions had a numerical loss in membership and that in 1962, 33 states showed a loss, and declared it is the responsibility of the Shrine to put Masonry back on a progressive growing basis.

Still, there was no single year since the war when the Shrine failed to record a net gain in membership. It reached a low point of 2,500 net gain in the calendar year of 1962, but the fact still remained that new creations were declining and losses, principally from deaths, were increasing; and it was not until 1963 that there was any significant shift in the trend. In New York in 1964, Imperial Potentate Harold C. Close was able to report a net gain in membership of more than 6,000.

At the Los Angeles extravaganza in 1950, Harold Lloyd was succeeded as Imperial Potentate by Hubert M. Poteat, a Wake Forest University professor, a musician and composer of some note, and recognized in the Imperial Line as the outstanding ritualist of the long list of Imperial Potentates. Poteat was also a stickler for Masonic conduct at all times, and set about to cure all the ills of the Shrine in one short year, but the Shrine was too big, the temples too far flung. He soon found that too many temples were headed by men who did not know Shrine law. They were interested in operating their temples for the benefit of their own nobility, and all too often became embroiled in affairs that never would have happened if they had known the law. In almost every difficulty that Poteat handled, he discovered it was not so much wilful disobedience of the law as it was ignorance of it. Perhaps Poteat's greatest achievement while in office came at the end of his administration when he insisted that the contribution of every Shriner to the hospitals should be increased from $2 to $5 a year. It had been forecast that he would run into opposition when the matter was put before the Imperial Representatives, but it sailed through the legislative process with little more than a murmur. The fact was—and the Imperial officers were not quite aware of it—that the Shriners themselves were in love with their hospitals, a fraternal love that perhaps has known no equal in the history of fraternalism. Shrine clubs, temples and regional associations had begun to take an active interest in them. Special nights were held at the clubs to collect toys and even food for the nearest hospital. Units gladly contributed their efforts to entertain the children, who were looked upon as guests and not as patients. Every Shriner became literally a committee of one to tell the story to "unbelievers" who might in their wills leave some bequest for the great charity so ably managed by devoted and dedicated members of the fraternity.

The result was an astounding growth of the Colorado Corporation's endowment funds, with which each succeeding Imperial Potentate must be concerned along with the members of the Board of Trustees. Then, too, each succeeding Imperial Potentate sought to develop an individual program and thus leave his contribution for posterity and history.

Roland D. Baldwin of Morocco Temple in Jacksonville, Florida, who had been scheduled to succeed Poteat, died suddenly a month before he was to take office. He had been a popular figure in the Imperial Line, and the Imperial Council for the first time took the unusual step of naming him posthumously as "Honorary Imperial Potentate." In his place, Robert Gardner Wilson, Jr., a Boston judge and a member of Aleppo Temple was elevated to the Shrine's highest office, and made it abundantly clear that he was interested in the Shrine's legal problems, including not only its position with respect to public law, but in Shrine law itself. He realized all too well that while the Shrine had its Imperial by-laws, and a code by which the Imperial Council controlled individual temples, there were times when it was a conglomerate that confused temple officers. This was understandable because there was not only the official law as written, but the unwritten law descended by decisions and edicts of each succeeding Imperial Potentate, which in turn were approved by each succeeding Imperial Council, and thus became law. Wilson worked at the problem all through his year and as a past Imperial Potentate in the years that followed, but it would be many years before there would be any recodification. In 1966, Imperial Potentate Rush appointed Morocco Past Potentate and a Justice of the U.S. Court of Appeals Warren Jones to effect recodification.

Then, in June of 1952, Harvey A. Beffa of Moolah Temple in St. Louis became Imperial Potentate and the first of several to realize that the Shrine and its hospitals had become big business. A top business administrator in his own right, Beffa realized that as the Shrine passed the 700,000 mark in membership, and quite likely would go beyond a million, that better records would be required not only in the national organization but in the temples themselves. Beffa did not endear himself to some temples in his visitations, when he discovered that membership lists and financial rec-

The late Gen. Douglas MacArthur wearing his Nile Shrine fez. He was created a Noble Aug. 10, 1936, in Manila. On Dec. 12, 1945, he became a life member of Nile Temple.

ords were in a deplorable state. His experiences convinced him that some kind of uniform records were required, and he ordered the Imperial Office to devise them, but it would be years before they were universally adopted.

Remmie L. Arnold of Acca Temple, Richmond, Virginia, a prominent and successful manufacturer with headquarters in Petersburg, Virginia, became Imperial Potentate in July 1953 at New York City. A co-chairman of his elaborate pageant was Orville F. Rush of Kena Temple who later was to become Imperial Potentate. Arnold had been the titular head of national, state and local organizations and was well prepared to assume the office of Imperial Potentate and to bring business practices into the order. He followed up on the records matter and sponsored some innovations. He proved to be a tireless worker.

Arnold was succeeded by Frank S. Land of Ararat Temple, a noted fraternalist and founder of Demolay, who was well prepared to head another fraternal organization. He left his mark on Shrinedom.

Walter C. Guy of Scimitar Temple, Little Rock, Arkansas, succeeded Land in 1955. A native of Indiana and a printing company executive, Guy inserted business practices in the Shrine and checked into the operations of the individual temples.

Gerald D. Crary of Naja Temple located in the famous frontier town of Deadwood in the Black Hills of South Dakota, became Imperial Potentate in 1956. A business executive who examined temple records and practices, Crary sponsored the acquisition of an international headquarters building, pointing out that the Shrine had grown too large to be operated out of rented space in an office building. His plea bore fruit when within two years after he went out of office a building at 323 North Michigan Avenue, Chicago, was purchased for a headquarters.

Thomas W. Melham of Tripoli Temple, Milwaukee,

Wisconsin, was elected Imperial Potentate at the 1957 Minneapolis Imperial Council Session and Orville F. Rush of Kena Temple, Alexandria, Virginia, a noted boyhood orator, was elected Imperial Outer Guard. A native of South Dakota, Melham received early business training in that state before entering the University of Wisconsin from which he was graduated in 1923 with a B.A. in commerce and business administration, immediately taking a position with the National Cash Register Company, serving at Dayton and Philadelphia. He returned to Wisconsin to enter the field of life insurance and was one of the first in that state to receive the professional degree of Charter Life Underwriter. In 1937, he joined the Prudential Insurance Company of America in Milwaukee and in 1952 transferred to New York City as manager of their Manhattan agency, receiving a president's citation for excellence in overall operation for 1956. He was involved in numerous civic activities and was appointed Wisconsin State Rationing Officer by the governor after Pearl Harbor. With this impressive background, Melham served splendidly as Imperial Potentate, with a business-like approach to all Shrine problems and activities. When he left office during the 1958 Chicago Convention, the Shrine had passed 800,000 in membership. In 1966 he was elected Imperial Treasurer and still serves in that capacity.

George E. Stringfellow of Crescent Temple, Trenton, New Jersey, took over from Melham as Imperial Potentate. An associate of Thomas A. Edison, he became executive vice president of Edison Industries in West Orange, New Jersey. He took two major steps, i.e., first, to improve and strengthen relations between the Shrine and Masonry, he appointed wherever possible each Grand Master as his personal representative in each jurisdiction, with all but six Grand Masters accepting the appointment. Then he conducted a Shrine symposium for Grand Masters attending the Annual Grand Masters Conference, a day prior thereto, in Washington

Norman Vincent Peale, Crescent Temple, Trenton, N.J., was Imperial Chaplain in 1958–59, appointed by Imperial Potentate George Stringfellow, Crescent.

February, 1959, to elicit suggestions as to how the Shrine could help them and they responded with a plethora of suggestions.

Stringfellow's second project was the holding of a seminar in Dallas, Texas, on April 6–7, 1959, for Potentates, Chief Rabbans and Recorders for an indoctrination course in Shrine law, temple management, relationships within the overall body of Masonry and relationships between Masonry and the public. Some 450 officers from 125 temples attended and heard enlightening presentations from Imperial Divan Officers, Past Imperial Potentates, Key Committee Chairmen and the Imperial Auditor. Similar future sessions were suggested.

26

Rendezvous with Destiny

On that afternoon of June 23, 1920 when Forrest Adair arose in the Portland, Oregon, auditorium and made his famous "bubbles" speech, he was more prophetic than he knew when he said, "The best alms you can give is that which will make alms unnecessary."

In effect, he was hoping that eventually the sight of crippled children on the nation's streets and in the alms houses could be eradicated. With the population in 1920 just over one hundred million in the United States alone, he pointed out there were 400,000 crippled children. Thirty years later at the advent of the decade of the fifties, population had risen to more than one hundred fifty million, but the Shriners could point with pride to the fact that while the sight of crippled children had not been eradicated, there certainly were fewer of them.

The Shriners could carry their heads high over the accomplishments of their Hospitals for Crippled Children, for while they had by no means achieved the great results alone, they had led the way. During the fifties, they not only were operating their own seventeen hospitals where miracles of healing were achieved almost daily, but they had seen units of government erect additional hospitals in centers of population. It was during this decade, too, that Salk vaccine was given to the public, thereby reducing drastically the number of children crippled by dread poliomyelitis.

The dedicated men to whom was entrusted the management of this "glory" toward which Shriners had been parading since that first straggling walk in Indianapolis so many years before, suddenly realized during that decade of the fifties that subtle influences were at work that could change or add to the route of the Shrine Caravan toward Mecca.

The Board of Trustees was aware, of course, that the Shriners were doing more for their great charity than the mere contribution of money to the operating funds. During the regime of Imperial Potentate Hubert Poteat in 1951, the annual contribution of every member for hospital operation was increased from $2 to $5 but, in addition, temples and units of the temples were raising huge sums of money for the hospitals through football games, circuses and other entertainment. And to these growing funds were added additional monies left to the hospitals in the wills of charitably inclined Shriners, and of individuals outside the Shrine, who had become impressed with the great work the hospitals were doing.

It was gratifying indeed when endowment funds climbed to the fantastic total of more than one hundred million dollars and kept climbing rapidly. It required more and more work on the part of the board members and their advisors, and it required an additional staff in the international office, to manage the funds, and even the estates themselves; but the endowment also assured the proper upkeep of the hospitals, the construction of four new buildings (St. Louis, Honolulu, San Francisco, and Mexico City) and the repair and refurbishing of others.

But as the endowment funds increased and waiting lists of patients declined it was apparent that the Shriners were reaching toward some new rendezvous with destiny. No one knows exactly when or where the Shrine leadership began to realize just what had been accomplished in slightly more than thirty years, but imperceptibly at first and then with a rush, they knew that the Shriners were in a position to once more offer to the world concrete evidence of their sincere desire to help suffering humanity.

How?

Well, it is a fascinating and sometimes complicated story of how divergent forces within the Shrine suddenly jelled and made possible on July 4, 1962, in Toronto, a program for the treatment of serious burns afflicting children, laboratory research in methods of treating burns and a teaching force to spread for all mankind the knowledge obtained.

In a sense, at least, the story begins with the appointment of Robert P. Smith as General Counsel, and with the election of Dr. Clayton F. Andrews as Imperial Outer Guard at the glamorous Los Angeles Convention in 1950. Ten years later, Dr. Andrews was to become the first physician and surgeon since Walter M. Fleming, to become Imperial Potentate. Andrews was a fraternalist and a devout Mason and Shriner, but he also was a doctor, and on his way up the ladder of Imperial Shrine offices to Imperial Potentate, it was natural that he should be devoted to the hospital program.

Thus it was that it became apparent to him in the decade of the fifties that while the hospitals had successfully and mercifully treated thousands of children afflicted with orthopedic deformities, not much use had ever been made of the wide background of knowledge obtained by the hospitals and doctors from all of the success and, of course, a few failures.

During the decade, Dr. Guy A. Caldwell, professor of surgery at Tulane University in New Orleans, had become chief of the advisory board of orthopedic surgeons, and as Dr. Andrews moved up the line became friendly with him. And so it was that at the mid-winter meeting of the Board of Directors and the Board of Trustees of the hospitals at the Astor Hotel in New York in January of 1958, Dr. Andrews presented Dr. Caldwell to make a long and detailed speech on the value that could be obtained from all of the hospital records if the board would approve a program of clinical research.

Dr. Caldwell and Dr. Andrews made a point of distinguishing between clinical research from the records alone and laboratory research where laboratory technicians sought answers to given problems. Dr. Caldwell was persuasive and the board approved the program and appropriated funds for it. Chairman Galloway Calhoun named as members of the research committee Illustrious Walter G. Seeger of St. Paul as chairman, Imperial Sir George E. Stringfellow and Past Imperial Robert Gardiner Wilson. He also appointed a sub-committee on research headed by Dr. Andrews and including Dr. Harold A. Sofield of Chicago, Dr. John R. Moore of Philadelphia and Dr. Frederick C. Bost of San Francisco, all chief hospital surgeons; Dr. Caldwell and Dr. Joseph S. Barr of Boston, representing the advisory board of surgeons.

The sub-committee went to work immediately, and in its first report, the committee recommended a uniform system of records and the international office was ordered to prepare it. IBM equipment was obtained and the long task begun of putting into punch cards the information from the records.

Dr. Andrews made regular reports on progress. So did Dr. Caldwell, and as a result some of the members of the board caught fire. The word "research" was synonymous with the times. The hospitals had the money that could be used only for the treatment of children or some related field. But it was not until the Board of Directors and the Board of Trustees met in Atlantic City in July 1959 that the spark of fire generated itself into a flame.

In a long discussion over research and what it entailed, Imperial Sir Marshall M. Porter out of a clear sky said, "My concept is that it should rival in appeal and effective work what the crippled children's pro-

gram did, and I think we have the money to do it."
Past Imperial Potentate Harvey Beffa sounded another
note when he said, "Sooner or later we have to determine the program." Dr. Andrews conceded in the discussion that his program of clinical research would not
need all of the funds the hospital corporation had available for research, and Porter replied that side by side
with the program of clinical research, the Shriners
should explore some other field that bears some relation
to the overall picture of the Shriners Hospital for Crippled Children.

But what field? No one knew.

In Atlantic City that July of 1959, Dr. Andrews became the Imperial Potentate. Together with the manifold duties of his office, he continued to watch over
his research project. Seminars for surgeons were conducted. Experts devised the punch-card IBM program,
and in Washington, Chief Counsel Bob Smith picked
up the telephone in his office and put through a call
to the United States Army Medical Research Command.

At some unrecorded date in the spring of 1959, Smith
had discussed with some of the top medical brass of
the Army, Navy and Airforce what the Shrine might
do in the field of medical research to help humanity
in general, and children in particular. And Army records reveal that a number of projects were suggested,
but Colonel Frederick Timmerman, deputy to Briga-
dier General Joseph McNinch in command of Army
medical research, recalls that he had become convinced, and told Smith, that the greatest single medical
need in North America was some facility for the treatment of major burns and research and teaching projects
connected with them.

While Smith had all of the suggestions in hand when
he went to Atlantic City, there is no recorded evidence
that he offered them to the trustees, but it is likely
that he talked about them behind closed doors, for after

that session was concluded he immediately asked the Army's medical research command if they would stage a seminar on burns for the Shrine's leadership. They would and did on August 24 and 25. Attending for the Shriners were Imperial Potentate Andrews, Trustee Board Chairman Calhoun, Imperial Chief Rabban Porter and Dr. Guy Caldwell. The Army doctors did a bang up job of showing the need for burn research. They went into every phase of their own research programs. Colonel Edward H. Vogel, Jr., the commanding officer of the Army medical research unit at the Brooke Army Medical Center at San Antonio, Texas, who was in charge of the only burn research center in the United States, was particularly impressive with a movie and slide presentation of the work his unit was doing.

But all of the military men said there was so much more to be done, particularly among civilians; and among civilians, particularly children, for burns were one of the great scourges of childhood.

In January of 1960, at the mid-winter meeting of the Board of Directors and the Board of Trustees in New Orleans, there was no doubt of the enthusiasm that had been generated among Smith, Porter and Caldwell, but Calhoun cautioned that so far it was just something for the board to think about, and that the entire matter for the time being should be held confidential among themselves.

However, the spark had begun to ignite into flame, and by the time the trustees met prior to the Denver Convention, it had grown into a bright blaze, and they unanimously improved a resolution that Chairman Calhoun should appoint a burns committee that would make extensive investigations into a burns treatment and research program for children and report to the mid-winter meeting in Las Vegas, Nevada, the following January. To that committee, Calhoun named Past Imperial Potentate Harvey A. Beffa as chairman; Marshall M. Porter, who was to become in Denver the

Deputy Imperial Potentate and Past Imperial Potentate Robert Gardner Wilson, Jr.

The committee wasted no time. They quickly called into consultation the doctors, the lawyers and the builders. The doctors and the committee visited at the Brooke Army Medical Center. So did the Shrine's architects so that they might report on just what would be involved structurally if a burns program was finally approved. The lawyers investigated the legal feasibility of the Colorado Corporation entering into such a program, and they quickly discovered from a search of the records that Shriners Hospitals for Crippled Children had been treating burns cases of children for years because burns created orthopedic problems. The Surgical Advisory Board was unanimous in its opinion that while burns created problems other than orthopedic, certainly burn cases were orthopedic in character because of bone and muscle contractures.

Progress was being made by the committee, but it was slow work for there were so few people to advise. They had talked, of course, with Colonel Vogel in San Antonio, and with Dr. Truman Blocker, another former Army burns specialist, and now a professor of surgery at the University of Texas Medical School in Galveston. Dr. Blocker and Dr. Vogel also recommended that they talk with Dr. Curtis P. Artz, associate professor of surgery at the University of Mississippi, who as an Army colonel had originally set up the Brooke burns program.

At the Imperial session in Miami in July 1961, the burns committee was able to make an interim report, but they were not quite ready to formalize a program. There was still much work to do. Dr. Caldwell needed to talk with the deans of important medical schools, so that when a program would be formally introduced there would be no doubt of its final passage. The delay in Miami was brought on largely through the death of Bob Smith in Boston on May 12, 1961, of a heart attack. He was visiting Robert Gardiner Wilson in con-

THE FIRST COUNCIL ON BURNS—(left to right) Dr. H. T. Merymann, Staff Member, Naval Medical Research Institute; Marshall M. Porter; Dr. Guy A. Caldwell; Dr. Clayton F. Andrews; Captain J. R. Kingston (MC) USN, Deputy Director, Research Division, Bureau of Medicine and Surgery, U.S. Navy; Captain O. E. Van der Aue (MC) USN, Commanding Officer, Naval Medical Research Institute; Robert P. Smith; Galloway Calloway (MC) USN, Assistant Chief for Research and Military, Medical Specialties, and Director, Research Division, Bureau of Medicine and Surgery; U.S. Navy; Dr. Ralph Muckenfuss, Scientific Director, Naval Medical Research Institute; Lt. Col. J. D. Galloway, Royal Canadian Armed Forces Medical Corps.

285

nection with his activities on behalf of the proposed burns institutes.

Still by January 3, 1962, the burns committee was ready when the members of the Board of Trustees, and the Board of Directors of the Iowa Corporation met at Lichfield Park, Arizona, outside Phoenix. Harvey Beffa, a consummate showman, arranged the affair so there would be no doubt of the eventual result. He, as chairman of the committee; Marshall Porter, who had become Imperial Potentate in Miami the previous July and Robert Gardiner Wilson, Jr., all believed devoutly in the cause for which their committee had been created—the acceptance by the Shrine of the challenge to do something to help children suffering from burns and their complications.

For the first time in the memory of any Shriner, the meeting at which the report was to be presented was held at night, and significantly the wives of the top men in all Shrinedom were invited to hear the report.

Galloway Calhoun presided.

"This," he said, "is probably one of the most momentous and important meetings the Shrine of North America has ever had."

It was just that, of course, but an even greater day was to come just six months later at the Toronto Convention, presided over by Marshall Porter, and Chairman Calhoun didn't live to see it. For that matter, neither did Past Imperial Potentate Thomas C. Law, who was vice chairman of the Board of Trustees.

Galloway Calhoun, who had lived most of his life at the center of drama, died the same way as he addressed the 90th annual conclave of the Knights Templar of Arkansas on the evening of April 16, 1962. He had begun his address slowly, telling more jokes than he usually did on such a solemn occasion during the week of Easter. His friends noticed as he proceeded that it was more difficult for him to speak, and that from time to time he clutched the lectern. Then he turned from a description of the hospitals and the children he loved so much, to his love of Masonry and Christianity. In tones of great compassion, he described the scenes on Calvary from which Holy Week came and to which the Templars are so devoted—and then he collapsed behind the lectern and died before help could reach him.

Past Imperial Potentate Law died three weeks later on May 4, 1962, in a private hospital in Atlanta, and thus three men who had had so much to do with the Shrine's hoped-for new philanthropy were not present when the Shriners began to arrive in Toronto on June 30.

It was to be a real wing-ding. Toronto had prepared well for the affair, and the Toronto *Telegram* on June 30 headlined their edition "Hold Your Hats, Here They Come." The Shriners came by lake steamer, by special trains and by automobile—100,000 of them, and for a purpose. There had been no Canadian Imperial Potentate since 1943 when Morley Mackenzie of Rameses Temple held the office, and the Shriners had not visited Toronto since 1930, when the peace monument was dedicated with international ceremonies.

Now the peace monument, refurbished and with an eternal circle of flame surrounding it, had been moved to a new location outside the Canadian National Exhibition Grounds, with the "lady of peace" looking out across Lake Ontario to the United States. To rededicate it was Marshall M. Porter, Justice of the Supreme Court of Alberta, and a member and Past Potentate of Al Azhar Temple of Calgary. The ceremonies took place on Monday, before the giant parade on Tuesday, which followed a night of revelry. There were impromptu parades, street dances and hilarious hi-jinx. And as for the parade, the *Globe and Mail* called it "the biggest, brashest parade in Canadian history."

Even while the parade was still moving in the streets of Toronto, Imperial Potentate Porter told the repre-

The Peace Monument, erected by Shriners outside the National Exposition grounds in Toronto. In its new setting, it is surrounded by a moat of water, and an eternal flame.

sentatives that there would be presented on Wednesday "what those of us who have studied it regard as a new breakthrough into another great charitable operation for the child in the field of burns." And he said the women and the public would be invited to see the presentation that Burns Chairman Harvey Beffa and all of his technical advisors had prepared.

Porter also had a few announcements to make. He told the representatives that to fill the chairmanship in succession to Galloway Calhoun, he had appointed Walter G. Seeger of St. Paul, already a member of the board. To fill the vacancy itself, Porter named Carl Rahn of Al Bedoo Temple in Billings, Montana, but a trustee would be elected to fill Calhoun's unexpired term. Porter also said that he had not filled the vacancy created by the death of Vice Chairman Law, since only a few weeks intervened between his death and the holding of the current convention.

Porter also announced the appointment of a new

General Counsel. When Bob Smith had died a year before, Galloway Calhoun himself and his law firm had been appointed. Now, Porter said, to succeed Calhoun, he had appointed Stanley Garrity, Past Potentate of Midian Temple in Wichita, Kansas, and a distinguished corporation lawyer in the middle west.

And then came that day of July 4, a day the Imperial officers hoped would go down in Shrine history equal in importance and glory to that day in Portland, Oregon, when the Shriners Hospitals for Crippled Children were created. Very briefly, Porter opened the ceremonies and concluded that "the report you are about to hear is the product of all of the considerations that your officers and advisors can give to this subject and we recommend it without qualification."

The lights dimmed, and with motion picture film clips, slides, and narration the presentation began. With photographs and art work, the narration traced the history of the Shrine from Knickerbocker Cottage, Walter Fleming, Billy Florence and all the rest, until the haunting strains of "I'm Forever Blowing Bubbles" brought into focus the Portland convention. There was the staged photograph of that wandering minstrel, film clips of parades and shots of the various hospitals where thousands of children had been treated.

The narrator said, "Now, today, we too, have the privilege to pioneer once more in philanthropy—to dispel, in our day, with the 'Sunshine of the Shrine' a great but practically disregarded danger to the present and future health and welfare of our nation. This growing and urgent menace stems from the presently inadequate stage of research and facilities devoted to burns therapy."

There was more, much more. Dr. Guy Caldwell gave the representatives the history of the Shrine research that had gone into the decision taken at Lichfield Park six months before. Dr. Curtis P. Artz with his gruesome slides of burns and their care, told the delegates that "the thermal burn is the most severe injury to which a man is liable."

There was so little known about burns or their treatment. Only Brooke Hospital in San Antonio was engaged in burn research in all of North America. He told of the tremendous expense in treating burns, of the 25 to 50 percent anticipated loss of life in Shriners institutes from burns, even with the best of care; but, he said the program presented was one of the great challenges to the nation, and for the Shriners, a great opportunity.

Dr. Caldwell returned to tell the Shriners that as projected, the burns institutes would provide three things—1. immediate treatment for burned children, treatment within 48 hours, which would require in many cases air travel for the patient; 2. total burn research in laboratories in each institute, which would be located on or adjacent to campuses of outstanding medical universities where vast facilities for treatments associated with burns would be available; and 3. the creation of programs for the teaching by teams of burn doctors and technicians, which could then take to all America training programs for other teams to be created.

Then Beffa took over and explained that a thorough canvass of the costs had been made for construction, equipment and operation; that outstanding businessmen and accountants had examined the Shrine income, and that unanimously the members of the Board of Trustees and the members of the Board of Directors, had concluded that the Shrine had the money for construction and for operation of three burns institutes.

But Beffa didn't let it go at that. He had a tear-jerker left, and with the lights once more dimmed, he began to tell the story of a horribly burned St. Louis boy named Billy Roach.

The boy had been severely burned in a fire while playing with other children. He had been taken to a

St. Louis hospital, where the burns had been treated, and after a short period in the hospital was sent home with prescribed medical treatments; but after a period of time, when the burns on his legs failed to heal, he was taken to a neighborhood doctor, who found serious infection. In addition, the leg muscles had contracted to the point where his legs and back were pulled out of shape.

The doctor, untrained in either orthopedics or burns, had told the parents that he saw only one solution and that was amputation of one of the legs. The boy's father had carried the story to his employer, a Past Potentate of Moolah Temple.

Even then Beffa was interested in burns. Perhaps this was a time when Shriners might find at least one of the answers to questions they were probing in their investigation of burns. By happenstance, Dr. Caldwell was in St. Louis at the time, and reached by Beffa by telephone, promised to look at the boy the following morning at the St. Louis unit of the Shriners Hospitals for Crippled Children. The employer hurriedly called his employe and said, "I'm sending an ambulance within an hour to put your son in our hospital. Have him ready."

After Dr. Caldwell's examination, he told Beffa that "if we had had this boy immediately after he was burned, this would not have happened. This is the very thing that your burn institutes will correct."

Even so, after a period of months in the St. Louis hospital, doctors eliminated the infection and by surgery restored his contracted muscles.

And at that moment, Billy Roach ran from the wings of the stage at O'Keefe auditorium and Harvey Beffa shouted: "Billy Roach."

The boy ran to a football on the stage, and kicked it into the audience. Then, taking a parchment scroll from Dr. Artz, walked across the stage and handed it to Beffa, himself crippled by polio.

Beffa turned to Billy, and asked: "Billy, if I gave you this microphone, what would you say to these people?"

And Billy replied: "Thank you, Mr. Shriner."

"There wasn't a dry eye in the house," said Harold Lloyd, "and some were openly weeping with joy and pride."

And it was at this point that Chairman Beffa opened the parchment Billy had handed him, and offered the burn center committee resolution. It read:

"Whereas, reliable medical surveys disclose that each year thousands of children are rendered actually or potentially crippled by burns, and

"Whereas, the facilities in North America for research, treatment and care of such burns are inadequate and limited, and

"Whereas, the Shrine, as a leader in child therapy in the field of orthopedics, can again make a contribution to medical science;

"Now, therefore, be it Resolved, that Shriners Hospitals for Crippled Children, a Colorado Corporation, do construct, establish and operate one or more hospitals for the care and treatment of curable crippled children afflicted with acutely dangerous burns, and for research activities and training programs related thereto, at such place or places in North America as the Boards of Directors and Trustees of the Shriners Hospitals for Crippled Children may determine, at an aggregate cost of not to exceed ten million dollars.

"And be it further Resolved, that the Boards of Directors and Trustees be directed to proceed forthwith to cause the first of the proposed hospitals to be built and put into operation."

Perhaps significantly, the resolution was dated July 4, 1962, and Beffa recommended adoption of the resolution signed by himself, Wilson, and the Imperial Potentate.

Almost before a discussion of the resolution could

get underway, there were cries from the floor of: "Question. Question."

However, as had happened in Portland when William Melish had asked for caution, and perhaps a year of delay for consultation with the temples, there was a word of caution from Louis Chackes of Ainad Temple in East St. Louis, Illinois, but it was obvious the representatives were in no mood for delay. They wanted the program, and they wanted it quickly, so that once more the Shriners could get at the business of helping children in a medical field no one knew much about.

The resolution was adopted without a dissenting voice, amidst tremendous cheering.

27

Tears of Pride and Joy

Among the 729 representatives at Toronto, there was a lot of laughter when Billy Roach kicked the football from the stage of O'Keefe Center auditorium into the midst of the Nobility on the floor, but there were a lot of handkerchiefs, too, to wipe away the tears of pride and joy.

Shriners are an emotional people. They salute their three national flags, stand at attention when national anthems are played, dress up in Arabic costumes and trim military uniforms and parade in strange cities behind flying emblems and stand absolutely subservient to their Imperial Potentate. But most of all, they worship at the Shrine of the Crippled Child. Now they would have another Shrine of the Burned Child.

It is likely that few of the representatives really understood just what they had done that July 4, 1962, or what the Boards of Trustees and Directors would do in the future. The leaders weren't sure themselves, any more than Imperial Potentate Garrison and his Divan had been sure in 1920 in Portland, Oregon. And the rank and file of the patrols, the bugle corps, the bands and other marching units didn't even know what had happened, and wouldn't for some time to come.

The Toronto papers printed only comparatively minor statements of the event. There was little more than brief mention in newspapers in the States, for actually what had happened was that the Imperial Council had voted an appropriation of ten million dollars to build three hospitals for the treatment of burned children, research in burn therapy and the international teaching of what the specialists might learn. And the ten million would not be enough.

What the Toronto papers played up were the parades on Younge Street, the high-jinx in the hotels and the mass of Shriners and their wives who were spending millions of dollars in monetary therapy for the Canadian city.

It would be four years before the first Burn Institute was in operation and still more years before they were all in operation and results achieved. It would be slow work, tedious in concept and there would be little noteworthy news to stimulate the Shriners themselves and even less to make the new project known to the public.

Four Imperial Potentates later, the first of the Burn Hospitals would be in operation and some of America's top business, scientific and architectural executives would have devoted countless hours, weeks and months in research and consultation to do the job right the first time.

George M. Klepper, a Memphis, Tennessee, lawyer was elected Imperial Potentate in Toronto, and it fell to him to appoint various committees to do that job.

In the first place, he had a new chairman of the Board of Trustees of the hospital corporation. Walter G. Seeger of St. Paul, appointed originally to succeed Galloway Calhoun, was elected in his own right. And while he had been a long-time member of the Board, the typical set-up left most of the work in the hands of the Chairman. Past Imperial Potentate Harvey Beffa, who had carried much of the burden of preparation of the Burn Program, was reelected Vice Chairman, and was immediately re-appointed by Imperial Sir Klepper as Chairman of the Burns Committee. Other members of the Burns Committee appointed by Imperial Sir Klepper were Past Imperial Potentates Porter, Wilson and Mattison; Imperial Sirs Harold Close and

O. Carylle Brock and Illustrious Sir Carl Rahn. Theirs would be the big job. In their visitations, from time to time, some member or members of the Imperial Divan would join them.

Imperial Sir George M. Klepper took his convention to· Chicago after a year of almost constant traveling to temples and to meetings with the Burns Center Committee, and it was to be a historic occasion. There were, of course, the big parades that the people of Chicago had learned to love. But it was in the tiled meetings of the Imperial Council that the real history was written.

Past Imperial Potentate Harvey A. Beffa made his report to the Colorado Corporation and, if it lacked the emotional appeal created in Toronto the year before, it was only because it had been a year of hard work. The Sites Selection Committee for the Burn Institutes had travelled more than 25,000 miles. It had contacted an original 101 medical schools and had narrowed the field to a secondary 21 medical schools from which to choose three. The Committee members talked with university presidents and deans of medical schools.

From all of these, the Committee had selected the three sites for the burn institutes and had even arranged for the purchase of some land or had been promised it as a gift. The Committee chose locations adjacent to and in conjunction with:

> The Massachusetts General Hospital and Harvard University at Boston
>
> Sealey Hospital and the University of Texas Medical Branch at Galveston
>
> The University of Cincinnati Hospital and the University of Cincinnati Medical School

Furthermore, the committee had selected as the Shrine Professors of Surgery at the new burn institutes:

Dr. Oliver C. Cope, Harvard University Medical School

Dr. Curtis Artz of the University of Mississippi, a designer of the Burn Center at Brooke Army Medical Center in San Antonio. Dr. Artz later resigned from his Galveston post.

Dr. Bruce Mac Millan of the University of Cincinnati

All were burn specialists.

This was real progress, even though not a spadeful of dirt had been turned. But architects had been busy. They had visited the Brooke Army Medical Center, and could submit plans and sketches.

As Imperial Sir Beffa neared the end of his report, he had a major suggestion. After talking with the new Shrine Professors of Surgery, he said that the treatment of severely burned children should get underway at once in wards provided by Sealey, Massachusetts General and University of Cincinatti hospitals.

The program was adopted immediately, of course, and thus before the first hospital for burns was opened in Galveston, the Shrine had provided treatment for scores of burned children.

In Chicago in July 1963 there was one additional and significant change in Shrine management. Walter G. Seeger announced that he could no longer occupy the position as Chairman of the hospital Board of Trustees and would decline reelection.

In his place, the representatives elected the great movie comedian Harold Lloyd, who was missing the first Imperial session since his original election from Al Malaikah Temple. He was in France putting together a movie, but after two telephone calls, he cabled the Imperial Council he would accept his new office.

Also elected in Chicago as Imperial Potentate was Harold C. Close of Scotland, Connecticut, a retired businessman and Past Potentate of Sphinx Temple

THREE BURN INSTITUTES

Galveston Unit, Burns Institute, Galveston, Texas

Cincinnati Unit, Burns Institute

Boston Unit, Boston, Massachusetts Burns Institute

in Hartford, who had an idea that the Shrine should establish a separate Department of Public Relations and employ expert counsel. He asked the Chicago convention to appropriate funds for the activity, which it did, and the inception of it was largely at his direction.

Imperial Sir Close took his convention to New York, and it was a big one. The city officials denied the Shrine the right to parade on Fifth Avenue before all the stores, where there was room for crowds to gather. Instead, the parade came from the edge of Columbia University, down Fifth Avenue to the Sixties. It was a big parade just the same, and on Thursday night, thousands more saw the night parade through the World's Fair grounds and through the new Shea Stadium.

Actually, the Shriners had more fun going in New York than they had had in many years, but it was all in good fun, and *Time Magazine* was able to report after it was all over (although some of their figures were not quite accurate) that:

> Accompanied by 50 brass bands, some 500 horses, and at least two camels, the Shriners swarmed into Manhattan 150,000 strong, occupied 85 hotels and motor inns, added to the traffic jam, monopolized sidewalks, held seven-hour-long parades and displayed a keen group sense of humor in a thousand hilarious ways, including occasionally entangling innocent natives in loops of invisible thread. They wore red fezzes, red and green floppy harem trousers, and red-embroidered jackets and looked like wandering extras from "The Forty Days of Musa Dagh.' They were the respectful and respected members of the Ancient Arabic Order Nobles of the Mystic Shrine. As representatives of an organization forthrightly dedicated to whoopee in a good cause, the Shriners are pranksters by profession. . . . By the end of last week, their fezzes askew and damp with humidity, their throats hoarse from laughter, they were plumb out of invisible thread as well. But all that was small fish compared to the whale of a time they had.

Obviously, this was an image of themselves the Shriners like. The words "respectable" and "respected" in a national magazine of the rank of TIME meant that whatever was left of an image created a half century and more before, was dissipated. Very simply, in the public eye, the Shriners had grown up, but still played at being Moslems and infidels to have fun and, in the process, help little children who, through no fault of their own, would not have much of any kind of fun out of life.

In the words of the late Noble J. Edgar Hoover "Freemasonry has for centuries meant constructive building in the hearts of men, in the life of institutions and in the souls of Nations."

Now, the bands, patrols, clowns and other funning units of the Shrine could go on to Washington for the next Imperial Council session in 1965, firm in the knowledge that only small minds would laugh or sneer at them for the outlandish trappings they might wear in the parades, the hotels and on street corners.

It was the new Imperial Potentate, O. Carlyle Brock, who had decided to take the Shrine convention to Washington the first time in 30 years that the Imperial Council had met in the nation's capital.

Brock was something of a he-man, a Canadian-born dairyman from Zem Zem Temple in Erie Pennsylvania, who had earned a wide reputation as one of the great big game hunters. He was a man of firm beliefs in individual freedom and the rights of man under domineering government. But most of all he believed that the Masonic fraternity, and particularly the Shrine, was the fraternity of destiny.

Purely as a matter of timing, it fell to the lot of Imperial Sir Brock to make several public appearances in connection with both the Burn and Orthopedic Hospital programs.

Imperial Sir Harold Close had turned the first shovel of dirt for the Galveston Burns Institute and Past Imperial Sir George A. Mattison, Jr., as chairman of the Building Committee, had the building under construction. Almost at the same time, Imperial Sir Brock turned ground at both Cincinnati and Boston with the same shovel used by Close. During his Hawaiian visit, Noble Brock turned ground for a new Honolulu orthopedic unit as part of the hospital refurbishing program. After 40 years of service, some of the orthopedic hospitals had grown obsolete. St. Louis had a new one. Philadelphia, Chicago and Greenville, were alloted funds for compete renovations and San Francisco was to get a new wing.

Perhaps emblematic of the new Shrine fervor was the ceremony arranged by Past Imperial Sir Robert Gardiner Wilson for the turning of earth at Boston. It was a staged affair, of course, as Julius Fedel, captain of Aleppo Temple's mounted patrol, dressed as Paul Revere galloped up to the Imperial Potentate and handed him a replica of the lanterns which were hung in the Old North Church to start Paul Revere on his midnight ride. Imperial Sir Wilson declared that he hoped "the lantern may symbolize the bringing of new light to the medical world today in the field of burn therapy."

Both the lantern and the silver-plated shovel now have been placed in the Shrine Rooms at the George Washington National Masonic Memorial in Alexandria, Va.

The Galveston building itself, a massive $3,500,000 structure just across the street from Sealey Hospital, was still under construction as Most Worshipful J. Caroll Hinsley, Grand Master of Texas Masons, delivered the oration preceding the leveling of the cornerstone to this new monument to Shrine charity. Imperial Sir Brock made an impressive speech.

Mementoes of the Shrine, the Burn Program, the day's festivities and a copy of "Parade to Glory" were placed in a steel box, to be sealed inside the cornerstone and opened at some unknown date in the faraway future.

And then, just as Forrest Adair had recalled a wandering minstrel in Portland, Oregon, playing in the early hours of the morning "I'm Forever Blowing Bubbles," Imperial Potentate Brock remembered the tears of joy and pride and hope that had dropped from the eyes of representatives at the Imperial Council session in Toronto.

To prepare for the 1965 Washington, D.C. convention, Noble Brock had chosen Orville F. Rush, Imperial Assistant Rabban, as Director General, the first time in the history of the Shrine that an Imperial officer had been chosen for that difficult task, and it had not been easy.

Washington itself had a number of new buildings,

including a Washington Hilton hotel, where the convention sessions would be held. The requests for hotel accommodations exceeded facilities, and some units were housed in Virginia and Maryland, some of them as far away as Baltimore. It took acts of Congress for permission to parade and erect the stands for those who wanted to sit down at the parade. As in 1935, Pennsylvania Avenue was again the parade route with the standard Shrine convention decorations in evidence.

Imperial Sir Rush had prepared well, and the parades were declared to be among the largest ever held in Washington. It was a wing-ding to be remembered and had innovations that made history. Rush always seems to have the answer ready before the question was born.

At the first business session of the Imperial Representatives, they approved in principal Imperial Sir Brock's program, for which he had worked all year, that the Shriners Hospitals for Crippled Children should take over two additional orthopedic hospitals that had been operated over the years by Arabia Temple in Houston, Tex., and by his own Zem Zem Temple in Erie, Pennsylvania.

Former Vice President
Hubert H. Humphrey

As guest of honor at the Imperial Potentate's banquet on Wednesday night in Washington, Director General Rush arranged for the appearance of Vice President Hubert H. Humphrey, a Mason who was to become a Knight Templar and a Shriner of Zuhrah Temple a month later on August 14.

It had been a hectic day for the Number Two Man in the government. There had been a cabinet meeting that morning and, during the day, the popular Adlai Stevenson, Ambassador to the United Nations, had dropped dead on a London street. The Vice President had been assigned by President Johnson to fly to London to return the body to the United States, but he remained at the banquet long enough to tell the Shriners that he had come from a Masonic family and that he was a Royal Arch Mason. Then he praised the Shriners for their great charitable work.

Earlier that day, the Imperial Council had elected Barney W. Collins of Mexico City as the new Imperial Potentate. But all the real emotion of the Washington session came on Thursday afternoon when Harold Lloyd made his annual report as Chairman of the Board of Hospital Trustees, after which traditionally he accepted gifts from Shrine temples for the great charity. There were checks representing personal gifts and profits from circuses, etc. There were checks from Shrine clubs and associations, and as usual Islam Temple came near the end of the line to present a check from the East-West game that sports writers had dubbed "Football's Finest Hour."

For forty years, as director of the game, Noble Bill Coffman had waited patiently to present the funds, this time more than a quarter of a million dollars, bringing Islam Temple's total contribution to more than five million.

"But this," said Coffman, "will be my last appearance before this body."

Instantly the entire audience came to its feet in a loud and lengthy tribute. Now eighty-two years old, Coffman was stepping down to become Director Emeritus of the game.

But there was still more. It was learned that in Los Angeles, Al Malaikah Temple had received from one of its lesser known members a bequest and with the bequest came a story.

The actual events had happened over a period of

time, and now they could be told. It concerned Albert MacDonald, now ninety-three years old, who had been a member of Al Malaikah for fifty-two years. A long-time farmer, and the first Ford dealer in Orange County, he was affectionately known as "the little old guy" from Pita Verde, California.

Some years before, he had established a trust fund of $20,000 for the hospitals, but as time went on, he and his wife decided their total estate should go for the benefit of the kids treated free by the Shrine. Then, his wife died.

"I didn't need all that money," Noble MacDonald said later, "and besides I was getting tired at my age making out my income tax returns."

And so it came about that "the little old guy" went to his bank, withdrew his securities from a vault and took them home. That night, he packed them in a shoe-box, covered the box with camellias so no one would know what it contained, for they were negotiable.

The next morning with the box under his arm he boarded a bus for Los Angeles, and walked into the office of J. Marion Wright, attorney and a Past Potentate of Al Malaikah.

"I want you to count all of this, and I want you to handle the details of giving it all to the hospitals," Mac-Donald said.

It took three months for the bank to count all of it and establish its current market value. It came to $1,900,000.

MacDonald said he thought it was over two million, but that he would bring more. The total to date is $2,020,669.85.

Imperial Sir Brock had ordered "the little old guy" flown to Washington so that the story might be told at the Imperial session. He went with Illustrious Sir Marion Wright. They attended the Imperial Potentate's banquet and every party to which they were invited.

Then on the stage of the Imperial session, while the

representatives gave another rising ovation, he was surrounded by all of the brass. And he enjoyed it more than anyone else.

Officially, the representatives granted a charter dispensation to a group of Nobles from Tucson, Arizona, who had selected "Sabbar" for their Temple name, and some of them had been so certain before the vote was taken that, as soon as it was official, they produced their own fezzes. It was the 168th Temple of the Shrine.

It had been thirty years since Washington had entertained the Shriners, but they liked the Capital City and Washington liked them, their parades and their frolic and really didn't expect to see them soon again.

But there were forces at work beyond the ken of mortal man that decreed a return of the Shriners only two years later and so Washington, together with Almas and Kena temples, prepared for another great influx of the Faithful, with their families in July 1967, with Orville F. Rush as Imperial Potentate.

The Imperial Year of 1965–66 might have gone down in the history of the Shrine as the "Year of the Serape" had it not been for other events that transcended it.

The "serape" is a blanket or shawl worn as an outer garment by Spanish Americans, particularly Mexicans, usually folded and draped over the left shoulder. Imperial Sir Barney W. Collins had told the Imperial Council that his two principal themes during his year in office would be De Molay and the Masonic significance in Mexico, and thus he wore the serape, wherever he went, and gave many away during his visits.

There was a pilgrimage to Egypt during his year. It was not the first pilgrimage of Shriners to Egypt. There had been one the previous year, but there had been no ceremonial. The Egyptian government provided entertainment, including a night in the desert under illuminated tents.

It also fell to the lot of Imperial Sir Collins to welcome the first patient into the new Galveston Burns Institute.

It was March 20, 1966, when five year old Miguel Angel Delgado of El Paso, Texas, was wheeled across the street from Sealy Hospital on a stretcher. The Imperial Sir talked with the boy in Spanish and wished him a full and complete life after the Shriners had completed their restoration of his badly burned body. Later on June 20, the Imperial Sir helped to lay the cornerstone of the new Burns Center in Cincinnati.

While there had been joyful events through the year of 1965–66, there also were sad ones. The Imperial Session in Washington had been over just three months, when the Imperial Divan was called to meet in Coronado, California. After the meeting was over, Imperial Sir Edgar L. Turner, the First Ceremonial Master, died of a heart attack. On December 4, Deputy Imperial Potentate Charles E. Merrill died in a bus while on his way to his office in Detroit. Imperial Treasurer and Past Imperial Potentate Leonard P. Steuart died after a lingering illness in January, 1966. He had served both the Iowa and Colorado corporations since 1937. Collins appointed Past Imperial Potentate Harold C. Close to succeed as Treasurer. Imperial Chaplain, Col. Reginald E. Clevett also died during the year.

The three deaths in the Imperial Divan marked the first time since its formation that the Imperial Council faced the election of four new imperial officers in a single election. But there was more to it than that. Deputy Imperial Potentate Merrill had expected to hold his 1967 convention in Detroit and had made all plans for it. But with his death, Orville F. Rush of Kena Temple, the new incoming Imperial Potentate, decided to hold the 1967 session in Washington, and the succeeding officers of the Imperial Divan necessarily moved their convention dates ahead for one year.

Past Imperial Potentate Thomas W. Melham of Tripoli Temple, Milwaukee, Wisconsin, won the office of Imperial Treasurer. Jake A. Wingerter of Salaam Temple, Livingston, New Jersey, Jack Streight of Gizeh

Temple, Vancouver, British Columbia, and W. W. Bennett of Ararat Temple, Kansas City, Missouri, were elected from among nine candidates for the offices of Marshal, Captain of the Guard and Outer Guard.

Most of the major airlines were on strike, and since travel in 1966 was considerably different from travel a score of years before, many of the Shriners in San Francisco were stranded; but some rented automobiles to drive a thousand miles or more, some waited it out, some took the trains, thinking of ways to have more fun at the next Imperial session, back in Washington again.

28

Extraordinary Happenings

The Imperial Year of 1966–1967 entailed over 250,000 miles of travels, colorful kaleidoscope of visitations and fellowship for Imperial Potentate Orville Findley Rush, Senior Past Potentate of Kena Temple, Alexandria, Virginia. He asserted "I will always look back on the year as one of rediscovery, if you will, not only of this great nation of ours, but of the entire continent."

It began with a beautiful and unusual pageant in San Francisco, presented before an overflow audience, with the finale-introduction of his wife Mary and seven children. The climax-participation in the Washington Convention, for the first time in the history of the Shrine, of the President of the United States Lyndon B. Johnson, Vice President of the United States Hubert H. Humphrey, and the First Lady of the Land Lady Bird Johnson. They were all together at the same time with Imperial Potentate Rush and the other Shriners. This was over the objection of the Secret Service who thought they should have divided their time in a public display and not be all together at the same time.

During this Shrine year, Imperial Potentate Rush participated in several ceremonials that marked the continued growth and progress of "The World's Greatest Philanthropy." He dedicated the new building of the Honolulu Unit of Shriners Hospitals for Crippled Children and on National Shrine Hospital Day, he dedicated a new out-patient wing at the Mexico City unit. The following Sunday, May 21, he made the dedicating

A historic photograph of the 1967 Washington, D.C. Convention. Right to left—Mary Rush, her husband Imperial Potentate Orville F. Rush, President of the United States Lyndon B. Johnson, the First Lady, Mrs. Lady Bird Johnson, Vice President of the United States Hubert H. Humphrey and Deputy Imperial Potentate Tom Seay. To left Deputy Imperial Marshal Edward E. Buckley and in the background can be seen Imperial Sirs Woody Bennett, Aubrey Graham, "Chick" Hogan, "Chick" MacGregor, and J. Worth Baker.

President Lyndon B. Johnson shaking hands with Imperial Potentate Orville F. Rush as Lady Bird Johnson looks on. In background, Bill Woodfield, Aubrey Graham, "Chick" Hogan, Tom Melham, J. Worth Baker, Vice Presidential Assistant, Jake Wingerter, and "Chick" MacGregor.

speech before a large crowd of Masonic, civic, university, and Shrine officials gathered in Cincinnati for the official dedication and opening ceremonies of our second completed Burns Institute, having participated in the Galveston Unit dedication soon before he became Imperial Potentate. There was a most colorful parade on the route from Syria Temple to the Burns Institute. Thousands were gathered at the site with an enjoyable afternoon of music, pagentry and ceremony.

On Saturday, July 1, 1967, Imperial Sir Rush made the principal address at the cornerstone ceremonies of the third Burns Institute in Boston, before a tremendous crowd. A sidelight—Elliott Richardson and John Volpe, soon to become presidential cabinet members, participated in this event. He also was present at several other dedications, including new Shrine temple buildings.

In the vital area of Shrine-Masonic relations, despite foul weather, attendance at the Frank S. Land Memorial Breakfast in February held coincidentally with the Grand Masters Conference in Washington was maximum, with distinguished guests invited by Imperial Sir Rush including members of the Senate, House, the Supreme Court, the President's Cabinet, and representatives from the White House and from the Vice President Noble Hubert Humphrey. Rush attended every conclave of major bodies within the framework of Masonry. He was on national television at several Shrine-related football games and appeared on other prominent national and international TV and radio shows. The Voice of America interviewed Rush about the Shrine and the interview was broadcast overseas.

Imperial Potentate Rush conducted the Shrine's second seminar school of instruction in Houston, Texas, March 27–28, 1967, with approximately 650 temple officers and Nobles in attendance. Thirty-two speakers covering a wide range of topics concerning temple administration appeared on the program. Enthusiasm ran rampant with the hearty endorsement of participants, evidenced by several commendatory resolutions introduced and passed at the conclusion of the final day's session, including adoption without a dissenting vote that a similar session be held as a matter of continuing practice on a tri-annual basis, and this has been effected.

Rush initiated and led interference for the Shrine exhibit at the Football Hall of Fame in Canton, Ohio, a sports shrine through whose portals pass exceedingly more than one million visitors annually. An invaluable showcase for the AAONMS.

A most pleasurable highlight of an unforgettable year was the exotic mid-east ceremonial held in the inner sanctum of the Sphinx at Gizeh, Egypt, with more than 500 Shriners from many countries present. Rush acted as the ceremonial potentate for the initiation of candidates. Picture, if you will, a procession of some 200 camels and horses slowly making its way for three and a half miles across the burning sands between the Sphinx and the Pyramids and Sahara City where a sumptuous Moslem feast of oriental splendor awaited the camel-hump and saddle weary Nobles and their families. An hour television program covering the Shrine pilgrimage was produced for Egyptian and nearby countries viewers.

The Imperial Banquet at the Washington Hilton featured as guests top Congressional leaders, White House, Cabinet, Supreme Court and governmental representatives, sports luminaries, famed aeronautical figures, prominent business leaders and many, many more. A galaxy of important personages and, in addition, Vice President of the United States Hubert H. Humphrey, who was to become a presidential nominee the following year, was present and gave a rip-roaring speech. He had acted as Rush's grand marshal in the Shriners Day Parade. Incidentally, the police reported that the two parades were witnessed by record crowds and that the conduct of the convention Shriners was exemplary.

Thomas F. Seay, real estate tycoon, of Medinah Temple, Chicago, was elected Imperial Potentate at the wonderfully enjoyable Washington Imperial Session, serving from July 1967 to July 1968. It was said in his biography that "Tom Seay accomplishes a lot of work and planning in his Lake Shore apartment, and, as he discusses real estate deals amounting to millions of dollars over the eleborate electronic communications systems installed there, it is almost beyond belief that this is the same country boy from Kentucky who arrived in Chicago in 1924, flat broke, with no higher education, and no skills beyond driving a taxi or working as a redcap and a switch tender at Union Station. His story of overcoming seemingly insurmountable obstacles in his climb to the lofty heights of success and influence in Chicagoland's world of business and finance is in the best Horatio Alger tradition, and has earned for him the reputation as Chicago's "Cinderella Man." In addition to his real estate interests, he is an officer and director of companies and banks.

Imperial Sir Seay emphasized a "four point program to strengthen our great fraternity and facilitate its continued growth," i.e., a return to the basic concepts of Masonry; improved relations with the other Masonic bodies; expanding the philanthropic work, particularly in the burns field; and building the Shrine's image through an expanded public works program. He established a Masonic advisory board and, as others, conducted the Frank Land Memorial Breakfast in conjunction with the Grand Masters Conference. To expand the philanthropic work, he formed a burns study committee, with Imperial Sir Orville Rush as chairman, and favored determining possible sites for future burns institutes. He accomplished a greatly stepped-up public relations program.

Seay visited 125 temples and held the 1968 session

in Chicago, which was well attended and numerous important matters formed the agenda. Peter Val Preda, an automobile dealer of Cairo Temple, Rutland, Vermont, was elected Imperial Outer Guard at the 1967 Washington session and Harvey W. Smith, a Past Grand Master of Masons of Sudan Temple, New Bern, North Carolina, was elected Imperial Outer Guard at the 1968 Chicago Convention.

Chester A. Hogan of Afifi Temple, Tacoma, Washington, with his business in Puyallup, was elected to succeed Imperial Sir Seay. He began his year with a visit to the newest temple, Hadji, in Pensacola, Florida, and then covered the continent and made an overseas jaunt to Frankfurt, Germany, where he participated with the European Shrine club in a ceremonial. Hogan and Harold Lloyd, Trustees Chairman, took part in dedicating the Boston Burns Institute on November 2, 1968, and in corner-stone laying ceremonies on June 1, 1969, of a new San Francisco Unit hospital building. During the year, the Black Camel appeared at the tent of Imperial Assistant Rabban C. P. "Chick" MacGregor of Al Malaikah Temple, Los Angeles, California, creating another vacancy in the Imperial line.

The 1969 Imperial Session was in Seattle, Washington, where J. Worth Baker of Murat Temple, Indianapolis, succeeded to the Imperial Potentate's throne. His business interests included bank supplies and an apartment building. Also elected at the same time were Fred R. Morrison of Moslem Temple, Detroit, as Imperial Captain of the Guard, and Warren F. Weck, Jr., of Zuhrah Temple, Minneapolis, as Imperial Outer Guard.

In 1957 when Imperial Baker was Potentate of Murat Temple, he called together civic and business leaders to propose that a "500 Festival" should be organized in connection with the 500-mile automobile race. When Baker ran into some opposition among merchants and others, he told them that "Whether any of the rest of you participate or not, the Murat units will parade the night before the race." Today, the festival is a month-long affair, including the election of a queen, the mayor's breakfast, the governor's ball and huge floats in the parade, together with Murat's units. Soon after taking office, the "moon landing" was accomplished and Shrinedom had a real "first" with Noble Astronaut Edwin E. "Buzz" Aldrin, Jr., of Arabia Temple, Houston, becoming the first Shriner to walk on the moon. He was the Grand Marshal of Baker's 1970 Indianapolis Imperial Convention Day Parade.

Following the Houston seminar 1967 resolution, when Orville Rush was Imperial Potentate, three years had passed and Imperial Sir Baker held an Imperial leadership seminar at Shreveport, Louisiana, in March 1970. Later, he participated in a Shrine ceremonial at Heidelberg, Germany.

Imperial Potentate J. Worth Baker and Edwin E. "Buzz" Aldrin, Jr., with his Arabia Temple Apollo II fez, the first Shriner to walk on the moon, at the Indianapolis 1970 convention.

Aubrey G. Graham, Norfolk, Virginia, postmaster and Past Potentate of Khedive Temple, was elected Imperial Potentate in July 1970 at Indianapolis, and Charles J. Claypool of Antioch Temple, Dayton, Ohio, was elected Imperial Outer Guard.

Imperial Sir Graham became a Master Mason in 1928, a Shriner in 1929, Potentate of Khedive Temple in 1938, served as treasurer for 19 years, was first elected as a representative to the Imperial Council in 1936. He became postmaster of Norfolk in 1945. He traveled extensively during his year as Imperial Potentate and accepted a recordmaking check of $500,000 for Shriners Hospitals during half-time ceremonies of the Annual Shrine Bowl of the Carolinas at Charlotte, North Carolina. During his year of service, Harold Lloyd, Chairman of the Board of Trustees of the hospitals since 1963, succumbed to the Black Camel in March 1971 and Deputy Imperial Potentate C. Victor Thornton of Moslah Temple, Fort Worth, was appointed as interim chairman until the next Imperial Session in Miami, Florida, where he was elected Imperial Potentate on June 30, 1971. Past Imperial Potentate Harvey Beffa was elected Chairman of the Board of Trustees of Shriners 22 hospitals.

The charismatic and versatile Dr. F. T. "Hogan" H'Doubler, Jr., of Abou Ben Adhem Temple, Springfield, Missouri, prominent physician and civic leader, was elected Imperial Outer Guard.

Imperial Sir Thornton, a native of Salt Lake City, Utah, was graduated in civil engineering from the University of Utah in 1935 and became president and chairman of the board of two steel fabricating companies. He is a past director of several civic, cultural, youth and business organizations. The Hundred Million Dollar Club idea in support of the hospitals endowment fund got well under way during his administration. He participated in the initiation of over 200 men into the Shrine at Heidelberg, Germany, sponsored by the Eu-

ropean Shrine Club, and on March 18, 1972, Shrine
Rooms West opened in the old San Francisco Shrine
Hospital building.

The 100th anniversary of the founding of the Shrine
and the golden anniversary of the first hospital in
Shreveport, Louisiana, were celebrated the entire year
of 1972, although the Shrine's founding was September
26, 1872, and the first Shrine hospital was opened on
September 16, 1922. The July 1972 Dallas/Fort Worth
Imperial Session was a lively convention and Imperial Sir Thornton was succeeded as Imperial Potentate by Henry B. Struby of Hadi Temple, Evansville,
Indiana, a board member and vice president of Credi-
thrift Financial Corporation. Randolph R. Thomas, a
popular and successful industrialist of Morocco Temple, Jacksonville, Florida, was elected Imperial Outer
Guard.

Imperial Sir Struby led the nobility at the start of
Shrinedom's second century and the 51st year of Shriners hospitals. One of the eventful programs was the
"Shrinetennial" and it was coupled with graveside
memorial services for the founders of the order, Dr.
Walter M. Fleming and William J. Florence, the seminar school of instruction in 1973, three years having elapsed since the previous seminar, and the "First
ceremonial of the second century of our noble order," all in New York City, the birthplace of Shrinedom.

The 99th Imperial Council Session was held in Atlanta, Georgia, July 3–6, 1973, with Yaarab Temple Potentate Gene Bracewell, now Imperial High Priest and
Prophet, serving as Director General. Jacob A. Wingerter of Salaam Temple, Livingston, New Jersey, was
installed as Imperial Potentate and Dr. Daniel E. Bowers of Mohammed Temple, Peoria, Illinois, who has
been in general surgery since 1937 and a graduate of
Bradley and Illinois universities, was elected Imperial
Outer Guard.

President Gerald Ford, a Noble of Saladin Temple, Grand Rapids, Michigan, played in the East–West Shrine Game at San Francisco.

Imperial Sir Wingerter, a Pennsylvania native, is a New Jersey professional engineer and president and chairman of the board of New Jersey Testing Laboratories, Inc., Newark. He had an active year of visitations and early in his regime on November 3, 1973, he attended the initial ceremonial of Jamil Temple, U.D., Columbia, South Carolina, when 863 crossed the hot sands, to add to the 1,442 members at the time of receiving dispensation at the Atlanta July session. In 1973, he received from the Pennsylvania Grand Master Elect the 100th Anniversary Medal, commemorating the dedication of the Masonic temple in Philadelphia in 1873. He assisted in laying the cornerstone of Alcazar Temple, Montgomery, Alabama, together with Governor George Wallace. During his year Shriner Gerald R. Ford, who had played in the Shrine East-West Football Game, became Vice President of the United States, later President. November 17, 1973 was Imperial Recorder George M. Saunders' 75th birthday and Imperial Potentate Wingerter spearheaded a mammoth birthday party celebration in his honor, attended by many distinguished Nobles.

29

The 100th Session

The 100th Imperial Council Session was held in Atlantic City June 23–28, 1974. Jack M. Streight, Q.C., of Gizeh Temple, Vancouver, British Columbia, Canada, barrister and solicitor of New Westminster, was elected Imperial Potentate and Richard B. Olfene of Kora Temple, Lewiston, Maine, a state senator, business executive, and civic leader, was elected Imperial Outer Guard in a spirited contest. Dispensation for Shrine temples in Alaska and Lake Worth, Florida, were granted.

Aahmes Past Potentate Earl Warren was thrice governor of California and Chief Justice of the U.S. Supreme Court for 16 years.

A community activist, Imperial Sir Streight designated "One of her majesty's counsel learned in the law" and as a "Queen's Counsel," Q.C., he is entitled to wear silk in the courts of law. He visited a multiplicity of temples and hospitals. Soon after his installation, a most distinguished Past Potentate of Aahmes Temple, Oakland, California, and a Past Grand Master of Masons, Earl Warren, mounted the Black Camel on July 12. He was a three-term governor of California and Chief Justice of the United States Supreme Court for 16 years. During Streight's tenure, the first federally recognized Burns Trauma Center in the United States was established at the Boston Unit, Shriners Burns Institute, and adjacent Massachusetts General Hospital. The National Institute of Health awarded the Burns Trauma Center a three year grant, to try to lift some of the shrouds obscuring medical knowledge about burns and thus bring innovations in treatment. Project Director named was Dr. John F. Burke, the Boston Unit's chief surgeon and chief of staff. Also, Imperial Sir Streight attended the ceremonial marking the opening of the new Shrine Genetics Research Center at the Montreal Unit, Shriners Hospitals.

The Toronto, Canada, Imperial Session June 29–July 4, 1975, was a pleasurable and exciting event long to be remembered, with record crowds for the "Queen City" viewing the antics of the paraders, and excellent publicity. Woodrow Wilson Bennett of Ararat Temple, Kansas City, Missouri, and operator of the Bennett Construction Co., Inc., was elected Imperial Potentate and personable, genial, efficient Gene Bracewell of Yaarab Temple, Atlanta, Georgia, president of National Chemical Co., was elected Imperial Outer Guard.

Imperial Sir Bennett is a native Missourian and as a civic-minded businessman, he has served on numerous boards to the betterment of his community. His year was an active one for the Shrine and hospital programs. August 28, 1975, was the departure day for the Imperial Shrine cruise to Alaska, a memorable occasion. At the beginning of his year, Bennett issued a special order to all of the temples regarding tours and cruises. In his message at the culmination of his term of office, he reported acceptance of same throughout Shrinedom. He also reported there were several ceremonials in Europe and in the Orient that produced many new Nobles. Dr. Carroll Larson, Director of Medical Affairs, gave an excellent hospitals report, stating partially that new regulations have added administrative chores to all units but that they had formalized affiliations to the operation of the orthopedic units in Montreal, Winnipeg, Honolulu, and St. Louis, as well as all of the burns units. Chief Surgeons were appointed on a full time basis at the Cincinnati and Chicago units. Imperial Sir Bennett was in the forefront of the triennial leadership seminar in Dayton, Ohio.

Sadness crept into the Shrine year with the passing of the popular and inimitable Harvey W. Smith, Imperial Chief Rabban, creating another vacancy in the "line," and Chairman of the Board of Trustees of the Hospitals Harvey A. Beffa died on October 20, 1975 and Past Imperial Potentate Barney Collins died January 6, 1976. Deputy Imperial Potentate Peter Val Preda was appointed interim Chairman of Trustees of Shriners Hospitals to serve until the upcoming Kansas City Imperial Session.

The 1976 Imperial Council Session was held July 4–9 in Kansas City, Missouri, with W. W. Bennett presiding. Several interesting election contests transpired. Past Imperial Potentate C. Victor Thornton was elected Chairman of the Board of Trustees of Shriners Hospitals. Peter Val Preda of Cairo Temple, Rutland, Vermont, ascended the "Top Step of the Ladder" to become Imperial Potentate. He came to the job with a splendid organizational background. Walker S. Kisselburgh of Al Malaikah Temple, Los Angeles, president of K and S Bearings, Inc., was elected Imperial Captain of the Guard, and Russell H. Anthony, D.V.M., of El Kahir Temple, Cedar Rapids, Iowa, veterinarian and sports organization activist, was elected Imperial Outer Guard. Both of these newcomers brought verve and enthusiasm to the imperial line.

Imperial Sir Val Preda, a native of West Virginia, operates automobile agencies in Rutland and Burlington, Vermont, and is a past president of the Vermont and National Automobile Dealers Associations. In 1976, he was elected chairman of the board of directors of the Vermont National Bank. The final year of World War II was spent as a prisoner of war.

During Imperial Sir Val Preda's year as Imperial Potentate, many temples were in the midst of constructing new or refurbishing present facilities and the Black Camel arrived at the door of Past Imperial Potentate Henry Struby in 1976 and at the door of Past Imperial Potentate Worth Baker in May 1977. Past Imperial Potentate Walter Guy died September 19, 1977.

In July 1976, the board of directors and trustees of both the fraternity and the hospitals unanimously adopted a plan for the reorganization of the Shrine's general offices in Chicago. Charles G. Cumpstone, Jr., was named Executive Secretary for Fraternal Affairs, and Lewis K. Molnar was named Executive Secretary for Shriners Hospitals for Crippled Children.

Val Preda placed special emphasis on the reorganization of the general offices, Masonic relations, public relations, membership, regalia and emblems, endowment, wills and gifts, the $100 Million Club, and the formation of the Research Advisory Board. He presided over the New York City July 3–8, 1977 Imperial Council Session.

New York City did not turn out the big welcome to the Shriners as it had in the past, nor did the convention receive the publicity it deserved, however, the fez-topped gentlemen and their families did have fun and considerable business was transacted. The "Big Apple" does have attractions that not any other city can offer and can house more conventioneers than other municipalities.

Fred R. Morrison, Sr., of Moslem, Detroit, owner of Morrison Carbonic Co., was elevated to Imperial Potentate at the New York session. This was to be the first time in Shrine history that a Noble served as Imperial Potentate at the same time his son served as Potentate of his temple. Moslem Temple recognized this with a special father-son testimonial September 14, and Fred R. Morrison, Jr., was destined to be the director general of the 1978 Detroit Imperial Session.

Voris King of Habibi Temple, Lake Charles, Louisiana, president of Kelly-Weber and Co., Inc., was selected as Imperial Outer Guard. With an effervescent personality, King is a member of a prominent Louisiana family. His father was governor of the state.

Imperial Sir Morrison's year included unique events and also the making of Shrine history. Imperial Council representatives voted to move the International Shrine Headquarters to Tampa, Florida, in an historic special session held April 10, 1978, in Tampa. This is the fifth city to serve as home for the Shrine since 1872. Predecessors were New York, Boston, Richmond, Virginia, and Chicago. The Florida site was chosen primarily because of Tampa's highly efficient airport facilities and an anticipated annual saving of $190,000 in operating costs. On May 25, 1978, ground breaking ceremonies were held on the 6.7 acre property, located a few miles west of the airport and overlooking the Bay.

On September 28, 1977, the Shrine officially opened an advanced research lab at Montreal. On June 11, 1978, Morrison presided over ground breaking ceremonies for the Chicago Unit new building. The addition to the Greenville Unit was progressing and plans were being drawn for a new Portland hospital building.

Four temples, Syria, Pyramid, Kaaba and Ziyara, celebrated their centennials during 1978. Seven temples, Gizeh, Salaam, Luxor, Abba, Abou Ben Adhem, Cairo, and Jaffa, reached their 75th anniversary. Joppa Temple, Gulfport, Mississippi received its charter at the 104th Detroit Imperial Session, to become the Shrine's 181st temple. The membership December 31, 1978, reached 941,799.

Edward E. Buckley of Kena Temple, Alexandria, Virginia, announced his retirement at the end of the current session, after 17 years as Chief Deputy Imperial Marshal, with all of the representatives rising in applause for his outstanding work. He was made Emeritus by the Imperial Potentate.

Warren F. Weck, Jr., assumed the Duties of Imperial Potentate on July 14, 1978, at the Detroit Session. He is a Past Potentate of Zuhrah Temple, Minneapolis, and a vice-president of Northwestern National Bank of Minneapolis. He received a law degree from the University of Minnesota.

Edward G. McMullan, C.D. of Al Azhar Temple, Calgary, Alberta, Canada, manufacturer's agent and business manager, was elected Imperial Outer Guard and proved to be of immediate value and assistance to the Imperial line.

Weck served during a year of transition, faced with complex and unusual challenges, because of the relocation of the Shrine offices. Operations were divided between Chicago and Tampa, where offices were rented. In November 1978, construction was started in Tampa. On December 31, 1978, George Saunders, who had served with distinction for 30 years, retired as Imperial Recorder. Robert J. Turley of Oleika Temple, Lexington, Kentucky, Chairman of the Jurisprudence and Laws Committee, was appointed as interim Recorder until the following Imperial Session. When the very able Jack H. Jones of Egypt Temple was elected to the post. Imperial Sir Weck's year included the entire panoply of Shrine events. He enshrined a heritage capsule commemorating 100 years of Kaaba Temple activities and participated in dedication of new facilities for Osman, Aladdin and Hadji Temples.

On February 22, 1979, Past Imperial Potentate George A. Mattison, Jr., Birmingham, Alabama, industrialist and philanthropist, passed away.

Charles J. Claypool of Antioch Temple, Dayton, Ohio, was installed as Imperial Potentate in July 1979. A West Virginia native, he is semi-retired, overseeing his real estate investments in the Dayton area.

The friendly, affable George W. Powell of Crescent Temple, Trenton, New Jersey, was elected Imperial Outer Guard. A tireless worker, he is a company presi-

New International Shrine Headquarters, Tampa, Florida (Dedicated Dec. 1, 1979)

Chuck Claypool, Imperial Potentate, at Dec. 1, 1980 dedication of the new International Headquarters—with Congressman Sam Gibbons—presenting Chuck with a memorial key to the building.

Imperial Sir Randolph Thomas, master of ceremonies and The Most Worshipful Grand Master Franklin C. Smith, Grand Master of the Grand Lodge of Florida, at the Cornerstone Laying Activities, Nov. 17, 1979, for the new International Shrine Headquarters.

dent and banker, with offices in Cherry Hill, New Jersey, and residences in Cherry Hill and Ocean City.

During Imperial Sir Claypool's year, major events took place. One of the milestones for the Shrine occurred December 1, 1979. The new International Shrine Headquarters at Tampa was dedicated by Nobles and government dignitaries. Previously, on November 17, a beautiful cornerstone ceremony was conducted by Florida's Grand Master, Franklin C. Smith. All of the corporate offices of the A.A.O.N.M.S. and Shriners Hospitals have been relocated to Tampa.

The triennial seminar school of instruction was successfully conducted March 10–11, 1980 at Columbus, Ohio, with several hundred in attendance. Imperial Sir Claypool, like his predecessors, felt it extremely important for temple officers to be fully informed and prepared to handle the unique and complex requirements and responsibilities of their duties as Shrine leaders.

June 20, 1980, was a red letter day for the Philadelphia Unit and the Shriners Hospital movement as a remodeling project began to provide special facilities for the new Spinal Cord Injury Center, the first of its kind for children in the nation. This could well be the forerunner for a new area of services to crippled children.

30

Three Decades of Service

George M. Saunders

Tribute to three decades of service to the Imperial Council and 58 years to Shrinedom to Imperial Sir George M. Saunders is deserving of an entire chapter.

As previously mentioned, George M. Saunders retired as Imperial Recorder as of December 31, 1978, and he was honored in a special ceremony at the 105th annual session at Minneapolis in July 1979. Past Imperial Potentate Jack Streight made the presentation.

A native of Kansas City, Missouri, George Saunders has been active in Masonic and Shrine activities all of his adult life. He entered the service of Ararat Temple and served as Assistant Recorder from 1920 to 1934 when he was elected Recorder; serving until he was elected Imperial Recorder in 1948. He was president of the Shrine Recorders Association and was one of the organizers of the Central States Shrine Association.

Taken from the proceedings of the 1979 Imperial Council Session:

STREIGHT: Now, I have here a plaque, a very simple one, but I believe it expresses all of our love, sincerity and devotion to you. Thank you for your many years of untiring service.

In behalf of all of the Shriners and Shrinedom, may I present this plaque to you, George, which reads as follows:

"Few men can say their work is their hobby because that is the way he felt.

"George M. Saunders, Imperial Recorder 1948 to 1978, is honored today for his thirty years of dedicated service and loyalty to the Shrine and its philanthropy. Let it be known he always lived with the satisfaction that many crippled children's lives were improved because he cared."

George, I present to you this plaque in behalf of all of Shrinedom.

. . . Presentation of plaque and standing applause by the Representatives ensued . . .

IMPERIAL SIR GEORGE M. SAUNDERS: You know, I did not realize this was going to happen, Imperial Sir, but I did want to be prepared to express a bit of appreciation to the members of this great Representative body as well as the Imperial Divan and so I prepared a few little bits of history and if you will put up with me, I am going to tell you something that you may not know about in relation to the things that concern me.

As I stand before you, many Shrine historical moments come to mind and fond memories of the men who participated in them and I am proud of the knowledge that I am a part of those events and, in many instances, the innovator.

I have devoted my efforts to forwarding the goals and exemplifying the teachings of the Craft.

As Master of Kodash, Scottish Rite Masonry, Grand Sovereign of the Red Cross of Constantine, a Thirty-third Degree Mason, the Royal Order of Scotland, Grand Secretary of the Order of DeMolay, Recorder of Ararat Temple and, in 1948, elected Imperial Recorder of the Shrine and Secretary of the Shrine Hospital Corporations, I have gained new light and inspiration and, in turn, contributed to the furtherance of these organizations by my presence at meetings and by influencing others to join.

Truly the abilities of Masonic men, coupled with the esprit de corps when the teachings of the Masonic principle is the common denominator is awesome. It is a humbling experience to know that you can be dead wrong in a situation and still be respected and cherished by Brother Masons. This, of course, is one of the rewards in human relationships.

At this age, of course, you can understand that I have slowed down a bit but aided by an excellent staff and a dedicated board, as well as more than 800 knowledgeable Representatives, the business of the Imperial Council has not suffered.

At this point I want to pay tribute to my wife, Mabel, who has given me moral support and comfort during the years I have devoted to the Shrine, because she believes in the great good of the organization.

Born in 1898, the year of the Spanish American War, I participated in World War I, serving as a member of the American Expeditionary Forces in France. In World War II, I was classified as 4-F but I did my civilian bit by organizing through the Fraternal organizations war bond sales and have several government awards in recognition of my efforts.

The Korean War was a different sort of military effort for the nation did not require anything of me other than paying taxes and voting.

Family life in the United States is one of its greatest strengths. My son, who is a graduate of the Naval Academy at Annapolis, is a career military man is now a Colonel in the Air Forces, serving in Viet Nam. He has also served our country during peace in both Japan and Germany. Due to my efforts, he is also a Mason and a Shriner. I have always felt it was important to Masonry and to the Shrine to bring along the next generation as it were. This record, I believe, qualifies me as a patriot of my country and a guiding parent.

As I view the past years, I realize I have lived through one of the most dynamic periods of history. This country, with the advent of the automobile and air travel, space shots to the moon, communications and technology, has experienced an industrial and cultural change that boggles the mind and there are more changes to come.

My life span covers more than three generations but the pressures of the last fifteen years have been most traumatic, as this has been a period of international involvement and the evolution of a new culture at home—in fact, throughout the entire world.

I count myself fortunate to have spent more than fifty years serving an organization which is influential, dynamic—an organization which provides, by private funds, treatment for crippled and burned children, the Shriners Hospitals. Perhaps this is why I have survived so long—the very nature of the work is an inspiration.

Here are a few facts to support my contributions as Imperial Recorder of the Shrine and Secretary of the Shrine Hospital Corporations.

At the time I was elected Imperial Recorder and Secretary of the Shrine Hospital Corporations, there were 160 Temples, now there are 181 Temples.

Membership in 1948 was 575,954. Membership now is over 945,000.

Despite two rather severe market recessions, the capital assets have increased from $40 million in 1948 to over a billion dollars.

There were sixteen Crippled Childrens Hospitals in 1948—today we are operating twenty-one hospitals; eighteen for crippled children, plus three hospitals for the treatment of burns.

In 1948, when I took over the Imperial Recorder's office, there were four employees. At the time I left the office on December 31, 1978, there was a Legal Department, an Accounting Department, an IBM Department, a Publicity Department, a Hospital Administration Department, Medical Records Department, Printing Department, Promotion Department and a Director of Medical Affairs.

Retirement benefits for all hospital employees and the employees in the Headquarters Office have been established by private funding. I leave behind me definite advancement which is documented.

I leave the organization in a promising condition—a new Headquarters building in a new location, with a new building not yet completed to house the high hopes of the future. May the Shrine and its great philanthropy continue to prosper.

My successor will find in order a well maintained set of records and operating procedure in the office, as well as a cooperative office personnel. I pledge cooperation and support to the new Imperial Recorder elected by the Representatives of the Imperial Council and will be pleased to assist him in any way in the transition of assuming the duties of the office.

As I review my tenture of office, I am overwhelmed

by evidence of devotion to the Order by many fine, able and noble men too numerous to mention here in the time allotted. It is a comfort to know that the "God spirit" touches us all in the Fraternity and it is this recognition that unites us in the Shrine. Divine thought, coupled with the highest principles of Masonic teaching, will guide the Shrine in the future as it has in the past.

For the benefit of my good and concerned friends, I wish to say that the years spent with them in the organization have been rich in experience and human reward. The Shrine life has become my life pattern and I shall continue to participate and look forward to greeting them and working with them in the future.

To the Representatives of the Imperial Council and to the Officers of the Imperial Council, I express my appreciation for being a part of this organization and wish to thank them for their confidence in me through the years and their support of the Imperial Recorder's office.

I relinquished the office of Imperial Recorder with a sense of accomplishment and a full heart because of the many kindnesses of friends who have given me much in personal support, a retirement and expectation of a pleasant future. I want to express my appreciation to the Imperial Potentate, the Imperial Divan and each and every Representative and Shrine worker for this personal recognition.

And my words to you are—God bless each and every one of you. Thank you.

. . . Rising applause on the part of the Delegates then ensued . . .

PAST IMPERIAL POTENTATE STREIGHT: Thank you George.

Now, Nobles, I move that George M. Saunders be elected an Emeritus Member at this Annual Meeting for life.

. . . The motion was severally seconded . . .

IMPERIAL POTENTATE WECK: All of those in favor will indicate by saying aye; opposed. It is unanimous. Thank you very much, George.

Three decades of service to the Imperial Council and 58 years to Shrinedom.

31

Versatility and Enthusiasm

The Cleveland, Ohio, 1980, Convention featured the election on July 9 of a dynamic individual as Imperial Potentate, Dr. F. T. "Hogan" H'Doubler, Jr., of Abou Ben Adhem Temple, Springfield, Missouri, a man of versatility and dedicated enthusiasm, simpatico with his associates and efficacious. On the same day, Joseph P. Padgett of Islam Temple, San Francisco, was chosen Imperial Outer Guard on the first ballot. A native of Georgia, he is a retired business executive, possessing imagination and leadership ability.

Imperial Potentate "Hogan" H'Doubler is a man of many facets, popular in his hometown and popular with his Shrine associates. An unusual, expertly produced, and beautiful pageant was held in his honor at the Cleveland Civic Center, drawing sustained applause from the large audience. A succinct but splendid biography accompanied the pageant program and is worthy of repetition herein, as follows: "Imperial Potentate-elect F. T. "Hogan" H'Doubler, Jr. has been a representative of the Imperial Council since 1967. In the following year, he became the Illustrious Potentate of Abou Ben Adhem Temple and in 1971, was elected Imperial Outer Guard.

He became a Master Mason in Solomon Lodge #271 of Springfield, Missouri, and is a member of Scottish Rite, Valley of Joplin, in which he holds the honor of Knight Commander Court of Honor. He is also a member of York Rite Chapter #15 Royal Arch Masons, Za-

Imperial Potentate "Hogan" F. T. H'Doubler, Jr., M.D., and the First Lady of Shrinedom, Joan.

bud Council #25 Royal and Select Masters and St. John's Commandery #20 Knights Templar. He is a past director of the Royal Order of Jesters Court #73. The Order of De Molay has conferred on him the Honorary Legion of Honor and he is a member of the Royal Order of Scotland.

Dr. H'Doubler was graduated from medical school from the University of Wisconsin. He served as a Navy batallion surgeon with the Marines during the Korean conflict and was decorated with the purple heart with an oak leaf cluster.

Since returning to Springfield, he has been engaged in the practice of medicine and has been involved in many civic, business and political circles. He is a past president of the Jaycees; received Springfield's "Outstanding Young Man Award" and the state's "Distinguished Service Award".

The medical organizations to which he belongs include the American Thyroid Association, the American College of Nuclear Medicine (founders group) and the American Medical Association. The latter presented a "Special Recognition Award" to the "Singing Doctors," of which he is a member, for their efforts to raise scholarship money for needy medical students. He is to receive the Sigma Nu Fraternity's distinguished "Alumnus-of-the-year-award" at their national convention in August 1980.

Imperial Potentate H'Doubler, his wife and four children are members of First and Calvary Presbyterian Church in Springfield, Missouri."

On October 18, 1980, Imperial Potentate H'Doubler dedicated the new Spinal Cord Injury Center at the Philadelphia Unit of Shriners Hospitals.

July 12–16, 1981, the Imperial Council Session will be held in New Orleans, Louisiana, with H'Doubler presiding.

The 1980–1981 Shrine year foresees the continued growth and enhancement of the fraternal and charitable arms of the order, something surely never envisioned by the founders. The Shrine and the hospitals are operated by men of vision. "One quality of greatness is singularity of vision—a kind of tunnel vision. Diversified thought tends to disapate itself."

Growth, expansion and improvement are priority objectives every year at the A.A.O.N.M.S. and at Shriners Hospitals for Crippled Children. The Shrine is nearing the one million mark in membership. Operation of the hospitals since inception approximate one half billion dollars, the current annual operational budget is in excess of $55 million that includes expanded orthopedic and burns research projects, but the endowment fund portfolio showed a healthy $877 million market value at 1979 year end. Tremendous public exposure is received from the operation of the hospitals, temple activities, and the good deeds of Shriners everywhere.

Yes, the founders would be proud of the Shrine of today. They knew not what they created. The Shriners have played and marched their way into a glory of fraternalism and continue on and on, making history all the while.

History does encompass time. The sands of time shift endlessly and tell a continuous story. "Time is the chrysalis of eternity." Richter.

Orville F. Rush

ORVILLE FINDLEY RUSH 33°

Parade to Glory was revised and updated by the Imperial Potentate of 1966–67.

Background was requested and this is taken from a biography in a publication which described him as "a man of leadership, man of action, man of many facets, and man of service. He is listed in a large number of Who's Who publications, including the International Who's Who and World Statemen's Who's Who.

Orville Rush received his college education in liberal arts, law and graduate law at five universities with LL.B, J.D., and LL.D degrees, plus several honorary degrees. He is a longtime member of the board of trustees of the famed George Washington University, Member of the Council of the University of Alabama for over two decades, served on the National Education Committee of his church, a member of the Academic Affairs Committee, and several other education-related organizations. He received the national "Man of the Year" award of his college social fraternity.

Versatility has characterized the distinguished career of Orville Findley Rush, and the mobility and brilliance of his mind became evident at an early age. When he was 15 he became editor of the only newspaper in his hometown of Bessemer, Alabama, acclaimed the youngest city newspaper editor in the U.S. His organizational abilities began at the age of eight with the Cub Scouts. He received straight A's through four years of high school. He was valedictorian and president of all four classes, voted the outstanding student. He was editor of all school publications, captain of the state championship debating team, and was active in sports. He was also voted the outstanding student at the University of Alabama, was elected to the highest honor of president of the student body, also editor-in-chief of the school newspaper, associate editor of the year book and humor magazine and student editor of the law journal. He captained the world's championship debating team. He was listed in the Who's Who in American Colleges and Universities and National Hall of Fame of Students. He served as president of the Alumni Association, D.C. In 1952, he received the honor award as outstanding alumnus. In 1959, a banquet was given in his honor, acclaiming him the outstanding Alabama citizen in the Washington area.

After being admitted to the practice of law, he served as a federal government attorney, resigning to become advisor, counsel and personal representative of Alabama's Governor Bibb Graves. He was Director of Projects and served on state commissions and boards, authoring considerable legislation. He served other governors as personal representative. He has been an officer and board member and chairman of the board of several internationally prominent business concerns, including one of the nation's largest banks, and as international president of the Special Industrial Radio Services Association. Earlier, he was a sports reporter and columnist and contributed to numerous prominent magazines.

Rush has been the titular head of a variety of organizations, serving on national committees in industry, sports, politics, and education. He is widely known as a public speaker and has been praised on the floor of the United States Congress by members of both major parties as an eminent citizen of our country."